Future of Business and Finance

The Future of Business and Finance book series features professional works aimed at defining, analyzing, and charting the future trends in these fields. The focus is mainly on strategic directions, technological advances, challenges and solutions which may affect the way we do business tomorrow, including the future of sustainability and governance practices. Mainly written by practitioners, consultants and academic thinkers, the books are intended to spark and inform further discussions and developments.

Raphael H Cohen

Pre-Project Excellence

Unleashing the Power of IpOp Model and ISO 56007 for Superior Project Selection and Outcomes

Springer

Raphael H Cohen
Geneva, Switzerland

ISSN 2662-2467 ISSN 2662-2475 (electronic)
Future of Business and Finance
ISBN 978-3-031-61773-7 ISBN 978-3-031-61774-4 (eBook)
https://doi.org/10.1007/978-3-031-61774-4

This Springer imprint is published by the registered company Springer Nature Switzerland AG
The registered company address is: Gewerbestrasse 11, 6330 Cham, Switzerland

Contents

About the Author

Raphael H Cohen is an expert in professional agility and "weapons of mass innovation." The IpOp Model he developed and presents in this book is taught in executive education seminars with a view to empowering project managers, entrepreneurs and intrapreneurs to identify, analyze, and seize projects or opportunities that can bring competitive advantages to their company. In large organizations, Raphael's tools boost innovation, entrepreneurial behavior, selling effectiveness, business development, and employee commitment.

Raphael has been one of the key contributors in drafting the ISO 56007 standard, which improves the early-stage calibration of projects. Since the content of the standard is partially inspired by the IpOp Model, this book explains the underlying logic and how to concretely implement ISO 56007.

His latest book in French "Levers of Engagement" maps the levers of just and humanistic leadership, as well as a simple and novel way to measure an executive's level of leadership, which, in turn, brings about a paradigm shift in terms of how people are managed.

Through his activity as professor and academic director of MBA programs, including the Executive MBA in Entrepreneurial Leadership at the University of Geneva, Raphael has acquired a robust experience in designing and running executive education programs. His innovative AgilityBooster/MicroMBA MB™ programs are customized to stimulate the agility and intrapreneurial behavior of middle management in large organizations and have been used by Nestlé, Microsoft, and Sanofi, among others, as well as banks and public sector organizations such as the Lausanne University Hospital (www.lausanneuniversityhospital.com). AgilityBooster/MicroMBA MB™ programs generate measurable profits that go way beyond their cost and represent a change of paradigm in executive education programs.

Serial entrepreneur, active CEO, and business angel, Raphael brings hands-on experience to his lecturing and consulting activities, providing training, mentoring, and management services for senior executives, bankers, directors, and entrepreneurs. He has served on the board of directors of several companies, including a Swiss bank, and is a regular contributor to several world-class business publications.

He obtained his Ph.D. in Economics in 1982 while managing an international group of companies, which is still flourishing today.

X RaphaelHCohen

in RaphaelHCohen

1

Introduction (and a Warning...)

Take-Home of This Chapter

This introduction emphasizes the importance of the pre-project stage and the analysis before resource allocation, which is pivotal for any project developer and for any decision-maker. Additional objectives of the book are to enhance the project selection process, assist organizations in gaining competitive advantages, and aid innovators in turning their ideas into realities. The book provides a structured model of the entrepreneurial and intrapreneurial process, highlighting the importance of discipline and process. It aims to equip project initiators, particularly intrapreneurs, with the tools they need to thrive. The chapter also highlights the need for large organizations to tap into their employees' innovative capabilities and properly set up the intrapreneurial process. The author also emphasizes the importance of a common vocabulary to facilitate effective communication around innovation and pre-project management.

To implement ISO 56007, readers can use the content of this book to understand and apply the best practices outlined in the standard. Each chapter concludes with a box featuring a grey frame and a white background that explains how its content relates to ISO 56007, providing guidance on how to implement the standard effectively. By following the structured model and utilizing the tools and methods presented in the book, individuals and organizations can align their practices with ISO 56007 and improve their management of ideas and opportunities.

R. H Cohen, *Pre-Project Excellence*, Future of Business and Finance,
https://doi.org/10.1007/978-3-031-61774-4_1

1.1 Why the Pre-project Is Essential

It has been found that roughly 3% of all projects never reach completion,[1] **representing a significant waste of resources** that could be drastically reduced with a more effective selection process at the pre-project stage. Furthermore, the same study indicates that:

- Another 30% of projects exceed their planned duration
- About 50% of projects surpass their original budget

Consequently, only 12 to 16% of all projects are completed on time and within budget, meaning 84 to 88% of projects encounter setbacks at some point. A more detailed pre-project evaluation and calibration could greatly enhance these performance metrics.

Given that this study encompasses all types of projects within organizations, innovative projects likely fare even worse in terms of performance. Thus, a better assessment of these projects prior to launching them is crucial for making more informed decisions.

The aim of pre-project analysis is to provide a finer calibration of each project, offering a more accurate perspective on what the project can achieve and with a realistic roadmap. The IpOp Model, as described in this book, guides how to accomplish this. The approach it advocates is endorsed as a best practice by the recently adopted ISO 56007 standard, which concentrates on the initial stages of innovation, covering ideation and pre-project analysis.

1.2 Implementing ISO 56007

Following unanimous adoption by 42 countries, the ISO 56007[2] standard was published in August 2023. This standard offers guidance on managing ideas and opportunities, providing best practices for analyzing and selecting the best concepts.

[1] The Standish Group's 1995 CHAOS Report. Later CHAOS Reports show similar patterns, i.e. the 2015 Report which can be downloaded on https://www.standishgroup.com/sample_research_files/CHAOSReport2015-Final.pdf.

[2] ISO 56007: Tools and methods for managing opportunities and ideas — Guidance.

ISO 56007 primarily focuses on innovation, but certain sections can benefit any project in its early stages. For example, the parts about handling uncertainties and project selection can enhance any project planning, regardless of its origin—top-down or bottom-up. Implementing these practices leads to higher project success rates and reduced resource waste.

ISO standards are divided into two categories: certification standards (like ISO 9001) and guidance standards. ISO 56007 falls under the latter category, serving as a guidance standard that requires no certification. It outlines the best practices for managing ideas and opportunities, agreed upon by seasoned experts from all countries involved in drafting this standard.

It is important to note that ISO standards are not designed to be instructional textbooks. Some parts of ISO 56007 may be difficult to understand due to a lack of justification. However, since certain sections of ISO 56007 have been inspired by the IpOp Model described in this book, its content can help clarify why certain practices are recommended.

Additionally, ISO 56007 doesn't always provide specific "how-to" instructions for its recommendations. This book guides practitioners in implementing ISO 56007's best practices in organizations, including the process of identifying uncertainties/unknowns in any project.

To aid readers in understanding how the content of this book can assist them in implementing ISO 56007, there is a box at the end of each chapter featuring a grey frame with a white background that explains how it relates to the standard. Readers that are particularly interested in ISO 56007 could start by reading the content of that box before reading the corresponding chapter.

1.3 A Real Alternative to Producing a Business Plan

In the grand scheme of things, generating ideas is relatively easy. It's the execution that proves to be the real challenge. As Theodore Levitt aptly put it, the key is turning those ideas into action. Before any idea can materialize, it requires careful analysis and the development of an actionable plan. That is the crucial missing link.

The aim of this book is to bridge that gap and empower individuals with good ideas to bring them to life. Feedback from readers of the earlier (French) versions, published in 2006 and 2016, revealed that it transformed their lives by propelling their careers and broadening their horizons.

This book has three primary objectives: to enhance the project selection process at the pre-project stage, thereby reducing the number of projects that fail to meet deadlines and stay within the initial budget; to assist organizations in gaining competitive advantages; and to aid innovators in turning their ideas into tangible realities. Tailored for action-oriented individuals, it offers a structured model of the entrepreneurial and intrapreneurial process.

Recognizing the abundance of ideas already circulating, this book does not delve into creativity methods, as there are many excellent resources available on that topic. Instead, it focuses on discipline and process. It urges project developers and innovators to approach their projects systematically rather than relying solely on intuition. In essence, creativity alone is not sufficient; a framework and discipline are indispensable companions.

The primary emphasis here is on the project initiator or the intrapreneur—a person who exhibits entrepreneurial traits and behavior within an existing organization. I firmly believe that large organizations stand to gain significantly from tapping into their employees' innovation potential. Far too many promising ideas never see the light of day due to inadequacies in the intrapreneurial process. The pre-project stage, especially the analysis just before resource allocation, is pivotal for any project developer, whether initiated by top management or an intrapreneur.

My goal is to equip project initiators with the tools they need to thrive. Given the tougher journey for intrapreneurs compared to projects initiated by top management, and the principle that mastering more enables one to handle less, this book concentrates on intrapreneurs. Large organizations, in my view, urgently need to harness their employees' innovative capabilities, and proper setup of the intrapreneurial process is crucial to achieving this.

Tools that boost intrapreneurs are also valid for entrepreneurs, project managers and start-ups. The few points that are less relevant for the latter (e.g. alignment of the project with the corporate strategy) can simply be skipped when they do not need to be addressed. The IpOp Model presented in this book can considerably reduce the burden of writing a business plan, and many start-ups have used it with success.

To illustrate the application of the IpOp model, I have selected a specific case study, which is shown in a grey box in several chapters: the launch of Nespresso Classic, focusing on the period during its introduction when the circumstances differed significantly from today's. Because the Nespresso adventure was already well in motion before I developed the model, I have reconstituted the IpOp Model logic behind it a posteriori. Since Nespresso relies on innovation to relentlessly increase the perceived value and coffee lovers' experience, it offers a magnificent example of what intrapreneurial approach can do in a multinational corporation (Nestlé). As you will see from these notes, its development called several of Nestlé's traditional managerial practices into question. I thank Nespresso for supporting me in this endeavor and for the information that permitted me to write the present "case study".

Nespresso *in profile*

1. Headquartered in Lausanne, Switzerland, with more than 14'000 employees worldwide, Nestlé Nespresso SA sells products in 75 markets directly to its customers. At the end of 2023, it operated a global retail network of more than 790 boutiques in key cities around the world. Nespresso is one of the fastest growing brands within the Nestlé group and one of its "billionaire brands". According to Nestlé annual report, Nespresso achieved global sales of over CHF 6 billion in 2023.
2. First launched in Switzerland, the Nespresso B2B channel (Nespresso professional) now operates in 75 countries through its own subsidiaries and distributors and with one exclusive objective in mind: To deliver the very best coffee solutions in the commercial sector. From small or large offices to gourmet restaurants, premium hotels, luxury retail and customer care outlets as well as upscale airline services, Nespresso has a winning formula to suit all categories of businesses and allow them to tailor their coffee offer to their own customers.

3. Nespresso is the pioneer and reference for highest-quality portioned coffee. The company works with more than 150,000 farmers in 18 countries through its AAA Sustainable Quality™ program to embed sustainability practices on farms and the surrounding landscapes. Launched in 2003 in collaboration with the NGO Rainforest Alliance, the program helps to improve the yield and quality of harvests, ensuring a sustainable supply of high-quality coffee and improving livelihoods of farmers and their communities.

   In 2022, Nespresso achieved B Corp™ certification—joining an international movement of over 7900 purpose-led businesses that meet B Corp's high standards of social and environmental responsibility and transparency.

1.4 The Target Reader

This book has been written for people who belong to one (or more) of the following groups:

- **Anyone who wants to implement the ISO 56007 standard (Tools and Methods for Managing Opportunities and Ideas - Guidance)** at the operational level
- **Decision makers and board members in both private and public sectors** who
  - Select projects (make Go/No Go decisions)
  - Allocate and monitor the use of resources
  - Need to manage and control the innovation process more effectively
  - Wish to promote innovation and the acquisition of competitive advantages
  - Are responsible for promoting a culture of innovation and change while raising the level of their team's commitment
- **Project leaders/managers** who should calibrate the roadmap of the projects that decision-makers have instructed them to launch
- **Executives and managers** who want to contribute to their organization and boost their own career through innovation and intrapreneurial behavior—the content of the book should help them become change agents

- **Innovators, entrepreneurs and intrapreneurs** desiring to present their project to their superiors or Decision-makers in a more convincing and reliable manner
- **Marketing, R&D and business development experts** who need a structured model to supervise and assess projects at the "ideation" stage
- **Fundraisers and anyone involved in non-profit or public sectors**, to help them obtain more support for their projects or initiatives
- **Anyone who wants to increase the chances of success** of existing or future projects in private or public sectors

1.5 Using the Book

As a business practitioner, I believe that presenting theoretical concepts does not necessarily require the use of jargon, convoluted explanations, or repetitions to hammer them home. My aim is to be as concise as possible.

Each chapter starts with a grey box outlining the key elements of its content. The reader can use this as a "threat" to prepare mentally for what is to follow.

To make the book easier to read (and remember), the beginning of each paragraph is set in bold type, generally summarizing its content. Later, this text in bold type should serve to enable the reader to quickly remember the main idea of the paragraph.

As I have created several terms simply for their memorability (e.g. KISs, Terminators, etc.), the vocabulary used is not very orthodox.

Because sharing a common vocabulary facilitates communication between various groups of people with a common interest, one of my objectives is to propose a specific vocabulary to enable people to communicate more effectively around pre-project management and innovation. I have usually spelt specific keywords or expressions used by the IpOp Model with a capital initial or its abbreviation throughout, and their definition will be found in the Glossary at the end of the book.

Finally, each chapter concludes with a box featuring a grey frame and a white background, detailing how its content correlates with

ISO 56007. This feature is intended to assist readers in effectively applying the book's content to implement ISO 56007 in practice.

1.6 Warning

Because I say what I think, my words may not always be politically correct. I therefore apologize to anyone who could be offended by some of the statements I make in this book. I have no desire to offend, or indeed to convince anyone. My intention is simply to stimulate thinking and the seizing of opportunities. To achieve this, I have sometimes taken the liberty of breaking the rule of politically correct statements in order to put forward a provocative view.

To maintain inclusivity without bias, this book employs masculine pronouns throughout. However, it is important to note that when using masculine pronouns, it encompasses individuals of all genders.

Acknowledgment, Sources and References This is not an encyclopedic presentation proving that I have read a hundred books and have now written the 101st incorporating all previous knowledge. I humbly acknowledge that I could not possibly have discovered all the information presented in this book by myself, because I do not live in a vacuum. In the course of the 40-plus years of my life as an entrepreneur and intrapreneur I have read many books and articles, attended a great many training seminars and lectures, and dealt with quite a number of "real" people and business opportunities in real time.

All my combined experiences have taught me many valuable lessons, yet I regret not always acknowledging their sources. The IpOp Model presented in this book integrates what I have learned from various sources, and I must apologize to academics, professors, writers, consultants and experts for not always crediting their contributions. It was never my intention to plagiarize; rather, as an entrepreneurship professor with limited memory, I simply overlooked proper attribution. When I was just a businessman, I never imagined I would one day become a lecturer, teacher, or writer.

I chose to expedite the publication of this book to ensure that innovators could benefit from the model as soon as possible. Regrettably, this meant that I was unable to include all academic sources, quotes, and references that deserve recognition. I invite readers to provide any information that would allow me to properly credit those who have contributed to this work. Please feel free to reach out to me at book@getratex.ch with details of individuals who should receive credit and for what contributions. I am grateful for any input received, and I will incorporate all sources, quotes, and references provided into future editions of the book.

I must nevertheless give credit to Richard E. Schroeder and Raymond P. Kasbarian, who inspired me during a strategic analysis workshop they facilitated many years ago. It is they who first exposed me to some of the concepts referred to in this book: the Driver/Satisfier distinction and the Definition of Success. I have expanded on these notions to build the IpOp Model and take this opportunity to thank them both for putting me on track.

I believe that my primary contribution is in the way all the concepts fit together into a model. The architecture of the model and the links between the various concepts has not been borrowed from any other source. What the IpOp Model does is to crystallize into an explicit architecture the underlying thought process that successful people use when they work on a new project or an innovation.

I also would like to thank all the people who have participated in an IpOp Model training session, whose challenging questions have helped me further improve the model and progressively mature it to its current level of development.

Acknowledging that the IpOp Model served as a foundational inspiration for drafting sections of the new ISO 56007 standard, "Tools and methods for managing opportunities and ideas — Guidance," I extend my gratitude to the group of experts involved in developing this standard. Their constructive challenges enhanced my contribution to the standard significantly.

Mentions of the IpOp Model within ISO 56007, along with references to content from the 2011 version of this book in its annexes, has motivated me to publish this updated edition, incorporating the latest advancements and improvements.

I am also very grateful to my wife, Ellen, and my children, who have been so understanding in face of my lack of presence and availability while I was working on the IpOp Model.

Special thanks also go to Professor Jerry Katz, to my daughter, Jessica Liah Cohen, and to my son, David Cohen, who helped improve the content.

I extend my special thanks to my wife Ellen and Brian Levin for their meticulous refinement of the English text, offering numerous enhancements, and serving as exceptional sounding boards and advisors.

2

In the Beginning, There Was the Opportunity

No Opportunity, No Entrepreneur

Take-Home of This Chapter

This chapter discusses the concept of opportunities in entrepreneurship and intrapreneurship. It introduces the IpOp Model, which focuses on Innovation by Opportunity, and the management practice of "Management by Opportunity" (MbOp). It emphasizes the importance of identifying innovative solutions to market needs and defines an Opportunity as the combination of a Solution that satisfies one or more defined Pain/Need/Desires (PNDs). Building an intimate relationship with customers to identify unrecognized Pains/Needs/Desires can lead to the creation of new Opportunities possibly with existing Solutions. Since innovation does not necessarily mean invention, the innovative Solution does not have to be brand new and can be brought in from another market.

It also highlights the role of creativity, market research, and customer intimacy in identifying and capitalizing on opportunities. The content of this chapter can be used to implement ISO 56007 by providing insights into managing opportunities and ideas, understanding customer pain/need/desire(s), and developing innovative solutions. However, it should be noted that ISO 56007 does not specifically address the concept of "solution" like the IpOp Model does.

R. H Cohen, *Pre-Project Excellence*, Future of Business and Finance,
https://doi.org/10.1007/978-3-031-61774-4_2

Nobody becomes an entrepreneur for the sake of doing so. Typically, an entrepreneur is someone who has the flair to identify an opportunity and the ability to evaluate its feasibility, gather the necessary resources and, finally, implement an Action Plan with a view to seizing it. We may define Opportunity as the existence of an innovative solution to a market need.[1]

Given the central role of opportunities in entrepreneurship and intrapreneurship, the model presented in this book is known as the IpOp Model ("Innovation by Opportunity[2]"). It follows that the management practice focusing on seizing opportunities is called "Management by Opportunity" (MbOp).[3]

Identifying the Opportunity is usually the easiest part, and many people come up with great ideas. The difficult part is to develop such ideas further into a realistic Action Plan that can be successfully implemented.

2.1 Identifying Pains, Needs and Desires

The concept of need is a very broad one in this context, embracing any need that has not already been satisfied or can be satisfied in a more satisfactory or less expensive way.

The Kano Model[4] for Customer Satisfaction, which defines three levels of need, is a good starting point for their identification:

- Basic needs that are often taken for granted: failing to deliver them may often lead to dissatisfaction
- Performance needs, which the customer recognizes and can usually express; they are useful but not critical (e.g. evaluation on a scale)
- Excitement needs, which customers may not be aware of, because they go beyond performance needs; once identified, they provide an opportunity to create products that change the rules of the game (the iPad is a good example)

---

[1] This will be refined below with the concept of Pain/Need/Desire.

[2] In French: «Innovation par les Opportunités».

[3] See Chap. 22

[4] Kano et al. (1996).

The greater the pain, the more the customer will be motivated to buy the painkiller. Identifying what hurts is also a very good way to spot Opportunities. A good illustration is the invention of the salad spinner. We can all live without one, but it makes drying the salad less painful. Since it can be argued that this device does not actually satisfy a fundamental or "real" need, and to avoid discussing such fine definitions, I prefer to simply make the point that it reduces the pain associated with drying a salad. Thus, besides needs, pains can also be a source of Opportunities.

People also acquire objects or services simply to satisfy a desire. Everyone can live without treatment to reduce wrinkles, but it may appeal to some who have the desire to look younger. Here again, it may be argued that this is related to other needs, such as the need to be attractive and loved. I prefer to avoid this discussion and simply state that satisfying a desire is not the same thing as satisfying a need or alleviating a pain.

The concept of "Pain/Need/Desire(s)" (PND) captures all these nuances, while avoiding the semantic confusion created by any personal interpretation of these words. Using any of them singly may prevent covering all the possibilities that PND encompasses, so I will use the expression PND throughout this book. The expression Pain/Need/Desire(s) is also used by ISO 56007.

A PND usually exists only in one or more specific contexts. Clarifying the context(s) is very important because it clarifies the scope of the Opportunity. For instance, the opportunity to offer for rent high-performance fishing gear only exists in a resort where fishing is possible, and which attracts fishing aficionados. In that context it would make sense to open such a business. When IATA airlines were the only players in Europe, introducing low-cost flights created a huge opportunity for easyJet, Ryan Air and other airlines. Low-cost airlines may not be successful in other regions of the world. It is in this sense that opportunities are by and large context related.

Unarticulated PNDs create the greatest opportunities. While some of them may be expressed explicitly ("We need faster computers", for example), others remain unperceived until someone demonstrates that they were waiting in the wings ready to be discovered (e.g. instant messaging software). They are also the most difficult to detect, and often require the interpretation of weak signals. Some Pain/Need/Desire(s) do not get expressed because they are not politically correct (e.g., recourse to sex-related web sites that generate at least one-fifth of the traffic on the Internet, while most users will not admit visiting them).

Identifying Pain/Need/Desire(s) requires a finely tuned sense of observation: asking people what their needs are is far from enough—you have to observe how they actually do things. This is illustrated by the finding that while 77% of French consumers declare being in favor of generic drugs, only 33% actually purchase them. Clearly, traditional market research can sometimes deliver unreliable results.

Observation is critical, and our best advice is to observe:

- Real humans
- Real situations
- Real products or services being used

Going after the "wrong" PND can turn out to be a very expensive exercise. Because doctors were calling out for a solution to treat diabetics who are allergic to animal-based insulin, Eli Lilly spent about $1 billion developing a very pure variety of insulin that did not trigger allergic reactions. This innovation did not become an instant money-maker because only a small number of people needed it. For its part, Novo, a much smaller company, came to the realization by observation that the traditional process of injecting insulin (calculating the required quantity and preparing the needle) was not very user-friendly. Novo developed a "pen" that delivered a preconditioned quantity of insulin in a very user-friendly manner. Unlike Eli Lilly, who were chasing the needs of the doctors, Novo made a fortune by satisfying the end-users' needs.

Corporate anthropology is an interesting and effective approach to a clear understanding of (internal or external) clients or customers, the market, the technology, or the stakeholders. For instance, Motorola radically expanded the range of colors available for its line of pagers when anthropologists observed that teenagers were using pagers not merely for utilitarian purposes but also as status symbols. When studying the logistics process, anthropologists do not limit themselves to interviewing the company's vice-president of logistics but will also "sit on top of a box" or travel with delivery trucks to discover where time is wasted.

Observation is a state of mind. To understand your customers, you need to spend time observing them in their own environment. Watching them use a product or service in situ can bring PNDs to your attention that no one is yet aware of. For example, it is astonishing that laptop chargers do not incorporate a rewinding device for the power cord: any attentive observer would have noticed that people like to roll up the power cord before packing their notebook away. There is no way engineers ensconced in their cubicle offices could observe (and so identify) such a "Pain". Many real opportunities can only be identified outside of your office. Other strategies that can be used to complement observation are:

- Asking potential customers to role-play using prototypes
- Developing products jointly with a lead client
- Using design-thinking and fast prototyping approaches
- Market studies, etc.

Intimacy with customers is achieved when they feel you sound like one of them, rather than like a supplier. Understanding their PNDs at this level itself creates opportunities. The cosmetics industry knows its customers well enough to realize that at bottom what they are buying is hope, not creams. Understanding this had a major impact on the way the industry runs its business (packaging, marketing strategies, etc.). In another sector, Rolex has developed such a level of customer intimacy and recognition that the quality of Rolex watches is never open to question.

It is important to identify the market segments most likely to ensure the greatest returns. Observation led McDonald's executives to focus their marketing campaigns on children instead of adults. They had noticed that, while parents have the buying power, it is the children who play a critical role in selecting a restaurant. Their good understanding of the influencers' psychology led them to go after the specifiers (in this case the children) rather than the actual buyers. Building an intimate relationship with the children paid off.

Observing how users are dealing with or handling competitors' products or services can also help reveal unsatisfied PNDs. For example, the Swiss entrepreneur Domenic Steiner observed that the breakdown of professional coffee machines presented a real problem for restaurant owners, who were losing out on the downtime incurred during servicing. He designed a modular machine with standard replacement parts, thus eliminating the need to send the whole machine back in the event of a problem. His company, Thermoplan, has become the exclusive supplier to Starbucks! The secret is to develop familiarity with the customers, the market, the technology, and the networks.

Structural changes often create opportunities. When the situation is stable, it is more difficult to find opportunities than when they are on the move. This is because when things are going well, Decision-makers are reluctant to change a winning recipe. When business gets tough, their mind becomes open to exploring new avenues. Changing environments and crises represent great hunting grounds for opportunity seekers. The emergence of artificial intelligence is a good example of paradigm shifts that challenge many industries.

Many corporations are affected by the disease of "opportunity myopia". Their employees are conditioned to do things a certain way and become immune to any idea that might challenge the status quo. Such a narrow-minded way of thinking is often occasioned by successes in the past because people are prone to believe that past success is proof that they will continue to be successful in the future. Unfortunately, it does not work that way, because success in the future depends on the ability to deal with future, rather than past, circumstances.

Challenging everything right across the board, including past successes, should help to pinpoint opportunities. Probing and trying to understand how things could be done differently ultimately leads to improvement. Progress stops when people give up challenging the status quo.

As a significant portion of ISO 56007 is dedicated to the finding and sourcing of ideas and opportunities, the standard and its annexes are an excellent source of inspiration, way beyond the few examples mentioned in this chapter.

2.2 The Innovative Solution

It is not enough to identify a PND. You also must come up with a way to satisfy it, in other words find a Solution. The Solution does not need to be brand new, and bringing in an existing one from another market may be good enough. EasyJet's introduction into the European market of a concept already successful in the United States (Southwest Airlines) ensured them instant success. The founder's stroke of genius was to realize that Europeans could use a formula that had been successful elsewhere.

Too often people believe that "innovation" means "first-time" invention. My definition of innovation also includes new Solutions brought to a market where they were not previously available. This might not satisfy the purists, but it has the advantage of opening the door to creativity in environments that are not exposed to innovations available elsewhere.

It is not necessary to reinvent the wheel or even invent anything new, because there are so many inventions or Solutions sitting around waiting for a new application. Finding a good use for something that has already been invented can create an excellent opportunity. Innovation sometimes lies in identifying Pain/Need/Desire(s) that others have not yet recognized, which can be satisfied by existing Solutions.

The definition of innovation I use is: "the creating and bringing into gratifying use of new technologies, new products, new services, new marketing ideas, new systems, new ways of operating and new interactions".[5] The gratification factor may be profit, personal satisfaction or any other benefit to the organization or individual. Who would waste time with an innovation that does not have some kind of added value factor?

Another definition of innovation that focuses on the value-added concept is: "the process of creating something new that has significant value to an individual, a group, an industry or a society".[6] Note that the value-added benefit does not need to be measured in monetary terms.

An innovation factor is necessary because without it you obviously cannot do better than your competitors, unless you are content to be a

[5] Gifford Pinchot.

[6] James M. Higgins (1995).

Fig. 2.1 Pain/Need/Desire + Solution = Opportunity

"me too". The fact that your predecessor is already in business gives him or her, a competitive advantage, riding ahead of you on the learning curve.[7] You must therefore make sure you bring something new into the equation, sufficiently substantial to overcome this handicap.

Opportunity is defined by the {PND} + {Solution} dyad. An Opportunity can only exist when there is a Pain/Need/Desire[8] that can be satisfied by a valid Solution. Neither alone is sufficient to create an Opportunity. Because they have to fit together, this is ultimately a match-making exercise (Fig. 2.1).

The question "Which came first, the chicken or the egg?" is eminently applicable to the PND + Solution couple. Does the Pain/Need/Desire prompt the discovery of the Solution ("pull demand"), or does invention of a product lead the inventor to seek the appropriate market ("push demand")?

Many technology-based innovations seem to belong to the push-demand category: a scientist discovers something in the lab, and then works on developing a marketable application for it.

A "pull demand" situation exists when a new Solution to a known problem (PND) is discovered. Here, the market already exists, considerably reducing the uncertainty level. This in itself is a good enough reason to use a Pain/Need/Desire as a starting point for seeking the Solution whenever possible. A good example of "pull innovation" is the packaged pre-washed salads sold in supermarkets. When the wish (triggered by the pain of washing salads) to buy salads that did not require washing was first identified, a French farmer gave an R&D mandate to the national research center INSERN, which eventually came up with the right mix

[7] http://en.wikipedia.org/wiki/Learning_curve.

[8] Almost everywhere else in this book the word *Need* can be replaced by *Desire*.

of oxygen and nitrogen to extend the shelf life of pre-washed salad. This Solution turned the idea into a tremendous business Opportunity.

Looking for the innovative Solution requires creativity. Brainstorming is one way to figure out THE Solution. A number of such tools are available to stimulate the creativity process.

At the beginning there will most likely be just the perceived possibility of an Opportunity, such as an idea that needs to be refined. While this early idea gives a hint to what the Solution could be, it usually does not correspond to the final Solution. It takes time and homework to fine-tune the initial idea until it is mature enough to become a fully-fledged Solution. Several steps of the IpOp Model[9] are specifically designed to provide a roadmap for the process of maturing the initial idea. As long as the initial idea has not become THE Solution, the probability of success for the Opportunity remains very low. This is why, until the Solution is clearly defined,[10] I qualify the Opportunity as apparent (Fig. 2.2). This refining process is also necessary for the PND until a very clear PND has been defined.[11]

Fig. 2.2 At the early stage the Opportunity is still fuzzy and is qualified as "apparent"

> **Link with ISO 56007 (Tools and Methods for Managing Opportunities and Ideas: Guidance)**
>
> In the IpOp Model, the 'Solution' is what you provide to the Customer to meet his 'Pain/Need/Desire(s)'. The Solution is what the customer receives. It may not cover all the other aspects necessary to make it suitable for everyone involved. These additional aspects could include access to raw materials or the need to partner with a key player in the market, which the Customer might not even be aware of.

[9] Particularly Chapters 4 to 10.

[10] See Chap. 9.

[11] See Chap. 7.

ISO 56007 also uses the concept of 'pain/need/desire(s)' to address customer/user issues in several parts. However, it does not specifically discuss the concept of 'Solution'. Instead, it looks at the 'concept', which encompasses not only what the IpOp Model refers to as the Solution but also everything else related to it, such as access to raw materials and partnering with key market players. The 'concept' is a broader term that aligns more closely with what the IpOp Model calls the 'Opportunity' or the 'Project'.

In the IpOp Model, an 'Opportunity' is defined as the combination of a Solution that meets one or more identified Pain/Need/Desires. On the other hand, ISO 56007 defines "an 'opportunity' as emerging from a set of circumstances that can lead to potential innovation. It can also lead to ideas or opportunity areas". From my perspective, ISO 56007 defines the concept of 'opportunity' at a more abstract level, whereas the IpOp Model offers a more practical and grounded definition. It is a matter of perspective.

References

Higgins, J. M. (1995). *Innovate or Evaporate.* New Management Pub. Co.. ISBN-13: 978-1883629014.

Kano, N., Seraku, N., Takahashi, F., & Tsuji, S. (1996). Attractive Quality and Must-Be Quality. In J. D. Hromi (Ed.), *The Best on Quality* (Vol. 7). ASQC, Quality Press.

3

Even Geeks Can Come Up with Non-tech Innovation

Non-technology-Based Innovation Is the Low Hanging Fruit That Is Waiting to Be Picked

Take-Home of This Chapter

To implement ISO 56007, organizations can use the content of this chapter to gain a deeper understanding of innovation and how it can be applied in various contexts. This chapter showcases various examples of business initiatives across different industries, highlighting the potential of non-tech innovations. Innovation can take various forms, such as new packaging, new services, new marketing schemes, or new management approaches. By studying the different forms of innovation and learning from successful business initiatives, organizations can align their practices with the principles outlined in ISO 56007 and enhance their innovation capabilities.

This chapter also mentions the role of technology in enabling innovation. It explains the difference between invention and innovation. It emphasizes the importance of democratizing innovation. It also explores the concept of non-tech innovation as the "low-hanging fruit" that organizations often overlook, leading to missed opportunities.

The notion of innovation is usually associated with technology, and is even restricted to high-tech most of the time. Technology-based innovation attracts media and public attention, so it is understandable that it is the first to come to mind. Tech-based innovation is also easier to protect with patents, thus providing a Competitive Advantage. But this does not mean that non-tech Solutions should be neglected out of hand.

R. H Cohen, *Pre-Project Excellence*, Future of Business and Finance,
https://doi.org/10.1007/978-3-031-61774-4_3

3.1 Invention ≠ Innovation

The confusion between invention and innovation is probably one of the main reasons why people associate technology with innovation. In fact, invention does not necessarily imply innovation. As we saw above, until the invention has found a market and value brought to the organization, no innovation has occurred. On the other hand, innovations have been introduced that did not require any invention and were not based on technology.

Non-tech innovation can be incredibly effective. Let us look at some examples of large, highly successful businesses that did not depend on technology for their success. While I.T. plays a role in most of these examples, it is not the main focus. Instead, it mainly improves efficiency and cuts costs. Computerized data processing has become a standard part of business operations, but true technological innovations still stand out, like quantum computing.

Artificial intelligence, blockchain, the Internet of Things (IoT), robotics, and drones are all significant game-changers in today's business landscape. These technologies are rapidly transitioning from niche to mainstream, thanks in part to advancements in artificial intelligence making them accessible even to individuals without a programming background. This accessibility blurs the line between "tech" and "non-tech" domains, as these innovations become increasingly integrated into everyday operations across various industries.

Industry	Example of business initiative	Customer PND Focus Statement	Initial non-tech innovation	Comments
IT	Michael Dell sold competitively priced PCs long before the internet became a selling channel	More favorably priced PCs custom built to customer specifications	Selling computers without use of the middleman	Tech-based improvements later helped Dell acquire additional competitive advantages
Finance	Credit cards	Purchasing without cash or the need to write a check	Combining a clearing system with a card permitting the seller to identify the purchaser	While IT helped reduce processing costs and accelerate verification it was not conceptually indispensable
	Credit cards issued by banks	Banks' existing customers want to spend money without signing checks	Creation of a consortium of banks to enable the system to reach critical mass	Rapid access to a large number of customers was a major competitive advantage to permit obtaining a market share
	Letters of credit	The need for secure payments in international trade	The purchaser's bank guarantees payment if certain conditions are met	Clarifying the meaning of the UCP[a] significantly contributed to the international deployment of L/Cs
Watches	Design of the Swatch	Fun and fashion	Treatment of watches as a fashion accessory	While low-cost production technology was very important, the commercial success derived from the marketing strategy

Industry	Example of business initiative	Customer PND Focus Statement	Initial non-tech innovation	Comments
Tourism	Loyalty mileage program	Free trips or other rewards	Introduction of redeemable mileage points in the tourism industry	Airlines' operating expenses are mostly fixed; redeeming points against unsold seats costs them almost nothing
Tourism	Time sharing	Bargain vacations	Long-term lease for fractions of the year instead of permanent use of the premises	Selling residence by the week yields a cosmetically low price which amounts when annualized to much more than the market price
Education	R&D services by engineering schools to finance the cost of their research staff	Private sector looking to outsource R&D tasks	Turning school engineering departments into profit centers	The Weitzman Institute in Israel generates a large portion of its budget in the private sector
Food	VOSS mineral water sold in designer shaped bottles	The taste for exclusive high-end products	A beautifully shaped bottle that attracts the attention of consumers	The exclusive design allowed VOSS to penetrate markets already well served with bottled water (including Danone's and Nestlé's home market)
Advertising and sport	Promotion of brands by sponsoring athletes or events	Media coverage of sports events	Paying athletes to use/display a brand	

Automobile industry	Monospace vehicles	6- to 7-seater cars for families	Designing limousines with more interior space	No major technological breakthroughs were required
Aviation	Low cost airlines (Southwest Airlines, easyJet, Ryan-air, etc.)	Low-cost, no-frills transportation	Dynamic pricing without intermediation by travel agents plus high efficiency operations	
Courier services	DHL/FedEx	Fast delivery of documents and small parcels	Human transportation of consolidated shipments	
Employment services	Manpower, etc.	Short-term employment	Acting as a clearing house between workers and enterprises and handling administrative issues	
Consumer goods	Suitcases with wheels	Reduce the effort of carrying a suitcase	Adding wheels to suitcases	
Clothing	Zara, Shein, etc.	Rapidly changing fashions and clothes trends	Reduction of the production cycle between concept and in-store availability to 30 days	
Art	Christies, Sotheby's, etc.	Create a more transparent market for artwork	Branding auctions and backing them with complementary services	
Entertainment	Loft Story, Survivor, etc.	Voyeurism	Reality TV	
Machine industry	Extended support/ warranty	Reliability and prompt repair	Users pay an additional fee to have priority support or a longer warranty	

Industry	Example of business initiative	Customer PND Focus Statement	Initial non-tech innovation	Comments
Sport	Beach volley	Beach sport activity	Adaptation of volleyball to the beach environment	
Media	CNN, CNBC, Euro news	Instant availability of news	Specialized TV channel providing continuous news	
Retailing	Mail order	Buying at any time without needing to go to a store	Printing of a catalog and its distribution to a large number of consumers. Catalogs have have now been replaced by webstores	
Retailing	eBay	Wider access to auctions (by both buyers and sellers) of used products	Connecting buyers and sellers who do not know one other through the internet	This application of the internet was not as such a technological breakthrough
Food & Beverages	Alco-pops	Alcoholic drinks	Ready mixed gin and tonic	
	Starbucks	Better quality coffee for affluent consumers	High-end coffee served in a cozy environment	

[a]The Uniform Customs and Practice for Documentary Credits (UCP) is a set of rules on the issuance and use of letters of credit (Wikipedia)

This list could extend for several pages because, contrary to common belief, there is a life beyond high-tech. This means that being a technological genius is not a requirement for innovating and being successful. I have no hesitation in declaring that non-tech innovation is the "low-hanging fruit" that organizations tend to neglect. Forgetting this leads to overlooking Opportunities.

3.2 Democratizing Innovation

Anyone can innovate. Innovation requires nothing more than imagination and creativity. For example, during a focus group discussing the potential application of a hair removal laser system, most participants were exploring applications for women. Then, some people suggested offering hair removal to male swimmers, weightlifters, and bikers. These ideas generated new opportunities for hair removal.

Innovation can take many forms. Here are a few examples:

- New intellectual property remuneration models (e.g., allowing the reader to set the price of a book[1])
- New packaging (perfume packaging is a critical success factor)
- New services (e.g., concierge or valet services)
- New ways to access information (e.g. ChatGPT that challenges the Google search engine model)
- New information databases (e.g., the OAG (Official Airline Guide) which, at one point, generated more profit publishing airline schedules than the airlines themselves)
- New ways to connect people (e.g. Facebook, LinkedIn, Instagram, etc.)
- New distribution channels (e.g., multilevel marketing, webstores)
- New image (e.g., B&O electronics or Burberry that rejuvenated and changed their positioning)
- New marketing schemes (e.g., offering special deals on mobile phones)

[1] It was the case of the previous version of this book "Winning Opportunities, proven tools for converting your projects into success (without a business plan)".

- New management approaches to improve employee motivation (e.g., implementing "Management by Opportunity"[2])
- New profit distribution schemes (e.g., adopting fair trade practices)
- New ways of making customers feel valued (e.g., providing VIP treatment for frequent flyers)
- New marketing concepts (e.g., Bestgem.com, the first website to sell diamonds on the Internet)
- New ways to reach potential customers (e.g., leveraging social networks, viral marketing)
- New consumer processes (e.g., implementing self-service check-in machines at airports and railway stations)
- New processes for innovation (e.g., utilizing the IpOp Model described in this book and mentioned by ISO 56007)
- New methods to reduce customers' hesitation to buy (e.g., retailers offering unlimited return policies)
- New strategies to cut costs (e.g., outsourcing call center services to low-cost countries)
- New organizational structures (e.g., transitioning from a product-based organization to a region-based one)
- New pricing strategies (e.g., providing last-minute deals for unsold vacation packages)
- New methods of financing products or services (e.g., crowdfunding, offering free downloadable software sponsored by adware)
- New methods for monetizing intellectual property or information (e.g., utilizing platforms like Shutterstock)
- New web applications (e.g., utilizing Upwork for subcontractor searches)
- New strategies for creating awareness (e.g., collaborating with patients' associations to inform about new medical treatments)
- New methods for sharing knowledge and information (e.g., utilizing websites like Patientslikeme.com)
- New tactics for increasing brand loyalty (e.g., implementing a closed architecture like Microsoft Windows)

[2] See Chaps. 21 and 22.

- New ways to enhance customers' convenience (e.g., offering ID or passport renewal by mail)
- New ways of interacting (e.g., teleworking, videoconferencing)
- New types of partnerships (e.g., Nespresso subcontracting sales and distribution of pre-portioned coffee machines to household brands)
- New features for an existing product (e.g., integrating artificial intelligence into appliances), etc

As illustrated above, significant technical breakthroughs are not always necessary. Much of the technology needed for these innovations was already available. Many of these ideas are not even protected by patents; instead, they rely on the strength of their unique Activity Chain for protection. The beauty of innovation lies in its limitless nature—it is only bound by your imagination. The more people are encouraged to innovate, the more ideas will surface. The key is to grant them permission to do so.[3]

Lateral thinking can also fuel innovation. Consider how enhancing athletes' vision could enhance their performance. Someone had the insight to suggest offering laser vision correction technology to athletes: a skier with improved vision can process shapes and colors faster, gaining an advantage over competitors. This connection between sports and vision correction, a classic example of lateral thinking, not only opened up a new market for laser vision correction technology but also enhanced athletes' performance. Making this link did not require technology skills—anyone could have done it.

Expanding an existing concept to other areas can create intriguing Opportunities. For example, leveraging peer-to-peer (P2P) networks introduced a fresh approach to finding and reserving hotel rooms or car rentals without relying on a central portal or reservation system. The Internet has already revolutionized the travel industry and many others by enabling price comparison and dynamic pricing. Similarly, peer-to-peer IP telephony services like Skype or WhatsApp have significantly reshaped the telecommunications landscape and business model.

[3] See Chap. 22.

All this illustrates that Opportunities are accessible to anyone open to new (and sometimes seemingly wild) ideas. Employing viral marketing might have seemed unconventional, yet it proved highly successful for companies like ICQ and Hotmail two decades ago. Now, TikTok has become the latest viral sensation. The true secret lies in the capacity to question everything and, most importantly, to recognize the underlying opportunity, especially one that others have not noticed. Nobody is immune to the innovation bug. We are all at liberty to explore opportunities and identify... Opportunities (PND + Solution).

Patents are not crucial for gaining a Competitive Advantage, though they do help establish protective barriers to entry. Non-tech innovation is seldom safeguarded by patents. In fact, it is relatively easy to replicate most non-tech innovations, especially the visible ones. Consider Amazon.com: anyone could mimic its website in a short time, but Amazon's Activity Chain extends beyond its website to encompass its brand, logistics system, product selection, marketing strategies, and more.

Copying a complete Activity Chain is more challenging than replicating just its visible components. While the visible part can be easily copied, it is best if it represents only the tip of the iceberg. The underlying mechanism that binds the various components together is harder to replicate. Therefore, for enhanced protection, it is advisable to build a complex Activity Chain.

As of a 2024 perspective, here are some innovations from Nespresso Classic:

The Nespresso Club

Nespresso states that "the Nespresso Club is an exclusive global community where we cultivate human connections, united by a shared coffee passion and desire to share elevated benefits from simple pleasures to money can't buy unforgettable experiences with our members. Nespresso takes pride in fostering these direct human connections to drive personalized experiences across the Nespresso ecosystem. Underlied within the Club, is Nespresso's foundational innovative spirit and pursuit of the highest quality experience from bean to cup."

This unique and dynamic Club enables the company to establish privileged and direct relationships with its more than 20 million members through three interactive channels: Its online e-commerce platform (www.nespresso.com), its global boutique network of more than 790 boutiques and its international network of customer care centers. Through these channels, Club members can access a wide range of information, advice and tailored services around the whole Nespresso experience, as well as a variety of other benefits and exclusive offers including early access to product launches. Consumers can expect a high level of service and purchased products are automatically shipped to the Club Member's preferred home or office address within 48 hours.

This is one of the innovations that has played a transformative role in the global coffee culture. The idea of this unique community of coffee lovers is a completely novel one and the total mastery of customer relations it provides permits Nespresso to offer first-class service at all times while developing personal connections.

Every purchaser of a Nespresso machine automatically becomes a member of the Nespresso Club.

The Nespresso Club exists all over the world, supported by a dedicated Customer Relationship Center. Open 24 h a day, 7 days a week, the Customer Relationship Center is always available for its members' comments and suggestions. It offers a personalized service, acts as an information centre on varieties of coffee, and provides advice on the use and maintenance of the machines. In so doing it establishes a direct human connection with consumers and at the same time obtains valuable information about them. The underlying principles are comfort and ease of use.

A single producer

Although sold under the brand names of four domestic appliance manufacturers, all the machines are in fact designed by Nespresso engineers and have, until 2010, been manufactured by a single company.

The idea of putting the sale of Nespresso machines in the hands of domestic appliance manufacturers through their own networks and under their own trademarks is a further non-technological innovation that has enabled the company to penetrate the market very rapidly.

Nespresso's control of both the machines and consumables represents a further innovative (and above all non-technological!) approach, while yet another is its business model based on partnerships with the manufacturers promoting the brand, the "machine partners".

A luxury product

Yet another non-technological innovation is the high-end positioning of the Nespresso brand, elevating coffee routine into a luxurious ritual thanks to uncompromising quality, high precision and quest for excellence redolent of Swiss watch industry standards. There are very few food products that are graced with a promotion worthy of luxury goods...

This high-end positioning is reinforced by a resolutely avant-garde and elevated design: The new "rounded" look introduced in 2001 revolutionized the appearance of the old chunky appliance-looking coffee machines, and with yet another innovation, the water tank became visible.

The advent of Nespresso machines in domestic appliance stores was an enlivening event. The idea of demonstrating the machines in the sales outlets (shop in shop) is yet another non-technological innovation.

The boutiques

The Nespresso boutiques worldwide offer customers more than just a shopping experience. They provide an exclusive and sophisticated environment where customers can discover, learn, and share their passion for fine coffee, food, lifestyle, and sustainability. These stylish and premium spaces bring together like-minded individuals who appreciate the finer things in life.

The Nespresso boutique concept has been evolving over the years to meet every possible customer need. The latest concept introduced in 2023, offers interactive experiences such as masterclasses where customers can immerse themselves in the world of coffee, learning about different beans and recipes.

Nespresso's new offering aims to share its coffee universe in a unique and distinctive way. The boutiques strike a balance between modern aesthetics and spacious areas, creating a warm and inviting atmosphere that encourages customers to explore and engage with the brand's ecosystem. Coffee tastings, Masterclasses, products personalization are all part of the experience.

The growth of Nespresso boutiques is a testament to their success. From just one retail location in 2000, there were nearly 800 boutiques around the world by the end of 2023. This expansion allows coffee lovers from all over the globe to indulge in Nespresso's ultimate coffee experiences. Each boutique also incorporates authentic design elements created by local artists, giving each store a unique and localized feel.

The decision to establish a chain of boutiques resembling luxury stores to sell an everyday consumer product is a bold and innovative move. It showcases Nespresso's commitment to delivering exceptional and unparalleled experiences for its customers.

A solid technological base

These non-technological innovations—and they are not the only ones—complement a number of technological innovations, for example:

- The use of pre-portioned aluminum capsules offering a storage period of up to 12 months (whereas ground coffee already begins to lose its flavor a few hours after exposure to air)
- The use of nitrogen to preclude all contact with the oxygen in the air, which very rapidly oxidizes the coffee

- The introduction in 2001 of the automatic capsule ejector, representing a fundamental break with the symbolic gesture associated with traditional espresso coffee machines (given that it is no longer necessary to screw the capsule holder onto the base)
- Complete mastery of the water temperature and pressure by a "thermoblock", a high-precision system controlled by a thermostat. This element assures that the water is poured onto the coffee at the ideal temperature, guaranteeing the flavor, milk froth, etc.

Once the pre-dosed coffee market was seen to be lucrative, other manufacturers jumped on the bandwagon. Nespresso however focuses on keeping its promise: cultivating coffee as an art and offering the highest quality, sustainable coffee to its customers.

As this book focuses on the initial Nespresso classic offering, it does not talk about latest innovations and developments, such as:

- Vertuo system with Centrifusion technology
- compostable capsules introduced in 2023

History of latest news about Nespresso is available on https://nestle-nespresso.com/latest-stories

Link with ISO 56007 (Tools and methods for managing opportunities and ideas — Guidance)

Sections 4.2 and 4.3 of ISO 56007 offer valuable guidance on identifying ideas and opportunities. Annexes A and C2 also provide concrete tools for this purpose.

The IpOp Model, on the other hand, is not intended to aid in finding ideas and opportunities. Its relevance lies in the subsequent step, once an 'apparent opportunity' has been identified and you're ready to explore it further.

The purpose of this chapter is purely inspirational. It aims to demonstrate to readers that:

- There exists a multitude of non- or low-tech innovations
- Non-tech or low-tech innovation is attainable for anyone with an open mind
- Adopting a mindset focused on seeking low-tech opportunities is valuable and worth cultivating

4

Think Carefully Before You Commit

Opportunities Are Like a Marriage

Take-Home of This Chapter

This chapter outlines the importance of conducting pre-project analysis to avoid wasting resources on projects that may not be successful. It explains how the IpOp Model helps to screen ideas and have a realistic view of the required effort before allocating substantial resources. It introduces the concept of the four IpOp Reviews, which serve as a decision-making process to assess the feasibility and potential of an Opportunity. The chapter emphasizes the need for iterations and the Quick and Dirty approach to gather information and refine answers to key questions. It also highlights the role of Unknowns or uncertainties. The IpOp Model can be used to implement the recommendations of ISO 56007 that stresses the need to identify and catalog uncertainties but without explaining how. A rigorous management of all uncertainties/Unknowns optimizes the use of resources.

As an entrepreneur or intrapreneur, it is crucial to evaluate your opportunity with the same rigor as an investor or decision-maker. Why? Because ultimately, you are a decision-maker too! Pursuing an opportunity will require allocating your own time and resources. Choosing the wrong opportunity could result in a costly waste of those resources, aside from the learning experience it provides.

R. H Cohen, *Pre-Project Excellence*, Future of Business and Finance,
https://doi.org/10.1007/978-3-031-61774-4_4

Always keep the concept of opportunity cost in mind. This means understanding that committing to one opportunity means forgoing other potentially more rewarding opportunities in the future. The cost of this commitment is the loss of the benefits from those missed opportunities. Therefore, it's essential to make informed decisions to avoid regretting later that you did not choose the best opportunity available.

Think of it like marriage: when you commit to a spouse, you (normally!) give up the possibility of being with other potential partners. Similarly, committing to an opportunity means sacrificing other potential opportunities. Just as you would carefully consider before getting married, it is imperative to think before committing to an Opportunity.

4.1 The 4 IpOp Reviews

Smart decision-makers streamline their decision-making process to minimize wastage of time and resources. Through years of observation, I have concluded that the most effective approach involves using four key questions at the pre-project stage. I have labeled each question a "Review" because, unlike a stage or phase-gate, a positive outcome of a Review merely indicates a temporary green light for further exploration. Each "yes" prompts a revisit during subsequent iterations, while a "no" is final and signals "game over." Once a "No-Go" is reached, exploration can cease immediately.

The first IpOp Review centers on hope. The question to ask is: "Is there any hope for this Opportunity?" This means assessing whether the opportunity aligns with the company's or investor's objectives and whether the offering is compelling enough for customers to adopt it.

No buy-in equals no deal: if no customers are interested in purchasing your offering, and/or you cannot secure buy-in from investors or company decision-makers, then there is obviously no hope for that Opportunity. In such a scenario, it is best not to invest any more time in it. However, receiving confirmation that there is indeed hope grants you permission to proceed to the next Review.

The second IpOp Review assesses whether It Is worth It. This involves comparing the outcome (the "prize") with the efforts required to attain it.

If the outcome is deemed not worth the effort, it doesn't make sense to proceed with the Opportunity. However, if the Opportunity is considered worthwhile, you can proceed to the next Review.

The third IpOp Review focuses on analyzing the Influencers to determine if you can navigate the Factors and Stakeholders that may positively or negatively impact your ability to obtain the "prize." If the project is deemed too risky or faces insurmountable obstacles, it might be best to abandon it at this stage. Once you are comfortable with the Influencers, you can move on to the next Review.

The fourth IpOp Review ensures that your two Action Plans—one for reducing uncertainties/Unknowns and one for delivering the "prize"—and their associated investments are convincing. Without positive responses to the first three IpOp Reviews, it wouldn't make sense to spend time on "how" to exploit the Opportunity, "who" will do it, and "how much" needs to be invested (this constitutes the Investment or the Resources). Obtaining a positive answer to the first three Reviews will require you to assess the feasibility of the Action Plans.

Once you are convinced that the two Action Plans will deliver the expected prize from an Investment you are comfortable with, then you can give the green light to proceed with the implementation of the project. At this point, you transition from pre-project mode to project-management mode.

Given that the answer to any of these IpOp Review questions is never clear-cut, it is crucial to exercise judgment. Understanding the underlying logic of each IpOp Review is critical for making informed decisions. The following chapters will provide a step-by-step explanation of what needs to be understood in order to provide a useful answer to each of these fundamental questions.

Iterate to Mature the Opportunity **The findings of each IpOp Review are akin to shifting sands—constantly evolving** due to the influence of subsequent IpOp Reviews. Given the inherent complexity of each project, it is crucial to acknowledge that all parameters are interconnected. For instance, altering the distribution channel can impact customers' perception, while changing a product's image might necessitate adjustments to its distribution channel, and so forth.

Iterations are indispensable because the answer derived from each question in the IpOp Review process is susceptible to being challenged by the outcome of subsequent Reviews. For example, consider a product initially intended for sale in supermarkets, which successfully passes IpOp Review 1 (indicating hope of obtaining buy-in). However, during IpOp Review 3 (Influencers), it is discovered that a competitor has secured an exclusivity deal, limiting access to that distribution channel. In light of this new finding, there is no choice but to revisit IpOp Review 1 and adjust the chosen distribution channel to accommodate this new parameter. This underscores the iterative nature of the IpOp Model, emphasizing its adaptability over a linear phase-gate approach (Fig. 4.1).

Before allocating resources to a project and once the multiple iterations have been completed, investors and decision-makers will apply a more detailed decision-making process than the four basic IpOp Reviews. While the IpOp Reviews provide valuable insights, they may be too high-level to reliably inform a well-thought-out decision. Therefore, additional information is necessary for making informed decisions. The more comprehensive decision-making process used by investors and decision-makers will be elaborated upon in Chap. 19.

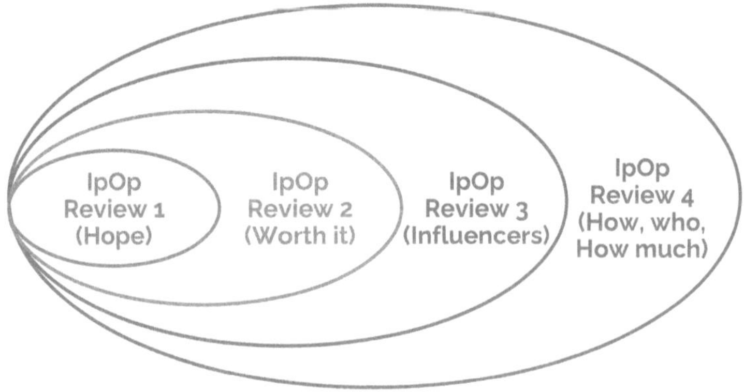

Fig. 4.1 The IpOp Reviews iterative process

4.2 No More Waste of Resources

The primary advantage of the four sequential IpOp Reviews is their ability to minimize resource wastage by preventing the launch of projects that should never have commenced. Avoiding resource wastage is crucial for both individuals and organizations (Fig. 4.2). This objective is relevant not only to innovation-related projects but also to any project or undertaking.

The four IpOp Reviews should in fact be applied to assess every project, regardless of its level of innovation. Many Project Management Offices (PMOs) within large organizations effectively utilize the IpOp Model as a filtering mechanism to weed out projects that should not proceed. This approach enables them to focus on projects that offer the

Fig. 4.2 Graphic representation of the 4 IpOp Reviews

most value, while also reducing their workload and enabling them to deliver better projects with less stress.

A rigorous selection process for projects is crucial to avoid burdening the workforce with too many initiatives, which can hinder their ability to perform effectively.

Killing weak Opportunities as early as possible is an obligation, given that it has been demonstrated that some 30% of projects never achieve completion and that only 12% are delivered on time and according to budget. The resources allocated to these unsuccessful projects represent a huge waste that could be significantly reduced by a more efficient selection process at the pre-project stage.

The IpOp Reviews sequence can also serve as a valuable tool for managing the ideation or conceptualization process. Some organizations, such as those in research and development (R&D), require innovators to first demonstrate that there is hope for their idea before allocating additional resources. Even scientists and engineers can conduct preliminary research to assess whether their idea or project has potential in the market and aligns with the company's strategy. They do not necessarily need expertise in marketing or corporate strategy to address the hope question posed in IpOp Review 1. Even if their initial assessment is incorrect, engaging in the process and facilitating discussions around it can help them develop a more client-centered approach and better alignment with the corporate strategy over time.

Exploring IpOp Review 1 ("Is there hope?") will never be detrimental. In fact, it can only yield positive and valuable insights, aiding tech-savvy individuals in gaining business acumen. This holds true even if the outcome reveals that there is no hope for a particular idea, as it signifies that further investment of time should be halted. Moreover, it fosters openness and readiness to explore alternative opportunities, considering the opportunity cost involved.

IpOp Review 1 thus acts as an initial filter once an Opportunity is identified. Only after demonstrating some "hope" should the question of whether it is worth pursuing (IpOp Review 2) be addressed. Since Review 2 typically requires more advanced business skills, it may be beneficial to supplement the R&D team with individuals experienced in financial projections and business models.

4.3 The Benefits of Being Quick and... Dirty

The main challenge is determining the appropriate depth of analysis for each IpOp Review and iteration, essentially deciding how thoroughly you want to explore. To save time, you can begin by making certain assumptions to offer preliminary answers to the key questions. This "Quick and Dirty"[1] approach provides an initial overview of the answers, which can then be refined in subsequent iterations.

Organizations seeking to optimize resource utilization often employ the "Quick and Dirty" approach to screen ideas before committing significant resources. Rather than diving straight into rapid prototyping or market testing, they initially ask inventors or intrapreneurs to spend a few hours going through the four IpOp Reviews in "Quick and Dirty" mode. This allows everyone to gauge the level of hope—IpOp Review 1—as well as gain some insight into the answers to the other Reviews.

The key to an effective "Quick and Dirty" approach is ensuring that each iteration maintains clarity regarding assumptions and areas of uncertainty. It requires disciplined cataloging of every missing piece of information, labeled as an "Unknown[2]" in the IpOp Model. Despite the challenge of acknowledging—and documenting—what is not known, it becomes clear that doing so is essential for progress.

Link with ISO 56007 (Tools and Methods for Managing Opportunities and Ideas: Guidance)

ISO 56007 also emphasizes the need to iterate the analysis.

ISO 56007 does not specifically use the concept of reviews like the IpOp Model but the Decision Tree and the template for the innovation concept case presented in the ISO 56007 annexes both mention the four IpOp Model Reviews.

---

[1] http://en.wikipedia.org/wiki/Quick-and-dirty.

[2] Unknowns will be described in Chap. 5.

5

Unknowns Are Your Best Friends

All Projects Have Uncertainties

Take-Home of This Chapter

This chapter provides a practical framework for managing uncertainties and implementing projects successfully, which aligns with the principles outlined in ISO 56007. It explains the process of assessing the effort required to reduce the uncertainty of Opportunities or projects. The first step involves identifying as many Unknowns/uncertainties as possible at the pre-project stage. The IpOp Model has been designed as a step-by-step process to facilitate the identification and prioritization of Unknowns, which are not to be confused with Risks. The list of Unknowns can then be used to calibrate the effort (time, money, and skills) required to reduce the level of uncertainty of the project. This chapter emphasizes the importance of drafting an Opportunity Case to demonstrate the merits of the Opportunity and obtain necessary Resources. It also highlights the need for two Action Plans, one outlining Tactical Moves for reducing critical Unknowns and a second one for delivering the Definition of Success. The process involves obtaining conditional buy-in from Decision-makers and Investors, spending Resources to reduce critical Unknowns, and obtaining later a final green light to launch the project. Since ISO 56007 recommends to catalog uncertainties as early as possible but does not explain how to identify them, the IpOp Model appears to be a very useful complement for operationalizing ISO 56007's recommendations.

R. H Cohen, *Pre-Project Excellence*, Future of Business and Finance,
https://doi.org/10.1007/978-3-031-61774-4_5

Every project inevitably harbors uncertainties. By minimizing our ignorance about any open issues/Unknowns present, we enhance our chances of success. It is unrealistic to expect to navigate in a completely predictable environment. Until a product has been fine-tuned and prepared for mass production, a certain level of open issues can for instance persist regarding its commercialization. Therefore, managing Unknowns is essential in both pre-project and project management.

Shareholders, investors, and lenders all despise Unknowns because they loathe uncertainty. Your credibility will significantly rise if you demonstrate to Decision-makers that you have thoroughly researched and are transparent about what you do not know. Including Unknowns in your presentation to Decision-makers is therefore warranted. It facilitates an informed decision by all parties involved, including yourself, as everyone can then assess the consequences of missing information or knowledge. Moreover, reducing the level of uncertainty will also enhance your ability to clarify your Definition of Success.[1]

Unfortunately, Unknowns are rarely explicitly outlined in a business plan. Surprisingly, few Decision-makers even inquire about them! Even innovators or project developers often neglect to catalog open issues, assuming they are already familiar with them. However, they later realize that overlooking an uncertainty at the right time can be a costly mistake. For example, numerous parameters can influence chemical reactions. As a result, producing a chemical compound in large containers may yield different outcomes compared to those observed in a laboratory pilot study. The potential transition from a laboratory pilot to industrial production exemplifies an Unknown that requires attention. It is crucial to account for this disparity when planning for production.

5.1 Many Unknowns Are Hidden

We tend not to like Unknowns. They are sometimes viewed as enemies to a project, and ideally there should be as few of them as possible. However, it's crucial not to overlook or conceal them, as this can lead to unforeseen complications down the line.

[1] See Chap. 11.

A common tactic is to portray Unknowns as risks. For example, it is often seen in lists like "the risk of sales falling below projections due to the product being too expensive or other factors". This simply indicates that the author lacks adequate understanding of the customer and/or market to confidently assess the product's attractiveness. Otherwise, there would be no doubt, and this supposed "risk" would not even be mentioned.

The main difference between Unknowns and Risk Factors[2] is that it is possible to reduce the level of ignorance (by testing, for example), whereas risks cannot be tested. What you do not know but could verify, at least partially, belongs to the realm of Unknowns. By definition, an Unknown is information that is or could possibly be available but which you do not (yet) have.

A key aspect of Risks is that each has a certain chance of happening. Unknowns, on the other hand, don't have a chance of occurring because they represent missing information, which is a definite fact. Sometimes, what might be uncertain and have a probability is whether we can find the information we lack.

The significant disparity between risks that are essentially unaddressed Unknowns and the Risks outlined in Chap. 12 is that the former arise solely because you have opted not to acquire the necessary information to mitigate certain critical Unknowns. In contrast, Risks cannot be mitigated through information gathering; their existence is beyond your control, and you cannot eliminate them. Instead, you can only implement suitable Tactical Moves to minimize their impact on your project. However, several Tactical Moves can be employed to reduce and potentially eliminate Unknowns. In the case of Risks, you are merely affected by them (and can only reduce their impact), while with Unknowns, you bear the responsibility for choosing to remain uninformed.

When making assumptions, you are essentially acknowledging the absence of certain information. If you had all the necessary knowledge, you would not need to make assumptions. The existence of doubt or assumptions signifies an Unknown. Assumptions in spreadsheets are often where hidden Unknowns can be found.

---

[2] For more information about Factors see Chap. 12.

Whenever a pilot, test, prototype, survey, or study is proposed, it indicates the presence of one or more Unknowns that require attention. The objective of any of these actions or their equivalent is to gather missing information, thereby reducing ignorance and the number of Unknowns. The very fact of including these Tactical Moves in the list of things to do implies the existence of Unknowns. But it is not sufficient to imply the existence of Unknowns: they also need to be clearly identified as such.

Since Unknowns cast doubt in the minds of Decision-makers, many entrepreneurs avoid bringing them to their attention lest they scare them away. This tactic may succeed initially, provided the investor or Decision-maker does not see through the ruse. However, once they realize the lack of transparency, trust in the entrepreneur diminishes. Sacrificing credibility for the sake of appearing clever comes at a steep cost.

5.2 Why Unknowns Are Your Best Friends

Unknowns are akin to blind spots in a car; awareness of their existence is crucial. While a car typically has only one main blind spot, a project may have numerous Unknowns, any one of which could lead to a crash if ignored.

Disregarding even a single Unknown can mean a death sentence for your project, making it imperative that you acknowledge and address all of them. Recognizing the limits of your knowledge will highlight potential obstacles and suggest ways to reduce your ignorance.

The more Unknowns there are, the less reliable the analysis of a project. Assuming all Unknowns have an equal impact, a project with many Unknowns is more precarious than one with fewer Unknowns. Conversely, fewer Unknowns inspire greater confidence. It cannot be stressed enough: identifying Unknowns is absolutely critical to assess the reliability of the analysis of the project.

To evaluate the reliability of the analyses presented to them, Decision-makers should always inquire about the number of critical Unknowns that still exist at this point in the analysis. No project evaluation should proceed without full knowledge of the corresponding

Unknowns identifiable at that moment. Making decisions without acknowledging the assumptions involved or the level of ignorance of the entrepreneurs/intrapreneurs presenting the project is very dangerous. Decision-makers should DEMAND to receive the list of Unknowns associated with any project proposal. This not only enables them to gauge the reliability of the presentation's information but also reveals whether the entrepreneurs/intrapreneurs have diligently assessed their own ignorance and are forthright in disclosing it.

Unknowns are your best friends because they help you make better decisions. As the primary Decision-maker of your project, they help you in assessing more clearly whether it is worth pursuing before presenting it to investors or Decision-makers. Embracing Unknowns also facilitates constructive discussions with investors, who can provide initial resources to address the most critical ones.[3] Moreover, they are your best friends because they contribute to your credibility, highlighting your transparency and commitment to thorough evaluation.

I recommend actively seeking out Unknowns rather than attempting to conceal them, as this knowledge will ultimately prevent potential pitfalls in the future. The more Unknowns are acknowledged, the clearer your project's parameters become, aiding both Investors or Decision-makers and yourself in making informed decisions.

Decision-makers greatly appreciate receiving a comprehensive list of Unknowns.[4] Presenting what requires further investigation boosts their confidence in the project, as it offers transparency about potential uncertainty. Without a thorough catalog of Unknowns, they lack the necessary information to make a sound judgment on the project's viability.

5.3 To Go or Not to Go, That Is The Question

Evaluating a project without being aware of its Unknowns is suicidal because it is impossible to gauge the reliability of our understanding about the project. For instance, consider a scenario where you plan to

---

[3] See below step 5 in "The Process from idea to launch".

[4] See Table 5.1

launch a service delivering meals to partygoers between 10 pm and 5 am. You might argue that there is a demand for such a service because many people get hungry during late-night hours. However, presenting this justification without acknowledging that it is merely an opinion (an Unknown) would be misleading. To address this Unknown, you should investigate how many partygoers would actually order food during late-night hours and how much they would be willing to pay for the service. Failing to do so could lead to the unpleasant surprise of discovering that the market is too small after investing in launching the service. By explicitly acknowledging this Unknown, Decision-makers (including yourself) can decide whether to rely on the initial assumption or to fund a market study to validate the market size. Ignoring Unknowns can thus jeopardize the project's success, especially when resolving them is crucial.

Some Unknowns eventually serve as Go/No-Go criteria. For example, to open a new restaurant you must find a suitable building in the right neighborhood. The availability and cost of such a place would be typical Unknowns. A No-Go criterion might be a higher rent than what you can afford or the lack of a suitable location. To reduce your level of ignorance you would check market conditions and the availability of an appropriate place (Tactical Moves to reduce this Unknown[5]).

The effort/resources required to reduce the critical Unknowns represent the price you pay for peace of mind. If you want to be on the safe side, you should allocate the necessary resources to reduce those Unknowns before committing to the project's launch. However, if you choose not to invest in reducing those Unknowns, you have two options: either abandon the opportunity or rely on intuition and...luck.

Cutting corners on the resources needed to address critical Unknowns increases the likelihood of your project's failure. Therefore, the decision involves striking a balance between resource allocation and accepting a certain level of ignorance, recognizing that embracing ignorance heightens project vulnerability.

Dangerous Unknowns persist solely due to your actions, or rather, inaction.

---

[5] See Chap. 14.

5.4 From Idea to Launch—The Process

To the greatest extent possible, the Go/No-Go criteria should be verified before launching the project. Indeed, identifying these criteria will assist in determining which Tactical Moves are necessary to secure the final approval. Their objective is to mitigate the critical Unknowns that are most likely to significantly influence the project's outcome.

As endorsed by ISO 56007, the recommended practice is to follow the following process from the initial idea conception through to the green light for project launch (see Figs. 5.1 and 5.2 below):

1. Once you have identified the opportunity (Pain/Need/Desire(s) and the corresponding Solution), a Quick and Dirty early-stage evaluation can prevent the waste of time and resources on an unviable Opportunity.
2. If step 1 provides encouraging results, analyze the opportunity with the IpOp Model to identify.
   (a) the critical Unknowns, those that are Go/No-Go criteria,
   (b) the Tactical Moves to lessen the critical Unknowns and the necessary resources needed to do so,

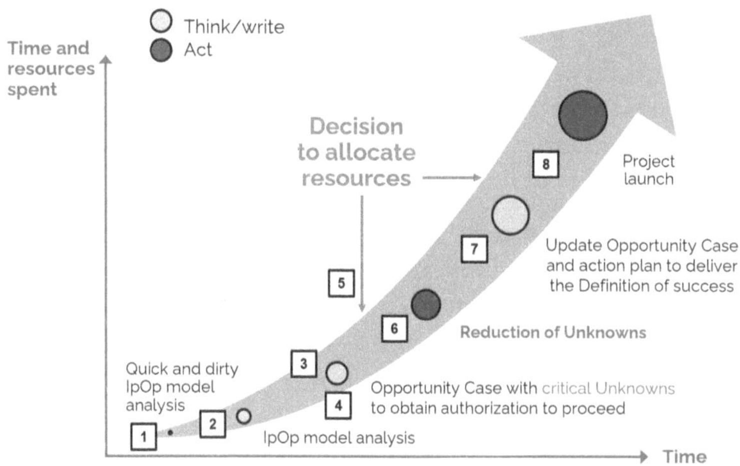

Fig. 5.1 Detailed process from idea to launch

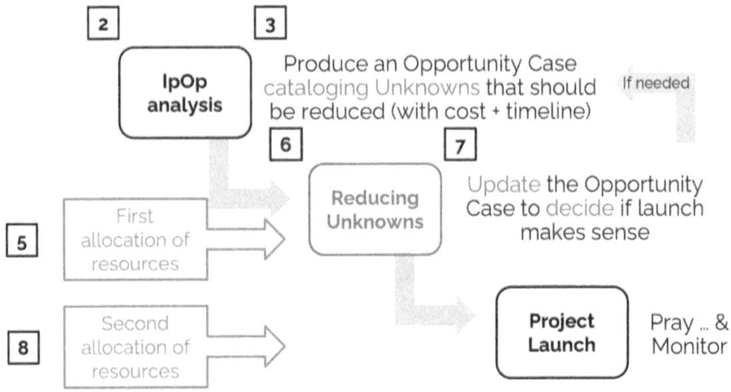

Fig. 5.2 Simplified process from idea to launch

(c) additional Tactical Moves to achieve the Definition of Success,[6]

The IpOp Model focuses on identifying, not reducing, Unknowns. This step should take no more than a few hours, as the lengthy part is reducing the Unknowns (step 6 below), not merely spotting them.

3. Drafting and presenting an Opportunity Case[7] with three objectives:

    (a) To demonstrate the merits of the Opportunity (why it should be seized)
    (b) To obtain what you want and/or need (investment, authorizations, etc.) provided you can reduce the critical Unknowns that bother the Decision-makers
    (c) To obtain the corresponding resources for reducing the Unknowns. A specific Action Plan for the reduction of Unknowns should be included in your Opportunity Case

Presenting the Opportunity Case aims to secure a conditional buy-in from investors or Decision-makers (step 5 below), whereby the understanding is to proceed only once critical Unknowns have been satisfactorily reduced (see steps 6 to 8). Additionally, a convincing Implementation plan may be required (step 4) as an extra condition.

[6] See Chap. 11.

[7] See Chap. 20.

4. Possibly drafting and presenting the main Implementation or Action Plan[8] describing how the opportunity will be implemented. This plan essentially outlines the "To Do" list. Including Tactical Moves for delivering the Definition of Success (identified in 2c above), while also considering feedback from Decision-makers after step 3.
5. Obtain the necessary resources to reduce critical Unknowns. These resources will only be allocated if the content of the Opportunity Case is convincing enough. This represents a conditional green light to the project, contingent upon the satisfactory reduction of Unknowns.
6. Allocate the resources (3c) to act and execute any Tactical Moves required to reduce critical Unknowns. Collecting information should be a controlled process with real customized phase-gates (Go/No-Go moments) to stop the project if necessary. These gates should be tailored for each project rather than being "one size fits all" as is often the case with a standardized stage-gate approach.[9]
7. Revisit the IpOp Model (step 2 above) with the information obtained in step 6 to update
   (a) the Opportunity Case (step 3)
   (b) the main Action Plan (step 4) that may also include Tactical Moves to reduce any remaining Unknowns that are not critical
8. Final green light to launch the project, provided that the critical Unknowns have been sufficiently reduced to reassure Decision-makers and Investors to allocate the required resources and authorizations for proceeding. The conditional buy-in obtained in step 3 above can now transition into a final green light to launch the project and implement your Action Plan.[10]

A simplified way to show this process is shown in Fig. 5.2:

The biggest advantage of this process is that resources are only utilized (step 6) after identifying the key success parameters (steps 1 to 4).

[8] See Chap. 15.

[9] See http://en.wikipedia.org/wiki/New_product_development.

[10] See Chap. 15.

This counters the prevailing trend of lean innovation[11] or early-stage rapid prototyping,[12] which encourage entrepreneurs to act swiftly. While there are numerous benefits to early action, the main drawback is that any action consumes resources (including your time). Another concern with early action is the opportunity cost[13]: committing to building a prototype or other early-stage Tactical Moves may hinder your ability to capitalize on potentially superior future opportunities.

It is useless to start spending resources to discover at a later stage (or gate) that there are one or more parameters that can kill the opportunity. In many cases, those Opportunity-killers could have been identified much earlier. For example, why invest in building a prototype if you later realize that market penetration is too challenging, the price point is unfavorable, or your project will alienate key influencers[14] within the organization? It is far wiser to first map out all potential parameters during the pre-project stage (such as pricing acceptability, access to distribution channels, or internal Stakeholder resistance) and make a comprehensive assessment before taking action. This holistic evaluation (step 2) might reveal that before building a prototype (which aims to reduce just one Unknown), there are other Unknowns that should be addressed.

5.5 Cataloging Unknowns

Early Cataloging marks the initial phase of addressing Unknowns. Once again, brainstorming serves as an effective starting point for identifying as many Unknowns as possible. Whenever uncertainty arises regarding a question posed by the IpOp Model, consider it an Unknown that must be addressed eventually. For example, if there is uncertainty about correctly identifying a certain Stakeholder's Aspirations, you should treat it as an unknown that requires attention. The IpOp Model has been designed as a tool for identifying Unknowns (Fig 5.3)

[11] See http://en.wikipedia.org/wiki/Lean_startup.

[12] Such as http://en.wikipedia.org/wiki/Rapid_prototyping.

[13] See the beginning of Chap. 4.

[14] They are Stakeholders as explained in Chap. 13.

Fig. 5.3 The 4 IpOp Reviews with Unknowns

Cataloging Unknowns often facilitates the identification of Tactical Moves, which are subsequently implemented to reduce the level of uncertainty. Like other parameters, potential Tactical Moves should be recorded in a list. As indicated above, a fundamental benefit of cataloging Unknowns is that it enhances the development of a more effective Action Plan for reducing them.

The sequence in which Unknowns are addressed significantly influences the efficient allocation of resources. For example, since securing customer buy-in is crucial for project success, it is unwise to invest in building a costly prototype before confirming customer interest in the product. When confirming customer buy-in requires fewer resources than developing an actual prototype, it's smarter to begin with market research and proceed to prototype development only after customer interest has been confirmed.

To minimize costs and effectively reduce Unknowns, it is essential to catalog all potential Unknowns or, at the very least, those that are identifiable. Only when this inventory is comprehensive can you determine the most logical sequence for addressing critical Unknowns while conserving resources. Uncovering critical Unknowns later in the process that could have been identified earlier through more thorough preparation may hinder optimal reduction efforts. Additionally, it hampers the realistic assessment and allocation of resources required for step 6 above.

The task of cataloging unknowns begins with identifying them. Given the difficulty of recognizing what you do not know, many people tend to accept their beliefs as facts. In other words, they make assumptions without realizing these are merely assumptions and not verified, reliable facts. The IpOp Tools[15] software assists in overcoming this obstacle.

Unknowns typically fall into seven categories, each with its corresponding set of questions:

Technological Unknowns:

- Will the product perform consistently as expected?
- Can you manufacture an industrial product economically?
- Will you be able to scale up production and delivery?
- What will be the environmental impact of the product or its production?
- Etc

Market-related Unknowns:

- Who will benefit and who will buy?
- At what price?
- How many people would be prepared to pay the price your Definition of Success requires?
- With what performance and Customer's Decision Criteria?
- How can you reach customers?
- Can you handle the compliance requirements?
- Etc

[15] See Chap. 18

Stakeholders Unknowns:

- Do you know all of your Stakeholders' Aspirations?
- Have you identified all of your Stakeholders' Resistances?
- Have you cataloged every one of the Constraints expected by your Stakeholders?
- Are you sure to know all the Decision-makers' criteria for selecting a Project?

Organizational Unknowns (these particularly affect intrapreneurs):

- Will you be able to defuse internal organizational resistance?
- Will you be able to build your "dream team"?
- What processes should be changed to implement this project?
- Etc

Resource Unknowns:

- What resources do you need for reducing critical Unknowns?
- What resources do you need for the Action Plan to deliver the Definition of Success?
- Can you obtain the necessary resources, and will they be available when you need them?
- Etc

Regulatory Unknowns

- Do you need a license to do what you intend to do?
- What are the conditions for obtaining such a license?
- In terms of I.P.[16] do you have the freedom to operate?
- What are the regulatory constraints?
- Etc

[16] Intellectual Property.

Network Unknowns

- Do you have access to the network of experts that you need?
- Do you have access to influential government officials?
- Do you have a good enough rapport with the key players in the distribution sector?
- Etc

Teamwork pays. Due to the diverse types of Unknowns, it is rare for a single individual to possess all the skills necessary to reduce the level of uncertainty across the board. In this realm, multidisciplinary teams are often more effective. It is critical to assemble a team that encompasses the relevant skills needed for addressing various Unknowns.

5.6 Prioritizing Unknowns

Assessing the impact of Unknowns on your Definition of Success is crucial.[17] Understanding which Key Indicators of Success[18] are affected by each Unknown helps pinpoint those most important for your Opportunity.

Deciding which Unknowns are critical allows you to focus on those with the most impact on achieving your Definition of Success. Each Unknown should be rated on a scale within the following range (identical to the one used for rating Factors):

- **Critical**: its outcome could make or break the project. They are Go/No-Go criteria
- **Important**: it could have a major impact on the project but probably not a critical one
- **Unimportant:** its impact on the project will be only negligible

Prioritizing Unknowns is essential for optimizing resources because you usually will not have enough resources to address them all. Critical Unknowns often get overlooked because individuals tend to focus more

[17] See Chap. 11.

[18] See Chap. 11.

on areas that align with their personal interests. For instance, scientists or engineers may devote most of their time and energy (a valuable resource) to refining product characteristics, as it aligns with their preferences and training, while neglecting commercial Unknowns, for which they may lack training or interest.

5.7 Reducing the Ignorance Level

Be humble enough to recognize what you do not know. Open issues indicate a lack of knowledge, which is normal because nobody can know everything. Cataloging these Unknowns demonstrates wisdom and honesty. Every Unknown is crucial to investors. However, it is far more effective to document them in writing rather than keeping them in the back of one's mind if you want to capture them all. Be willing to recognize (and admit) what you do not know.

Cataloging Unknowns can provide insights into the Tactical Moves required to acquire missing information. While it may not always be feasible, you can often gain valuable knowledge without expending significant resources. Gathering knowledge is the bread and butter of business intelligence experts.

Breaking down each Unknown into smaller subordinate Unknowns can simplify them and make them easier to address. This approach is especially beneficial for technological Unknowns, where solving a technical issue may involve addressing several sub-problems.

Testing assumptions is often the key to reducing the level of ignorance. An effective approach is to identify inexpensive and quick Tactical Moves to test your assumptions. For example, conducting a simple survey among a small group of potential customers can provide valuable insights into their level of interest and the price they would be willing to pay. Since comprehensive investigations are usually costly and time-consuming, you may need to settle for approximations and extrapolations. However, this approach still allows you to gain more knowledge than you had before.

Pilot studies can help to come to terms with Unknowns. For instance, you may discover that scaling up production is much more challenging than initially assumed. Soldiers learned this the hard way:

chemical reactions in a cooking pot depend on the size of the pot and the amount of food in it, therefore a recipe that produces a great soup for four people is unlikely to work well if you need to feed 400 soldiers. Altitude is known to affect taste perception in airplanes, creating an Unknown for airlines. The only way to fine-tune recipes is to evaluate how each meal tastes at cruising altitude.

Design-thinking[19] *is a prime example of a very useful and effective tool for mitigating some Unknowns.* Through hypothesis testing with potential customers/users and employing rapid prototyping, it is possible to validate assumptions and learn extensively about your Customers, their Decision Criteria, or product characteristics. Since design-thinking can resolve many Unknowns in a series of sessions, cataloging all potential Unknowns beforehand as provided by the IpOp Model is crucial. This preparation helps avoid the necessity for additional design-thinking sessions to tackle unknowns discovered later.

Some may also successfully use design-thinking to identify Unknowns. Despite its benefits, design-thinking is not a standalone solution. It is a very valuable tool but cannot substitute the comprehensive approach of the IpOp Model, which covers a broader range of parameters than design-thinking alone can address.

Only 20% of the information is typically required to make 80% of the decisions. This general statement, inspired by the classic Pareto rule, holds significant implications for managing Unknowns: reducing the level of uncertainty by 20% is often sufficient to make significantly better decisions.

5.8 Measuring Unknowns

Measuring the overall effort required to reduce Unknowns is essential for determining the time, money and other Resources needed for a project. This is achieved by adding the resources (mainly time and money) required for each Tactical Move aimed at reducing critical and other main Unknowns.

[19] https://en.wikipedia.org/wiki/Design_thinking.

The list of unknowns[20] **shown in** Table 5.1 *serves as a highly effective tool for evaluating the Resources* needed to obtain missing information or knowledge. It also outlines the timing, effort and due dates associated with each Unknown. This list is one the best practices recommended by ISO 56007.

No decision to launch a project should be made without reviewing this list or an equivalent version. This list helps Decision-makers understand:

- What information or knowledge is not sufficiently reliable
- The vulnerabilities of the project
- Which Unknowns can kill the project
- What information or knowledge is missing and still needs verification
- The total expenses required to collect the information or knowledge

Table 5.1 List for evaluating the effort for reducing critical unknowns

Ref	Critical Unknowns	Impact	Tactical Move to reduce the Unknown	Out-of-pocket Expenses	Man-days	Due date	Opportunity Killer
			Total resources				

[20] The software described in Chap. 18 automatically produces this list. It also outlines the level of reliability of each section of the Opportunity Case according to the team analyzing the project.

- The total time needed to acquire the missing information and knowledge
- When all these Unknowns will have been reduced

To determine if reducing these Unknowns is worthwhile, Decision-makers should compare this information with the project's merits and the availability of resources.

5.9 Monitoring Unknowns

Like Factors, the list of Unknowns will never be exhaustive since not all Unknowns can be immediately identified. Any Unknowns that arise later can be added to the list. Additionally, Unknowns may evolve over time and vary in their relative importance. For instance, the introduction of a new ISO standard or regulation automatically generates Unknowns regarding its acceptance until you can ascertain whether your current product will remain compatible.

Unknowns must be monitored over time because the level of uncertainty will inevitably fluctuate. For some Unknowns, uncertainty may increase, while for others, it may decrease.

Managing Unknowns is a dynamic process due to the constant evolution of knowledge and situations. Priorities will also change over time. Therefore, it is essential to periodically check the status of your Unknowns and adjust your focus accordingly. Gathering information is crucial and should be consistently pursued (Fig. 5.4).

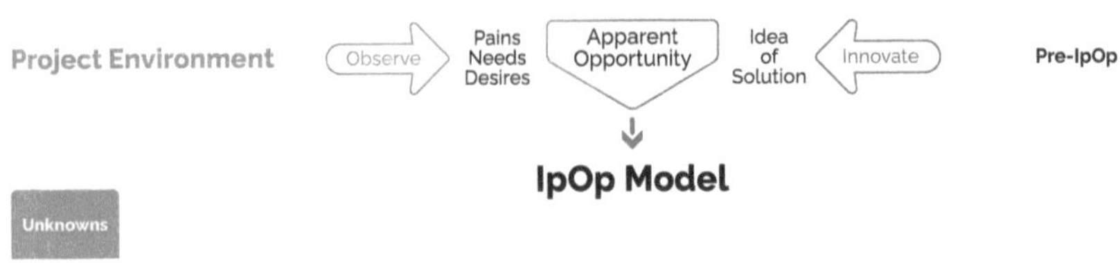

Fig. 5.4 Unknowns express the level of ignorance

Unknowns for Nespresso Classic

Unknowns	Possible Tactical Moves to reduce the level of uncertainty
Obtaining resources from head office	Prepare a good Opportunity Case[a] that minimizes risks (especially any that are liable to harm Nestlé's image)
Consumer acceptance	Market studies, focus groups, etc.
Cooperation with machine manufacturers	Sound out manufacturers
Process reliability	Endurance tests, in-house research and development, partial subcontracting
Formation of a strong team	Psychological profiles, training, team building tools, coaching, etc.

[a]See Chap. 20.

Link with ISO 56007 (Tools and Methods for Managing Opportunities and Ideas: Guidance)

As mentioned previously, Unknowns are referred to as 'uncertainties' in ISO 56007 to align with another ISO standard,[21] drafted earlier, which states that "an 'uncertainty' is a lack of knowledge or understanding across a wide range of considerations that increases the unpredictability of a desired/potential innovation". ISO standards require... standardized terminology; hence ISO 56007 adopts the same expression to denote a lack of knowledge or information.

However, the term 'uncertainty' could be interpreted as indicating a lack of knowledge, understanding, information, but also lack of predictability,[22] leading to potential confusion. Therefore, I prefer using the term 'Unknowns' to avoid this ambiguity. In addition to addressing this terminology issue And

[21] ISO 56000.

[22] I refer here to the lack of predictability of a Factor that may be triggered by an external event with a probability to happen, which is different from 'the unpredictability of a desired/potential innovation'. For a deeper analysis of the semantic differences between uncertainties and unknowns, and their respective implications, refer to "Uncertainty in innovation", Raphael H Cohen, Chapter 73 of World Encyclopedia of Entrepreneurship, second Edition", Léo Paul Dana, 2021, Edward Elgar Publishing Limited, Cheltenham.

like the IpOp Model, ISO 56007 also distinguishes between 'uncertainties' and 'risks'.[23]

Uncertainty and uncertainties are central components of ISO 56007.[24]

As expressed above for the IpOp Model, ISO 56007 also recommends[25] the early cataloging of uncertainties to identify the total resources needed to obtain missing information or knowledge. This mirrors the exact process outlined in this chapter. Since ISO standards are not supposed to be textbooks, the standard does not explain the underlying logic as is the case in this chapter. However, ISO standards are not intended to serve as textbooks, so the standard does not delve into the underlying logic as is done in this chapter.

ISO 56007 does not explicitly outline how to identify as many uncertainties as possible. Instead it suggests using the IpOp Model for this purpose.[26] Additionally, it proposes in its annexes[27] useful checklists of questions to ensure that key issues are being addressed. These checklists serve as valuable complements to the IpOp Model, which is designed as a process to identify as many Unknowns as possible during the pre-project stage. By offering practical processes for managing uncertainties in line with ISO 56007 recommendations, the IpOp Model serves as a practical or operational complement to the standard.

ISO 56007 also recommends[28] sorting uncertainties by their level of... uncertainty.[29] These levels are beneficial for evaluating the challenges confronting a project. Since exercising judgment is essential when examining any parameter related to a project, considering the level of uncertainty is an important aspect to keep in mind.

---

[23] ISO 56007, section 4.3.2.

[24] See section 4.3 in ISO 56007.

[25] ISO 56007, section 6.3.4.

[26] ISO 56007, annex B5.

[27] ISO 56007, aannex B.

[28] ISO 56007, section 4.3.4 and annexes B2 and B3.

[29] Defined in section 4.3 of ISO 56007 as "Uncertainty arises from a state of deficiency of information, understanding or knowledge that increases the unpredictability of a desired or potential outcome."

6

Fit to Be Adopted

Verifying the Investor or Corporate Fit

IpOp Review 1

Chapters 6 to 9 will guide you on how to respond to the IpOp Review 1 question: **Is there hope?**

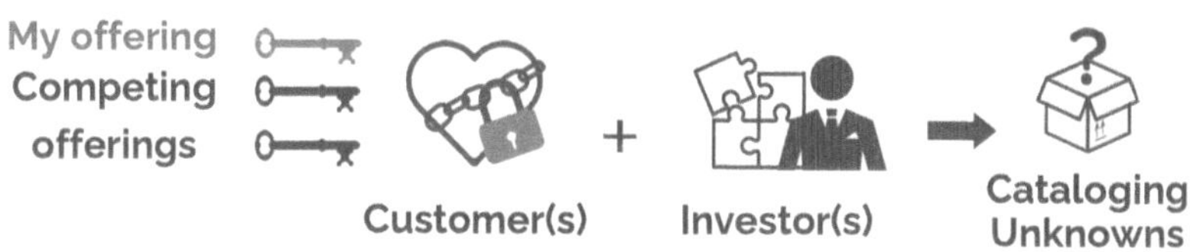

Reminder: Hope entails aligning with the company's or Investor's objectives and ensuring that the offering is compelling enough for Customers to buy-in. If Customers are not interested in purchasing your offering and/or if you cannot secure buy-in from Investors or company Decision-makers, then there is evidently no hope for this Opportunity. In such cases, it is advisable not to invest any further time in it. Conversely, if you receive confirmation that there is indeed hope, you are encouraged to proceed to the next IpOp Review.

R. H Cohen, *Pre-Project Excellence*, Future of Business and Finance,
https://doi.org/10.1007/978-3-031-61774-4_6

Take-Home of This Chapter

Since ISO 56007 recommendations include several selection criteria for ensuring company alignment, this chapter provides additional insights on the concept of Strategic or Investor fit. It stresses the importance of verifying the Strategic fit as a prerequisite for Investor buy-in and the need for the project to align with the Investor's Mission, strategy, image, and brand. The chapter also highlights the contribution of the Opportunity to the company's Key indicators of Success (KISs) and/or key performance indicators (KPIs). It suggests that organizations should establish criteria to verify if a project fits their strategy and emphasizes the need for a Mission/KPI filtering process to guide employees and encourage innovation. Failing that can hinder innovation and performance. Sharing these criteria with employees gives them permission to take initiatives that are collectively aligned with the strategy.

To secure the required support from Decision-makers, a project must be sufficiently appealing. Decision-makers may include top management of a company, venture capitalists, business angels, or even family members. However, there is one more decision-maker that should not be overlooked: yourself, the entrepreneur or intrapreneur. Even if you do not need to raise funds or obtain someone else's approval, you are still a Decision-maker because you are investing your own time and/or money. To streamline references to these various categories, I will collectively refer to them as Decision-makers or Investors.

Since this book primarily targets intrapreneurs, the focus is on the corporate world and its Decision-makers. However, the same principles apply to entrepreneurs as well. From their perspective, the crucial issue is ensuring that the opportunity they are pursuing aligns with their personal objectives and aspirations. When they are working alone, they often do this intuitively. However, as soon as they have partners, matters are likely to become more complicated, and their situation is not very different from that of intrapreneurs. To provide an entrepreneurial perspective, the words "corporate," "management," or "company" may be replaced by "personal" or "Investor."

Compatibility with the corporate Mission is also a prerequisite for maintaining organizational focus. Management must ensure that corporate resources—which are typically scarce—are used optimally to implement the corporate strategy (reminder: a primary function of managers is to optimize the use of the resources allocated to them[1]). This could become challenging when individuals pursue too many different types of opportunities simultaneously.

Employees can use a clear corporate Mission as a selection or elimination tool. Once they are confident that the Opportunity they have identified aligns with the corporate Mission, employees are more inclined to propose seizing it compared to when they are in doubt. An unclear Mission is one of the most effective ways of killing off innovation, because individuals cannot verify that their idea is relevant to the organization. However, very few companies succeed in articulating their Mission clearly enough to inspire their employees to know it by heart and propose compatible innovations.

As such, the existence of a Mission Statement serves as an innovation enabler. Therefore, it is incumbent upon senior managers and owners to issue a written Mission Statement to guide their staff in evaluating the relevance and benefits of any Opportunity (and the corresponding innovation/solution).

This might be less of an issue in a startup or small company, where individuals are more likely to naturally consider these aspects. Mission Statements in small organizations may be more personal or even very simple and straightforward, such as "making money". However, above all, they need to be clearly expressed.

In large organizations, senior management typically does not tolerate any project that is not aligned with the corporate strategy, which is designed to achieve the company's Mission. This requirement represents a typical Constraint[2] imposed by these Decision-makers, who are obviously critical Stakeholders. In an environment where such a Constraint is rarely negotiable, you should ensure that your project aligns well with the corporate Mission and strategy. This is called the Investor Fit, as shown in Fig. 6.1.

The concept of Strategic or Investor fit should be clear, not vague as it often is. Many understand the basic idea of strategic fit but find it hard

---

[1] See Chap. 19.

[2] See Chap. 13.

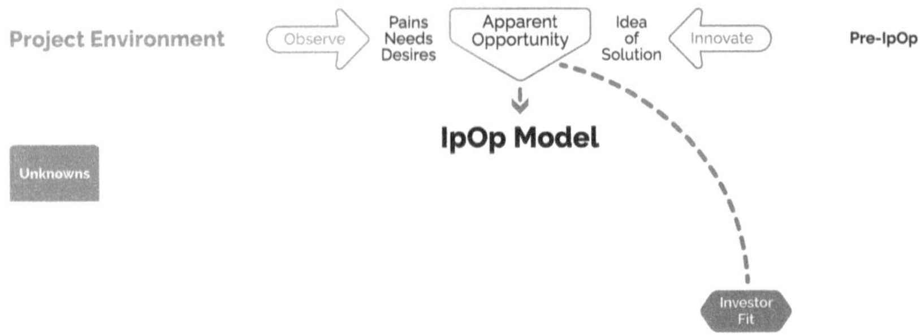

Fig. 6.1 The Opportunity must fit the corporate or Investor's Mission

to apply. To make it practical, an organization must define its strategy and list all criteria for determining whether an innovation aligns with this strategy. For each criterion, it should also specify the minimum threshold to confirm a fit. Having assisted companies in defining these criteria and thresholds, I can attest to the difficulty of this task. Regrettably, few companies put in the effort to translate their strategy into concrete criteria and thresholds.

6.1 Contribution to the Corporate KISs or KPIs

But compatibility with the Mission and strategy is not enough. If employees are to persuade senior management that an Opportunity is worth pursuing, they must demonstrate that it serves the objectives of the corporation or business and contributes to its Key Indicators of Success (KISs[3]) and/or Key Performance Indicators (KPIs). However, this is easier said than done! The most convincing way to impress management is to show:

- Which company indicator(s) will be improved by the Opportunity
- And (if possible) how these indicators will evolve over time (this means attributing values to the changes)

[3] See Chap. 11

This is a very concrete, down-to-earth, check which acts as an effective filter. If you can demonstrate that your idea will increase the market share (assuming this actually is a corporate indicator), and if possible, quantify by how much, your Decision-maker will find it difficult to reject your proposal, provided the required resources are available. Conversely, if you are unable to demonstrate this, it is time to question whether the Opportunity is truly worth pursuing.

For this self-regulating mechanism to function, management must make sure that corporate and business unit level KISs and KPIs are clearly defined and, just as importantly, known to their staff. Based on my hands-on experience, managers who fail to provide a clear Mission Statement often find it challenging to choose the appropriate KISs for measurement in practice. The issue is similar with Strategic fit. The use of indicators often comes with a substantial burden, as it requires a functioning measurement and reporting mechanism. However, this is easier said than done, especially when the Management Information System (MIS) is not as fully developed as it should be (which is often the case).

Vertical deployment of the strategy and the corresponding indicators is critical. Once the Key Indicators of Success and Key Performance Indicators have been decided upon—at either corporate or business unit level—and they meet the criteria of the MIS, management must ensure that they are communicated to all relevant employees and are accepted by them. To achieve this, employees must understand the KISs and KPIs and be aware of their own personal impact on them. This necessitates education and training, which is an essential aspect that is too often overlooked.

The absence of a Strategic or Investor fit/indicators filtering system will prevent employees from fully understanding the focus of the organization. This not only undermines their desire to innovate but also diminishes their ability to perform and innovate effectively. Without a clearly stated target (the Mission) and indicators, nobody, including employees, can accurately assess performance.

People need to understand how they can contribute to the overall picture, as this is the primary guide for determining which Opportunities are worth seizing. Clear and appropriate indicators will inspire employees to seek innovative solutions to achieve them. Therefore, all managers should ensure that these exist, and that people are familiar with them.

Link with ISO 56007 (Tools and Methods for Managing Opportunities and Ideas: Guidance)

The IpOp Model simply mentions that any project aligns with the Investor's strategy, which includes fit with the investor's image and brand.

ISO 56007 also includes the strategic fit in it list of selection criteria[4] but it expands on this concept by including fit with additional criteria such as scope, business/mission model, pipeline and portfolio objectives, risk exposure and other factors. All these criteria are grouped under 'Organization alignment' in ISO 56007, which essentially represents the same idea as the 'Investor fit' in the IpOp Model. ISO 56007 suggests some subcriteria with one of them being 'strategic fit' while the IpOp Model encompasses all this alignment under the term 'Investor fit'. Ultimately, whether to use "organization alignment" or "Investor fit" depends on personal preferences.

Given that each investor has its own specific strategy, and it is impossible to provide a complete list of criteria covering all possible strategies, the IpOp Model asserts that it is up to each Investor to define which criteria should be used to assess alignment with its strategy. This is why the IpOp Model does not suggest which sub criteria should be used to verify alignment with the strategy.

This implies that when an Investor/organization adopts a strategy, it should immediately define the criteria to be used for verifying if a project fits that strategy of not. Unfortunately, very few organizations establish such a list of criteria. Most organizations rely on management's judgement without a rigorous and systematic list of criteria.

---

[4] Decision criteria are mentioned in ISO 56007, Table 1 in section 6.4.3.5.4 with additional details in annex C5. As there are many references to ISO 56007 decision criteria, this source will not be repeated.

7

PND Before R&D

A Written Customer PND Focus Statement Creates Commitment and Keeps Entrepreneurs Focused

Take-Home of This Chapter

This chapter focuses on the importance of understanding and verifying the Pain/Need/Desire(s) (PNDs) of the target Customers in order to verify the Customers' buy-in. This requires to know who the target Customers are as well as the Pain/Need/Desire(s) of each them, as outlined by ISO 56007. It emphasizes the need for project initiators to clearly express the PNDs through a Customer PND Focus Statement. The chapter also highlights the significance of focusing on a limited number of PNDs and the potential risks of trying to satisfy too many PNDs at once. By providing more detailed insight of the concept of Pain/Need/Desire(s) than what is expressed in ISO 56007, the content of this chapter can be used to practically implement ISO 56007.

Once the opportunity has been identified, it's crucial to write your "Customer PND Focus Statement." This is a highly effective method for ensuring that the supposed Pain/Need/Desire(s) actually exist and that customers are interested in satisfying them. The numerous start-ups that have failed because they wrongly assumed the existence of a PND serve as ample proof of this.

R. H Cohen, *Pre-Project Excellence*, Future of Business and Finance,
https://doi.org/10.1007/978-3-031-61774-4_7

Many innovators become so enamored with their own ideas that they overlook the importance of clarifying and verifying the PNDs. Instead, they focus on extolling the virtues of their innovation without adequately developing Customer familiarity. However, a comprehensive understanding of the PNDs enables you to focus on what truly matters to your target Customers.

7.1 Writing the Customer PND Focus Statement

The Customer PND Focus Statement should succinctly summarize (in one or two sentences at most) the Pain/Need/Desire(s) to be satisfied by the Solution. If the PND is not clear, the fine-tuning of the Solution will lack focus, potentially leading to the delivery of a Solution that addresses a different Pain/Need/Desire as a coincidental side effect.

Expressing the Pain/Need/Desire is not as straightforward as it appears. From my experience, the Customer PND Focus Statements presented by individuals or groups often require fine-tuning or further analysis. This highlights the challenge people face in expressing the Pain/Need/Desire(s) that their Solution aims to address. Let us consider the example of the Short Messaging System (SMS), which is extensively used by teenagers. Was its success because:

- It is less expensive than a phone call
- It provides a way to reach someone whose phone is not answering
- It gives the recipient more time to draft his answer
- It offers a one-way communication mode that spares the sender direct interaction with the receiver
- It allows for silent communication, among other possibilities

The answer to this question will determine the focus, which, in turn, will significantly impact the final outcome. Therefore, having a genuine understanding or familiarity with end-users' Pain/Need/Desire(s) is essential.

Any difficulty in expressing the Pain/Need/Desire(s) in the Customer PND Focus Statement should be interpreted as a significant warning. It raises questions about the existence of the Opportunity. If there is no clear market need, the entrepreneur will recognize that the Opportunity is less compelling than initially imagined.

Pinpointing a wider range of PNDs can boost business. Take pagers, for example. In addition to their communication function, they were also viewed as status symbols. Recognizing this, companies began presenting pagers as fashion accessories, where factors like color, shape, and design played crucial roles in purchasing decisions. With the Customer PND Focus Statement "Teenagers want to make a social statement," affordable customization opportunities were opened up. This led Motorola to dramatically expand its pager color options and spawned a new industry supplying skins, ringtones, and graphics for personalizing mobile phones. Such lucrative opportunities would not have arisen if the PND had been limited to communication alone.

Attempting to satisfy too many PNDs at a time can kill an Opportunity. There is a common misconception that if one PND is less important, others will make up for it. However, this leads to a lack of focus and drains resources needed to address additional PNDs. With limited resources, some PNDs will inevitably be inadequately addressed, putting the entire project at risk. Given the principle of choice in life, smart resource allocation is crucial for gaining competitive advantages and determining which PNDs to prioritize. The key is to focus on a limited number of PNDs.

The proposed Solution must not only address a genuine Pain/Need/Desire but also clearly express it. A vaguely defined Pain/Need/Desire will result in an unclear Opportunity and, consequently, an ambiguous outcome. Documenting the Customer PND Focus Statement compels the entrepreneur to conduct a more comprehensive analysis of the Pain/Need/Desire(s) than relying solely on mental assumptions or intuitive understanding. We are more committed to what we write than what we merely say.

The components of the Pain/Need/Desire(s) outlined in the Customer PND Focus Statement need to be verified. Relying solely on the project initiator's perspective could be misleading, hence verification assists in pinpointing the most critical issues. Pain/Need/Desire is seldom singular or straightforward; rather, it typically encompasses multiple factors that the entrepreneur must explicitly understand. Enumerating these sub-needs ensures none are overlooked.

Identification of the target Customers for the Solution is obviously a prerequisite for expressing the Pain/Need/Desire(s) (Fig 7.1). How can you understand the PNDs of a target population that you have not identified clearly? Moreover, attempting to cater to the needs of too many Customer segments often results in failure. For instance, Ferrari's success stems from its establishment of customer intimacy within narrowly targeted market segments capable of affording its cars. Consequently, Ferrari remains attuned to the PNDs of these segments and concentrates on addressing them, disregarding the PNDs of other potential customer groups.

Sometimes, a provider serves multiple Customers. For example, Nestlé sells its products to consumers mainly through retailers. This setup means Nestlé has at least two Customers for its products: the consumer/end-user and the retailer. In the case of baby food, there are three Customers: the baby consuming the food, the mother purchasing the product, and the retailer selling it. Each of these Customers has their own Pain/Need/Desire(s).

A Customer PND Focus Statement is not a slogan. When asked to write a Customer PND Focus Statement, people very often come up with

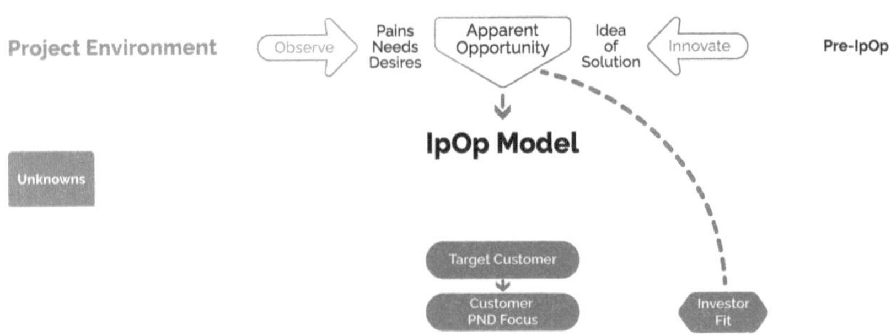

Fig. 7.1 The Customer PND Focus Statement expresses the Pain/Need/Desire(s) of a target Customer to be addressed by the Solution

a slogan or a statement focusing on the proposed Solution. This confusion may indicate a lack of thoroughness in the analysis.

The Customer PND Focus Statement must comprise a description of the Pain/Need/Desire(s), without reference to a solution. Since it is intended for internal, not advertising purposes, it is crucial to keep the explicit definition of the Pain/Need/Desire(s) separate from the definition of the Solution. This ensures that there is at least one Pain/Need/Desire, and customers indeed desire its fulfillment.

Finally, a firm understanding of PNDs is the first step to identifying the most critical Customer's Decision Criteria and Benefits that the Solution is intended to provide. This topic will be explored further in this chapter.

Nespresso Classic's Customer PND Focus Statement

The epicurean consumers of espresso coffee desire:

- The pleasure and self-gratification of indulgence (enjoying a range of refined coffee aromas comparable or superior to those offered by espresso machines in cafés and restaurants)
- Belonging (to a community of discerning gourmets who value excellence)
- Sharing (special moments with friends and visitors)
- Freedom (to enjoy these experiences at home or work, anytime)
- Convenience without hassle (without requiring special knowledge or complicated procedures)

Link with ISO 56007 (Tools and Methods for Managing Opportunities and Ideas: Guidance)

In various sections, ISO adopts the expression Pain/Need/Desire(s), mirroring the terminology of the IpOp Model. This chapter offers detailed insights into the meaning of this concept and guidance on its application.

8

Are You Competitive Enough?

A Prerequisite to Get Ahead

Take-Home of This Chapter

This chapter focuses on the importance of Customer intimacy and competitive advantage in exploiting successful Opportunities. It emphasizes the need to identify and understand Customers' Decision Criteria (CDCs) and highlights the significance of brand recognition and customer connection. The chapter introduces the concept of Customer Benchmarking, which involves comparing the proposed Solution with Alternatives to demonstrate Customer fit. By thoroughly knowing the Customer and their buying patterns, entrepreneurs and project developers can fill the Customer Benchmarking table and compare the proposed Solution with Alternatives based on the Customer Decision Criteria. To obtain Customer buy-in, it is necessary to identify and understand all the Customer Decision Criteria of each customer to tailor the Solution that best meet its needs. Additionally, it mentions the role of market analysis and competitive intelligence in assessing the strengths and weaknesses of key players in the industry. The chapter concludes by emphasizing the need to define areas of excellence and make strategic decisions accordingly. The Customer Benchmarking demonstrates to what extent there is hope to obtain Customer buy-in.

Since ISO 56007 mentions customer fit but without explaining how it should be done, the IpOp Model Customer Benchmarking described in this chapter is a practical way to demonstrate ISO 56007's customer fit.

R. H Cohen, *Pre-Project Excellence*, Future of Business and Finance,
https://doi.org/10.1007/978-3-031-61774-4_8

A "me too" strategy can sometimes work, especially for those with modest ambitions. The key is to enter an unsaturated market with room for newcomers. However, merely opening a new grocery store is not enough; competing with established competitors demands offering some form of "extra benefit".

The main purpose of innovation is to gain Market Advantages that allow you to outpace the competition.

Understanding your Market Advantages requires a solid grasp of:

- The Alternative solutions available to your target customer who has the identified PNDs (this includes competitors, but the status quo is also an Alternative)
- The Customers' Decision Criteria (CDCs, see below) crucial for market dominance

Once these parameters are clear, it is essential to benchmark your ability to meet these CDCs against that of your key competitors or Alternatives.

8.1 Identifying the Alternatives

Your competitors are not just companies with a similar approach and intentions, but also anyone aiming to engage the same market segment by meeting the same PNDs. The competitors of someone operating a glass bottom boat at a seaside resort are not limited to other glass bottom boats but anyone vying to entertain visitors during daytime. This includes other marine attractions as well as activities on land, including museums, supermarkets, and shopping malls.

The most effective way to identify Alternatives is to build customer intimacy. By closely engaging with your clients or Customers, you can uncover who is vying for their attention and possibly who is working with them. It also provides valuable insights into your competition. Keep an eye out for potential competitors who are not yet in the game: Netscape is a good example. Despite benefiting from the famous "first mover's advantage", Netscape was essentially wiped out of the market by Microsoft, who was nowhere in the running when Netscape launched its original browser. Late entrants can be deadly, particularly those with muscle and deep pockets. The iPhone is a notable example; even with its delayed market entry, it swiftly rose to become a leading entity in the mobile phone industry, surpassing Nokia, the top player at the time.

Business intelligence can play a crucial role in understanding the strengths and weaknesses of key competitors. Resorting to illegitimate information sources is often unnecessary: strategic internet research can yield up to 80% of the needed data. By properly employing competitive intelligence tools, much of the remaining information can be deduced in a legitimate manner.

The Principal Competitors of Nespresso Classic When the operation was launched, the main competitors of Nespresso were:

- Home traditional espresso coffee machines
- Instant coffee (including Nestlé's own Nescafé)
- Filter coffee
- Bars and restaurants
- Tea and other hot drinks

New competitors have since emerged:

- Other portioned espresso with capsules compatible with Nespresso machines
- Other portioned espresso for other machines (not compatible with Nespresso machines)

Nespresso Classic's Operation "Competitor Watch" Nespresso was quick to realize that the internet offers a unique source of information about the market and potential competitors. To take full advantage of all its facilities the company called upon a specialized company[1] which provided it with the following competitive intel-

[1] Digital Luxury Group SA: www.digital-luxury.com.

ligence practices enabling Nespresso to react more sensitively to new trends:

- A market analysis indicating the true perception of its products by consumers
- Tools to better exploit Nespresso's competitive advantages
- Up-to-date information on offer and demand
- Proactive protection of Nespresso's image (monitoring on the web to detect any illegal use of the brand; offensive action designed to dissuade any with such leanings)
- Monitoring and interaction through social networks (in 6 months the Nespresso fan club went from 50,000 to 450,000 members)

8.2 Identifying Customers' Decision Criteria (CDCs)

Customers' Decision Criteria (CDCs)—those they use to prefer one product or service over another—come in various levels of importance (Fig. 8.1). Establishing Customer intimacy not only aids in identifying the key players but also in pinpointing these CDCs. The crucial aspect is not necessarily whether features are essential, since some are

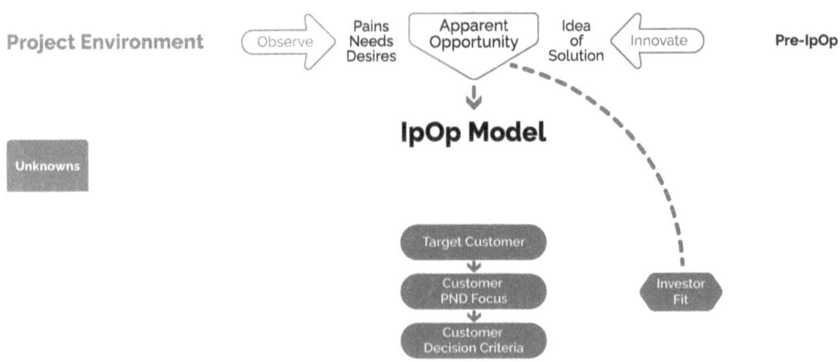

Fig. 8.1 Customers' Decision Criteria (CDCs) are critical characteristics of the Solution for winning over customers

intrinsic to the product itself, but rather how much they impact customer buy-in. For instance, a car without brakes would not attract buyers because brakes are indispensable. However, merely including brakes is not enough for success; it is considered a standard practice, not a CDC.

CDCs are essential to the customers' decision-making process and can contribute to increasing your market share. As previously mentioned, being close to your clients or end-users provides a significant advantage in identifying them. Relying on unverified Customer Decision Criteria can lead to misleading conclusions, and guesswork can prove to be perilous and costly.

CDCs include anything that can help tilt the scale in favor of a particular supplier such as brand reputation, user-friendliness, pricing, availability, product variety, design, customer intimacy, clear communication, technological advancements, and more.

Different markets may have different CDCs. Consumers in certain countries, for instance, are more attentive to the environmental footprint of a product compared to those in less environmentally conscious countries (where this impact will not be considered a CDC). Similarly, the acceptance of genetically modified organisms (GMOs) differed significantly between Europe and North America. Monsanto's failure to recognize this disparity resulted in substantial financial losses.

Understanding the relative impact of CDCs on customers' minds can be a very powerful source of inspiration for building Competitive Advantages. For example:

- **Price is not necessarily the major selection criterion**. Mobile phones achieved remarkable success despite being five to ten times more expensive to use than landlines at the time
- **Perception may overshadow reality**. Real convenience corresponds to the level that is actually demanded by customers. In this respect, convenience serves as a satisfier, and exceeding the perceived necessary level of convenience is unnecessary. For instance, home delivery of milk has become obsolete as most people now purchase groceries from supermarkets, rendering the added convenience of milk delivery at home unjustifiable. Understanding customers' PNDs is crucial in this context

The main challenge in pinpointing Customer Decision Criteria is achieving a comprehensive list. While many can identify some criteria, a complete enumeration is rare. Incompleteness poses the risk of missing a crucial criterion, which could be detrimental. This situation is exacerbated as people often focus on criteria their Solution addresses well, overlooking those it does not. Furthermore, they may believe they understand the customer's Customer Decision Criteria, but these beliefs are just that—beliefs. Only Customer Decision Criteria that have been verified hold relevance.

Thus, having a comprehensive and verified list of Customer Decision Criteria is crucial. The most effective strategy to fulfill this stringent requirement involves cultivating the deepest level of customer intimacy achievable and confirming through field verification that their buy-in decisions are solely based on this list of CDCs and nothing else.

Additionally, always treat your list of Customer Decision Criteria as an Unknown to be verified, as relying on assumptions is risky.

Nespresso Classic's CDCs in the Pre-portioned Coffee Market (in Descending Order of Importance)

- Trust in the brand
- Flavor and quality comparable to hot drinks prepared by the best professionals
- Choice among several varieties of flavors
- Reliability and consistent quality
- Image
- Machine design
- Comfort: Ease and availability of production (fast, practical, simple, clean, individual portions, etc.)
- Ease of purchase, after-sales service
- Price

8.3 Classic Pitfalls in Identifying CDCs

Believing that certain characteristics qualify as a CDC when they do not is a recipe for disaster. The most common mistakes are:

- **Combining Customer Decision Criteria from different customers, rather than addressing them individually**. Each Customer operates based on their own decision criteria, unconcerned with those of other Customers. Therefore, it's essential to maintain separate lists of Customer Decision Criteria for each target Customer, tailored to their specific Pain/Need/Desire(s)
- **Wanting to apply technological breakthroughs to PNDs that are already well served.** A notable example is Boo.com,[2] which spent over €100 million using high-tech software trying to sell fashion wear on the Internet.
- **Offering simpler or improved solutions that involve substantial cost shifting**, especially true in B2B[3] scenarios where new equipment needs to replace existing ones. For instance, the introduction of digital movies in theaters faced significant delays until a compelling reason, such as the appeal of 3D movies, emerged to enforce the new standard
- **Imagining unserved PNDs that are not real PNDs or that are already served**. Iridium, the satellite phone network, illustrates this category well
- **Supplying a better process that proves challenging to integrate into customers' existing Activity Chain**. For example, the introduction of significantly improved fast trains, such as the French TGV, requires substantial infrastructure adjustments, such as replacing or installing new rail tracks. This hurdle prevented Swiss railways from adopting the modern French system
- **Relying on the first mover advantage without possessing critical size or support from lead customer/partners**. Book Stacks,[4] launched online in 1992, was the first online bookstore. Amazon launched in 1995. Who remembers Book Stacks?

---

[2] https://en.wikipedia.org/wiki/Boo.com.

[3] business to business.

[4] https://en.wikipedia.org/wiki/Book_Stacks_Unlimited.

- **Introducing an innovative solution that can be easily replicated by larger competitors.** Despite the challenges faced by many early players in online trading services, Charles Schwab managed to secure a significant market share despite entering the market later

8.4 The Five F's—CDC Checklist

As an excellent checklist to ensure that a product addresses all the important criteria, I suggest using Rhonda Abrams's[5] list of the Five "F's" in Table 8.1, which motivates customers, and also serves as an excellent checklist for verifying a product's alignment with essential criteria. A product or service that fulfills all of the F's stands a better chance of success compared to one that does not. Moreover, the Five F's help to clarify Customers' Benefits[6] as well as Benefits brought to other Stakeholders.[7]

The Five F's should not be the sole basis for Customer Decision Criteria; they are too broad and conceptual. Customer Decision Criteria need to be much more specific. Use the Five F's only as a supplementary guide.

The following Table 8.2 illustrates the importance of these Five 'F's as applied to portable MP3 players:

[5] www.rhondaonline.com.

[6] See Chap. 9.

[7] See Chap. 13.

Table 8.1 List of the 5 F's

	Five 'F's	Explanation	Examples of questions to verify if the 'F' is addressed
1	Functions	Indicates the product functionalities that meet customers' real desires including emotional ones	How does the product or service meet customers' concrete PNDs?
2	Finances	Indicates all the financial implications for customers; these encompass not only price but other financial dimensions such as savings or productivity improvements	How will the purchase affect their overall financial situation—Not just the price of the product or service, but other savings and increased productivity?
3	Freedom	Expresses the impact that the product will have on customers' freedom and quality of life	How convenient is it to purchase and use the product or service? How will customers gain more time and less worry in other aspects of their lives?
4	Feelings	These cover all the emotional parameters associated with the product	How does the product or service make customers feel about themselves, and how does it affect and relate to their self-image? Do they like and respect the salesperson and the company?
5	Future	Takes into account a long term view of the impact of the product	How will they deal with the product or service and company over time? Will support and service be available? How will the product or service affect customers' lives in the coming years, and will they have an increased sense of security about the future?

Table 8.2 The 5 F's applied to audio streaming services, such as Spotify or Apple Music

	Five 'F's	Example of questions to verify if each 'F' is addressed	Relevance to portable digital music players
1	Functions	Does the product do the specific things that the customer really PNDs right now?	To store and play music on the go; additional functions such as convenient search, personalized playlists, suggestions based on personal taste/history, easy interface, etc.
2	Finances	How will the purchase affect the customer's overall financial situation?	Freemium model that can be tried free of charge Low monthly subscription with unlimited streaming encouraging spontaneous purchase No need to purchase individual records
3	Freedom	How will customers gain more time and less worry in other aspects of their lives? How convenient is it to purchase and use the product?	... to store only selected songs. ... to listen anywhere and at any time. ... to use the same playlists on different devices ... to obtain pieces any time thanks to the internet ... to share playlist with friends
4	Feelings	How does the product make customers feel about themselves and how does it affect and relate to their self-image?	Positive feelings resulting from the fact that • Music makes people feel good • Subscribers have immediate access to any piece any time anywhere • Streaming is cheaper than buying records • Streaming is trendy
5	Future	How will customers relate to the product or the supplier over time? How will the product affect customers' lives in the coming years and will it give them a greater sense of security for the future?	Digital music is here to stay the ability to back up stored music adds security New features can be added to the service

Nespresso Classic's five F's (reminder: The typical Nespresso customer is a private consumer who owns a machine adapted to the capsules. The ensuing reasoning would be different in the case of a professional restaurateur.)

Functions

To prepare espresso, cappuccino and caffè lungo.

Finances

Economic argument: While individual portions of coffee cost more than ordinary coffee, they permit the consumer to drink a quality espresso at any time of day or night without having to go to a public establishment where the cost would be still greater.

Long-term storage avoids wastage: Ordinary coffee loses its flavor after being exposed to air.

Home delivery 24/7 of the coffee ordered saves consumers the chore of having to go out to stock up. The time saved can be put to more productive use. As Nespresso can also be prepared faster than regular espresso, it saves time and we all know that... time is money.

All things considered, the Nespresso system in fact works out less expensive than alternatives offering a comparable quality of espresso coffee.

Freedom

The Nespresso system permits a real gain in time and effort, guaranteeing a quality result without complicated manipulations.

No learning process is needed, in contrast to the other ways of preparing an espresso.

The possibility of drinking an espresso at any moment frees the consumer from the constraints of coffee shops' opening times and distance.

The choice from among a wide variety of coffees offers freedom to drink a coffee according to personal taste without having to bow to the preferences of the group.

Feelings

The luxury of indulging in a self-gratifying experience.

The feeling of generosity while sharing this gratifying experience with others.

The pleasure of drinking a cup of coffee with exceptional aroma and texture makes the customer feel like a connoisseur.

The possibility of offering a choice of high-quality coffees to guests adds a further source of pride.

Nespresso puts out the image of the pleasure that consumers can experience through the accessibility of a high-class product.

Not having to prepare the coffee and clean the machine is a luxury available only to those who can afford it.

Future

The time saved by Nespresso can be put to more productive activities having an impact on the future.

Being perceived as a more attentive host can create opportunities in both the work and the private sphere.

8.5 Customer Benchmarking

Customer Benchmarking, as shown in Table 8.3 for Nespresso, **allows you to identify the relative strengths of the various Key Players**. After identifying all the CDCs, it is crucial to evaluate how effectively each Key Player or Alternative (including yourself) delivers them. This involves conducting a straightforward assessment exercise where each Key Player is assigned a score for each CDC. The following example of a scale defining the level of their delivery is sufficiently sophisticated for most purposes:

4 = Outstanding
3 = Good
2 = Fair
1 = Poor
0 = Not provided

Avoid the pitfall of creating a single Benchmarking table that mixes the Customer Decision Criteria of various customers. Each Customer bases their buy-in on their own unique Decision Criteria, independent of other Customers' Criteria. Therefore, you should prepare a distinct Benchmarking table for each Customer. This separation enables you to grasp the behavior of each Customer accurately. Consolidating different

Table 8.3 Customer Benchmarking table for Nespresso

No.	Customers' Decision Criteria (CDCs)	Alternatives for the Consumers: Nespresso	Home espresso machines	Instant coffee	Filter coffee	Bars and restaurants	Tea	Non compatible portioned espresso	Compatible capsules
1	Love/trust in the brand	4	2	2	2	3	3	2	2
2	Aroma and quality comparable to coffee prepared by top professionals	4	3	3	3	4	4	3	3
3	Choice of different varieties of coffee	4	2	2	3	2	4	2	1
4	Image	4	4	2	1	4	4	2	2
5	Machine design	4	2	1	1	NA	1	3	NA
6	Ease and availability of production (fast, practical, simple, clean, individual portions, etc.)	4	2	3	2	1	3	4	NA
7	Ease of purchase and after-sales service	3	2	2	2	3	3	3	3
8	Reliability and constant quality	4	2	4	3	3	3	3	2
9	Price of a cup of coffee	2	3	4	4	1	2	3	3

Benchmarking of Consumers Decision Criteria (CDCs) for Nespresso Classic and its main competitors

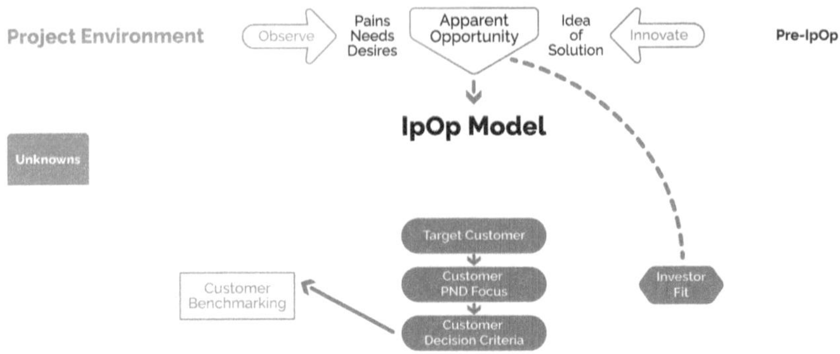

Fig. 8.2 Customer Benchmarking helps identify the areas of excellence that have an edge over the Alternatives

Customers' Decision Criteria into one Benchmarking table obscures your understanding of individual Customer behavior.

It is seldom possible to provide outstanding delivery of all the CDCs, and it is not wise to challenge a competitor who has achieved this feat. Since few can excel on all counts, it is necessary to prioritize which CDCs to focus on. This raises the question: how will underperforming in certain Decision Criteria impact Customer buy-in??

Ranking CDCs is one method to determine their relative importance. Another interesting approach is to identify which combination of CDCs generates a synergy of Market Advantages. For example, low price (a typical CDC) will become less important for a laptop computer if it can combine small size, lightweight, long battery life, a fast processor, and a large storage capacity. DVD/CD drives, not deemed critical CDCs for a certain target clientele, will sometimes be replaced by external units to reduce price, size, and weight.

The Customer Benchmarking is the most effective way to show to what extent there is hope to obtain buy-in from the Customer (Fig 8.2).

8.6 Defining the Areas of Excellence

Because trade-offs are inevitable, it is imperative to choose the CDCs in which you aim to excel, enabling you to outperform the competition or Alternatives. As a general, but not absolute rule, it is difficult to be the best provider for more than four CDCs. Selecting these (one to four) CDCs is a critical strategic decision. Focusing on the wrong areas significantly increases the likelihood of failure. Polaroid's instant development technology serves as an illustration. This CDC helped the company establish itself as a multinational powerhouse. However, the empire could not withstand the emergence of affordable digital printing. This not only posed a challenge to Polaroid's instant printing technology but also introduced additional synergistic CDCs, such as the ability to edit and print at home, and even email pictures.

Relying solely on price is risky, especially when lacking additional factors crucial for market domination, such as extensive distribution networks, brand recognition, and marketing strength, among others. With the escalating aggressiveness and sophistication of low-cost countries supplying goods, it is inevitable that someone will eventually challenge you on price.

Ideally, price should not even rank among your top four CDCs. These top CDCs should provide so much value that price becomes a secondary issue. The Swatch (watch) serves as a perfect example. The manufacturing cost of a basic Swatch is likely less than five dollars. While it could feasibly be sold for considerably less than the retail price (as of 60 Euro), other CDCs such as brand, design, image, or fashion justify the higher price.

Interestingly, the strategy of choice for most companies is product superiority, particularly for those in the technological field. However, this strategy demands that the company's product consistently remains the best, necessitating substantial investments in research and development (R&D). Maintaining technological leadership is challenging in today's fast-paced world, where newcomers can swiftly challenge the incumbent with superior solutions. Both Polaroid and Xerox struggled to maintain their positions as technology leaders. While opting for product superiority can be an effective strategy, it can also prove to be exceedingly costly in the long run. Apple may be an exception to this rule, but its success also depends on its brand superiority.

Customer intimacy is an interesting area of excellence, for it reduces the importance of weak operational efficiency and/or product performance. In other words, customer intimacy can enable a business to succeed despite offering products or operations with subpar performance. Thanks to their robust brand recognition, certain US car manufacturers managed to sell technologically outdated cars for extended periods.

Brand recognition stands out as one of the most powerful levers for building customer intimacy, which is reflected in brand valuations often reaching billions of dollars. However, even the most renowned brands are susceptible to challenges. Another critical aspect of customer intimacy involves staying connected with customers and understanding their (changing) PNDs. Swissair, for instance, was a prestigious airline with numerous qualities, including product superiority and excellent brand recognition. Nonetheless, it failed to establish sufficient customer intimacy to identify the market opportunity that easyJet eventually seized. Furthermore, Swissair struggled to achieve a sufficient level of operational efficiency, particularly in terms of cost-effectiveness.

Choosing the area(s) where you plan to excel is a crucial strategic decision, whether made implicitly or explicitly. Often, these decisions remain implicit, unfortunately. Your choice will shape the Solution you develop and may also affect the Resource model you choose.[8]

Customer Benchmarking plays a crucial role in refining your Solution and Customer Unique Experience.[9] Therefore, its importance extends beyond just assessing if you can outperform the Alternatives (including your competitors). It also guides you for establishing your uniqueness.

Link with ISO 56007 (Tools and Methods for Managing Opportunities and Ideas — GUIDANCE)

As part of the Customer/Mission alignment criteria outlined in ISO 56007, one of the sub criteria mentioned is 'customer/user fit.' However, the standard does not provide guidance on how to verify this fit.

The IpOp Model recommends demonstrating the fit using a Benchmarking table that lists all available Alternatives addressing the same Pain/Need/Desire(s). This Customer Benchmarking involves comparing the proposed Solution with the Alternatives using Customer Decision Criteria. To fill the Customer Benchmarking table effectively, the entrepreneur/intrapreneur/project developer must have a comprehensive understanding of the Customer and his purchasing pattern/profile.

Therefore, Customer Benchmarking serves as a practical method to verify what ISO 56007 refers to as 'customer/user fit.

[8] Refer to Chap. 10.

[9] Refer to Chap. 9.

9

Give Them Their CUE

The Customer's Unique Experience Is Your Key to Success

Take-Home of This Chapter

This chapter discusses the importance of a compelling and easy-to-communicate Elevator Pitch in presenting the Solution to potential Investors and/or Customers. The Elevator Pitch is a short presentation that captures the most impactful Benefits of the Solution and is designed to generate interest and excitement. It is compared to the trailer of a movie, enticing the audience to learn more. The chapter also emphasizes the need for a detailed Customer Unique Experience (CUE) Description as well as a detailed description of the Solution, which outlines all the key characteristics and benefits of the solution in clear terms. Anchoring the CUE Description and the Solution description in the minds of the team ensures alignment and focus on delivering the desired Customer experience. The solution should bring Benefits not only to customers but also to other Stakeholders, including social and environmental Benefits that support the corporate social responsibility.

The Crystallized Opportunity is achieved when the solution is clearly defined and fine-tuned for the target Customer's experience to address their Pain/Need/Desire(s). The chapter concludes by mentioning the link with ISO 56007, highlighting the importance of delivering Benefits to Stakeholders to obtain "acceptance by interested parties" that ISO 56007 sees as one selection criterion.

R. H Cohen, *Pre-Project Excellence*, Future of Business and Finance,
https://doi.org/10.1007/978-3-031-61774-4_9

To achieve success, it is insufficient to have devised the perfect Solution; you must still obtain Customers buy-in. To accomplish this, you must convince them that what you offer provides an Outstanding Superior Perceived Value (OSPV).

The key to your success hinges on a very simple equation:

- The outstanding benefits must be perceived by the (internal or external) Customer as having a greater value than their cost

where the terms *benefits* and *cost* include intangibles and feelings. "Outstanding" means exceeding all Alternatives available to your market segment. A performance that is merely "good enough" falls short of what is required.

The following check list will help verify that your reason to buy is a compelling.

Does your offering:

- provide a unique, preferably sustainable, and compelling way to satisfy the Customer's PND
- persuade the Customers to spend their money, grant you their attention, or adopt your perspective
- in an honorable and ethical way
- in exchange for the value you propose to deliver?

Every Opportunity must be subjected to this checklist. If the answer is not positive on all four counts, the chances of success are reduced. If the answer is an unconditional "yes", you have much greater chance of succeeding.

9.1 The Compelling Reason to Buy

Defining a valid compelling reason to buy requires a thorough understanding of the Customer's psychology (familiarity here is again crucial). It must be seen as able to satisfy the Pain/Need/Desire(s) expressed in the Customer PND Focus Statement.

It must be compelling in the customer's eyes. Assuming your beliefs are the same as your Customer's is a common mistake that can be costly. Merely thinking a reason is compelling is not enough. Customers buy-in must be verified.

Certain compelling reasons to buy stem from the product's quality or the company's market penetration. Microsoft's Windows Operating System, for instance, is inherently compelling because it offers optimum compatibility with other users' files in office environments. Except for the Vista disaster, each new release of a Windows operating system tempted its users to upgrade their software. With this "Wintel alliance" each software upgrade created a compelling reason for them to upgrade or replace the hardware with a more powerful processor (delivered at the time by Intel).

Industry standards (e.g. (ISO 9001) often provide compelling reasons to buy, as do government regulations on occasion. Certain companies, like Adobe, have successfully transformed some of their products into industry standards without official involvement (e.g., the PDF file format).

Another effective method of incorporating a compelling factor is to enlist specifiers to encourage customers or clients to purchase your product. Specifiers are individuals or organizations that recommend the use of specific products. They possess the credentials to support their recommendations and are perceived as authorities in their field. For example, doctors serve as specifiers for drugs, while architects act as specifiers for building materials.

Focusing on specifiers who assist customers in making purchasing decisions can significantly impact market penetration. To achieve this, the first step is to identify who the specifiers are. Customer intimacy and observation are valuable tools in this regard. Examples of specifiers include influencers, magazines, specialized websites, salespeople, and consumer associations. In his book *"The Tipping Point"*,[1] Malcolm Gladwell classifies specifiers as *Mavens* and *Connectors*. Mavens are people

[1] The Tipping Point, How Little Things Can Make A Big Difference, Malcolm Gladwell, Abacus Books, 2001.

in the know. They are trusted and listened to; their expert advice is reputed to be independent and not subject to influence; they are charismatic enough to convey the message. Mavens recommend restaurants, stereo systems, cameras, etc. Connectors, on the other hand, are highly sociable individuals with extensive networks. They connect people to Mavens or forward the Mavens' recommendations to a broader audience. Mavens and Connectors may not always be recognized by those they influence since they often operate behind the scenes. Despite the challenge, it is worthwhile to find ways (i.e., Tactical Moves) to influence them.

9.2 The Customer Unique Experience (CUE)

The CUE Description outlines what each Customer segment should perceive as unique about what you have to offer, from their own perspective. By empathizing with the Customer and writing their customized CUE Description, you can crystallize the key components of the compelling reason to buy for that customer segment.

It goes without saying that each Customer segment requires a distinct CUE description that caters to its specific Customer Decision Criteria. The one-size-fits-all approach to Customers simply does not suffice. The Customer Unique Experience must convincingly show that each Customer segment has compelling reasons to buy-in. Achieving this necessitates an analysis from the unique perspective of each Customer segment, independent of other Customers who do not share the same buying profile.

A Customer's buying profile, defined by the Decision Criteria they apply and the importance they assign to each criterion, is the most effective way to segment the market. The manner in which individuals make purchase decisions is what truly determines whether they are your Customer. This approach to market segmentation, based on buying behavior, is far more insightful than relying on socioeconomic factors, which may group together individuals with divergent buying profiles.

The CUE Description sets itself apart from the Unique Selling Proposition (USP) and Unique Value Proposition (UVP), though all three aim to clarify the offer's nature. The CUE emphasizes the customer's desire to obtain the experience, whereas the USP highlights the vendor's desire to sell, and the UVP centers on the benefits to the Customer. Despite the prevalence of USP and UVP in literature, I advocate for focusing on the Customer's Unique Experience because it places the customer perception at the forefront, unlike the USP. It also concentrates on the customer's perceptions rather than just the benefits highlighted by the UVP.

The recommendations for writing a CUE Description are straightforward. It should be:

- **Descriptive.** Clearly explain what the proposed Solution is
- **Convincing.** Include the compelling reason to buy and address the Pain/Need/Desire(s) expressed in the Customer PND Focus Statement
- **Unique.** Ensure your claim is unique, highlighting differentiation based on Customer Decision Criteria that represent Market advantages, as detailed by Customer Benchmarking.[2] This should ideally be so convincing that it makes the competition irrelevant
- **Clear and concrete.** Avoid jargon and buzzwords, which can undermine credibility as they are often perceived as hollow and disconnected
- **Simple and straight forward.** Get to the point without unnecessary repetition

Other useful qualities of a good CUE include:

- **Sustainability:** ensure it is sustainable unless you do not intend to remain in business
- **Difficult to copy:** make it hard for competitors to replicate to limit their impact on the market
- **Well written:** ensure it is well-written to be easy to understand and perceive

The CUE Description is a detailed description of your Solution, not a marketing slogan.[3] Marketing strategies for conveying the message to customers will be addressed separately by the marketing team. The

---

[2] See Chap. 8.

[3] See Elevator Pitch below.

CUE Description focuses solely on describing the characteristics of your Solution that will make the Customer perceive your offer as convincing.

A useful test of a good CUE Description is whether it adequately completes the following sentence as might be expressed by a (satisfied) Customer: "I strongly recommend this… (product, service, etc.) because it is the only one which…". This formulation is highly effective because it obliges you to focus on what really counts for the Customer.

Drafting a Customer's Unique Experience (CUE) Statement is more complex than it seems. Similar to Customer PND Focus Statements, experience has revealed challenges in crafting a strong CUE Description. A practical approach to begin is by identifying key words to incorporate and then stringing them together into a sentence (or more). Collaborative efforts often yield better results than individual attempts. Artificial intelligence, like ChatGPT, can also aid in enhancing the description of the Customer Unique Experience.

A written CUE Description provides a coach or an innovation leader in a large organization with a clear understanding of the Opportunity's nature and potential. Moreover, since the CUE Description is documented, physical presence may not be necessary. Similar to the Customer PND Focus Statement, the CUE Description serves as a valuable tool to determine:

- If the Opportunity merits pursuit based on the CUE's terms
- Whether the entrepreneur has conducted thorough research to ensure Customer buy-in
- If the CUE is genuinely unique and addresses a real and verified Pain/Need/Desire situation

After drafting the CUE, it is crucial to subject it to scrutiny against skeptical perspectives. One effective method is to present it to clients and gather their feedback. Customer testing is a valuable step in ensuring the CUE's resilience.

The toughest part is ensuring the CUE's genuine uniqueness and robustness. To achieve this, enlist particularly knowledgeable or skeptical individuals to scrutinize every aspect. Encourage them to highlight any potential objections or shortcomings, subjecting the CUE to the

Mean CUE Crash Test—a ruthless examination aimed at uncovering weaknesses. While this exercise may provide some amusement for the "devils," you, as the CUE author, stand to gain the most. Anticipating objections or resistance from Customers or Investors through this process allows you to refine your CUE or recognize its shortcomings early on. This saves you from persisting with a weak project.

The next step is to firmly embed this CUE Description in the minds of the team working on the Opportunity. This ensures that everyone comprehends the key deliverables and remains fully aligned with the project. This will prevent some team members from pursuing their own sometimes conflicting ideas about what should be delivered. Memorizing the CUE Description helps focus the team's efforts on ensuring that the customer experiences exactly what the CUE promises.

9.3 Make the Solution Explicit

Understanding the Customer Unique Experience is vital, but it's just one piece of the puzzle. The Solution's other attributes, even those not directly tied to the Customer's perceived experience, must be clearly defined. For example, a key aspect of a streaming service like Spotify is its intellectual property agreements with music owners. While end users might not be aware of or concerned with these agreements, they are crucial for providing access to the music. Similarly, technical aspects like Spotify's server capacity and performance are essential, though not directly noticed by users.

To align your team, the next step is to document a comprehensive description of the Solution's characteristics that you've refined over time. Experience shows that without this, team members often have varied understandings of the Solution, leading to misalignment, wasted efforts, and disagreements over what the Solution entails.

To avoid these issues, your Solution's description should be exhaustive, detailing every characteristic. Since this document is meant for internal clarity, it can be as detailed and lengthy as needed to cover what is included and what is not in the Solution. Documenting the description of your Solution in writing is also more reliable than verbal communication, minimizing the chance for misinterpretation. The primary benefit of a detailed Solution description is that it provides a clear and common understanding for all stakeholders, from the project team to Investors.

The CUE description, while a crucial aspect of the Solution, is just the tip of the iceberg. It is the most visible element to the Customer, who bases their purchase decision on it. However, the Solution encompasses many other parameters, such as the logistics required to deliver the CUE or the involvement of other Customers.

This highlights that the Solution extends far beyond the Customer Unique Experience, influenced by various other parameters of the IpOp Model. These could include outcomes from the Activity Chain, the Resource Model, or the necessity to meet the demands of key stakeholders.

This suggests that the comprehensive design of the Solution will most likely only be realized after all components of the IpOp Model have been thoroughly explored and integrated. This is because, although the Customer Unique Experience might be clearly outlined, the remainder of the Solution often requires additional refinement through the course of working with the IpOp Model.

9.4 Forget the "Apparent Opportunity"

Once the Solution has been clearly defined, what you have is a "Crystallized Opportunity". This term signifies that the characteristics of the Solution have been fine-tuned for the explicitly identified PNDs of a specific Customer and your Opportunity is no longer merely "apparent".[4]

At this stage, you can set aside the concept of "Apparent Opportunity" since nobody (except you) is concerned with the original idea. Customers and Decision-makers are only interested in the Crystallized Opportunity and the corresponding refined Solution (Fig. 9.1).

[4] See Fig. 2.2 of Chap. 2.

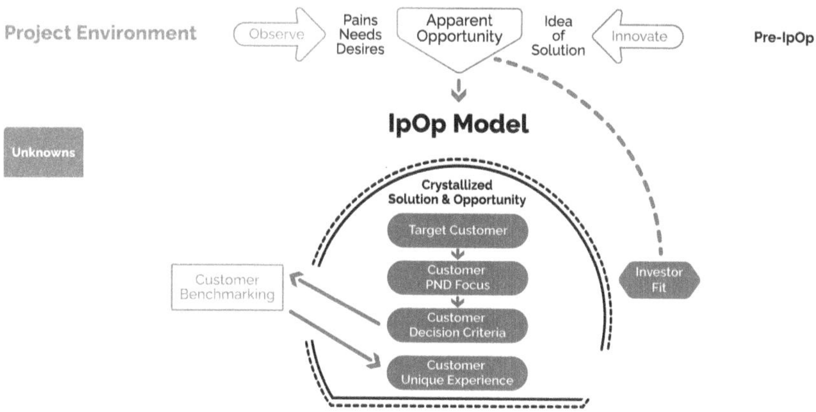

Fig. 9.1 The Crystallized Opportunity is defined by the Customer PND Focus Statement and the CUE Description, which expresses the Customer's compelling reason to buy

Nespresso Classic's CUE Description

"I recommend Nespresso because it is the only trustworthy system that guarantees lovers of gourmet coffee and their guests the possibility to experience the most self-indulging pleasure of enjoying a high-quality coffee to be individually selected from a wide selection of grand-cru flavors. This can be rapidly prepared without any skill or effort thanks to a user-friendly compact machine at an acceptable cost. The flavor and caffeine content of the coffee can be selected according to the whim of the moment from among a large selection of capsules, available for purchase 24 h a day directly through the very responsive Nespresso Club."

Nespresso Classic's Solution

Given that Nespresso classic involves a complex and proprietary solution, I'm restricted from detailing it here.

However, it's important to note that in addition to the above customer unique experience of Nespresso Classic, numerous parameters outlined on page 31 are integral to the solution. Examples include the production of capsules in dedicated factories in Switzerland, logistics, the Customer Relationship Center, boutiques, the website, and the recycling of capsules, among others.

9.5 The Elevator Pitch

The "Elevator Pitch" is a brief presentation of the Solution; so short that it can be made during an elevator ride with a stranger. It should capture the most impactful Benefit(s) that will excite and interest people, sparking their imagination and prompting them to want to hear more. It is akin to the trailer of a movie, designed to entice the audience to watch the whole thing.

Imagine you are in an elevator with a potential investor or a lead customer, and you have less than a minute to pitch your idea. Design a compelling elevator pitch that prompts that person to schedule another meeting to discuss your idea further. This pitch should succinctly explain the key benefits of your project in simple terms. Remember, the goal is to leave a lasting impression and spark interest in your idea before the elevator doors open.

Writing an elevator pitch is the next step, once you have completed the CUE Description. This concise, persuasive, and easy-to-communicate version of your CUE Description will be invaluable for future use. An example of an elevator pitch for the IpOp Model might be, "*Considering that 88% of projects fail to meet their expected outcomes on time and within budget, the IpOp Model offers a systematic approach to help innovators and organizations better calibrate their projects for timely delivery without exceeding the budget. This leads to a significant decrease in resource wastage from poorly calibrated projects. By minimizing frustration for everyone involved, the resources saved can be allocated more effectively.*"

It might be necessary to carry multiple elevator pitches, one for each type of audience. Pitching to the board of directors at Nestlé will differ significantly from pitching to appliance manufacturers that Nespresso aims to partner with. Each audience requires a pitch crafted specifically for their aspirations, interests, or concerns. Being prepared for each scenario is crucial.

The inability to deliver a convincing elevator pitch may indicate that your CUE is not easily communicable, posing a significant obstacle to success. A prime example of this is VoIP (Voice over IP), a technology enabling voice communication over the Internet instead of traditional phone lines. The challenge in explaining and conveying its benefits hindered its market penetration and acceptance initially. While the first application was launched by Vocaltec (an Israeli company) in 1995, it did not take off until years later with the introduction of Skype. Skype's straightforward elevator pitch, "Share the love and get your friends to download Skype so you can talk, instant message (IM) or make video calls for nothing," played a crucial role in its success. Just like a movie trailer, the elevator pitch captures the essence of the product or service in a brief and convincing manner.

Entrepreneurs often struggle to succinctly describe their project within 30–60 s in a manner that leaves their audience wanting to learn more. They usually delve into lengthy explanations of features rather than focusing on the most striking benefits of the innovation. They tend to express themselves in terms of their own interests and concerns rather than considering their interlocutor's perspective. The elevator pitch obliges them to adapt the presentation to their audience, providing a valuable opportunity to assess how easily communicable the CUE is.

The Nespresso Classic Elevator Pitch

For Nespresso's elevator pitch, I have opted to demonstrate how artificial intelligence can assist you. The following two elevators pitch were crafted by ChatGPT 4, without any modifications from me or Nespresso:

Elevator pitch 1

"Imagine a world where every coffee lover can indulge in the luxury of gourmet coffee, customized to their taste, anytime, anywhere. That's what our Nespresso system offers. With our sleek and user-friendly machine, users can savor a wide range of premium coffee flavors, meticulously crafted for the perfect brew. No more waiting in line at cafes or settling for mediocre coffee. Our system brings the café experience right to your fingertips. Plus, our responsive Nespresso Club ensures round-the-clock access to your favorite capsules. It's convenience, quality, and indulgence all in one cup. I'd love to discuss how we can revolutionize the coffee experience further. Can we schedule a follow-up meeting to explore this opportunity?"

Elevator pitch 2

"Good morning! Have you ever dreamed of a coffee experience that's both luxurious and convenient? Our Nespresso system delivers just that. Picture this: a sleek machine that brews premium coffee tailored to your taste, right in the comfort of your home or office. No more waiting in line at cafes or compromising on quality. With our system, you'll enjoy a wide range of gourmet flavors at the touch of a button. Plus, our Nespresso Club ensures you always have access to your favorite capsules. It's convenience, quality, and indulgence rolled into one. I'd love to discuss how we can bring this revolutionary coffee experience to more people. Can we schedule a follow-up meeting to explore this opportunity further?"

Not bad for a… machine!

9.6 Stakeholders' Benefits

A robust Solution delivers Benefits to several Stakeholders.[5] The CUE specifies the Benefits that the Customer will receive, which are directly tied to the outcomes of Customer Benchmarking using the CDCs and the Five Fs.[6] Additionally, the Project will yield Benefits for other important Stakeholders, such as the organization and/or its distributors. For example, when Apple chose to distribute its iPhone through selected operators, the business model generated Benefits not only for phone users but also for the telecom operators (and, of course, for Apple!).

Stakeholders' Benefits include social Benefits and what is commonly referred to as CSR (Corporate Social Responsibility). When an organization delivers Benefits to stakeholders beyond its customers, investors/owners/shareholders, it is usually for social purposes. This social objective can take many forms, but the underlying logic should be that the organization does not expect anything in return. The decision to allocate resources to support a social cause is generally driven by a desire to do what is right or to act in a socially responsible manner. The extent of social Benefits to be delivered will vary based on the threshold established by each group of decision-makers. For instance, those who prioritize delivering "shareholder value" are likely to have a minimal (or even non-existent) commitment to social Benefits. Conversely, "non-profit" organizations or NGOs will focus their efforts on providing Benefits to their target population, even though an excessively altruistic approach might threaten their own sustainability. To maintain coherence, decision-makers should ideally express the target threshold for social Benefits, ensuring that only projects meeting this requirement are implemented.

[5] See Chap. 13.

[6] See Chap. 8.

Clarifying who receives Benefits and what those Benefits entail is crucial because it helps to understand who gains from the project. Moreover, some entrepreneurs become so fixated on their own Benefits that they overlook the needs of other key Stakeholders.

The Five F's tool[7] *can be instrumental in identifying Benefits for Stakeholders by applying it to each Stakeholder*, rather than exclusively for each Customer. Examining how each dimension of the Five F's influences each Stakeholder can reveal Benefits, including some that may be unexpected. It's important to remember that the Five F's should be applied to one beneficiary at a time.

It's not uncommon for managers to start projects that align more with their personal interests or those of their employer, overlooking the actual Pain/Need/Desire(s) of the Customers, especially when these customers are internal, like employees. When personal or organizational desires take precedence over addressing the Customers' PNDs, it frequently leads to frustration and, in many cases, failure.

Decision-makers must understand the potential Benefits for each Stakeholder to determine which projects merit implementation (Fig. 9.2). Mapping out these Benefits provides them with a comprehensive overview.

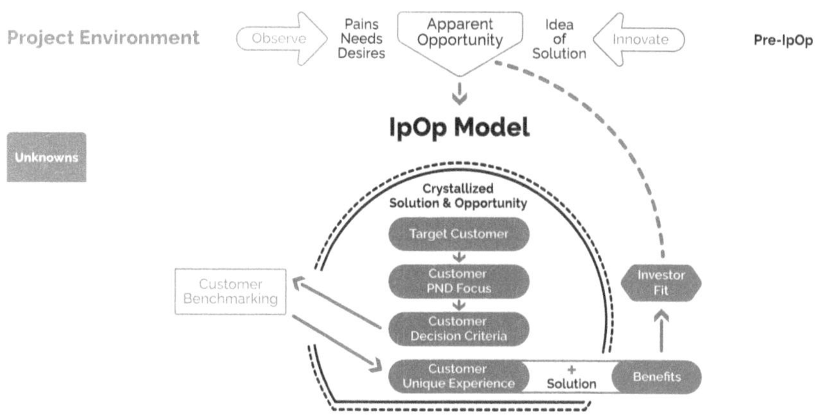

Fig. 9.2 The Opportunity delivers Benefits to other Stakeholders in addition to those for Customers

[7] See Chap. 9.

Link with ISO 56007 (Tools and Methods for Managing Opportunities and Ideas: Guidance)

ISO 56007 does not specifically refer to the Customer Unique Experience (CUE) or the Benefits brought to Stakeholders.[8] However, it does mention 'customer/user fit' and 'acceptance by interested parties' as important selection criteria.

Acceptance by 'interested parties' hinges on their satisfaction with the Benefits a project delivers to Stakeholders. The IpOp Model make these Benefits explicit.

The Customer Benchmarking within the IpOp Model acts as a powerful and dependable method for assessing what ISO 56007 terms as 'customer/user fit'. Without Benchmarking grounded in specific Customer Decision Criteria for each Customer, the concept of 'customer/user fit' remains vague and undefined. The IpOp Model's approach to Benchmarking introduces clarity and precision to this assessment.

By defining the criteria for acceptance for both customers and stakeholders, the IpOp Model clarifies what drives buy-in from customers/users and interested parties, as recommended by ISO 56007.

[8] ISO 56007 does not use the term 'stakeholder' but talks of 'interested parties'. Same idea, different terminology. As explained in Chap. 13, the IpOp Model clarifies what stakeholders are. The number of people who fit the IpOp Model definition of stakeholders is usually smaller that those who fit ISO 56007 definition of interested parties.

10

The Effort Model Can Be the Top Model in Your Life

What Does It Entail?

Recap of IpOp Review 1

Reminder: the objective of IpOp Review 1 is to confirm that there is hope – hope to obtain buy-in from the Investor[1] and from the Customers.[2] To determine if your offering will be appealing enough to the Customer, you must compare it with other available Alternatives that satisfy the PNDs you are targeting. This comparison, or Benchmarking, is meaningful only when you apply all the Customer Decision Criteria that your target Customer would use to select the most appropriate Solution to address those PNDs. Since your offering cannot excel against all the Customer Decision Criteria, you will need to select a subset of CDCs where you can outperform the Alternatives. This differentiation will enable you to offer a Customer Unique Experience and additional Benefits to your other Stakeholders. IpOp Review 1 analysis will also help identify the Unknowns to be cataloged.

Once IpOp Review 1 (Fig. 10.1) has shown that there is hope you can proceed to IpOp Review 2.

[1] Chap. 6.

[2] Chaps. 7 to 9.

R. H Cohen, *Pre-Project Excellence*, Future of Business and Finance,
https://doi.org/10.1007/978-3-031-61774-4_10

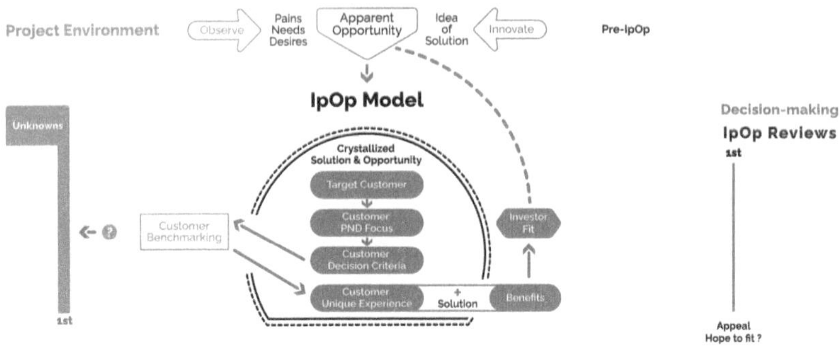

Fig. 10.1 IpOp Review 1 ("Is there hope?")

IpOp Review 2

Chapters 10 and 11 will guide you on how to respond to the IpOp Review 2 question: **Is it worth it?**

Reminder: To determine if an Opportunity is worth seizing, you should compare the outcome (the "prize" or "success") with the efforts required to obtain that prize. Naturally, when the outcome is not worth the effort, it makes no sense to continue with the Opportunity. If the conclusion is that the Opportunity is worth it, then you can proceed with the next Review.

Take-Home of This Chapter

This chapter focuses on the effort required to deliver the customer experience. The effort is defined by the Scope of the project, the required Activity Chain and the Resource model. The Activity Chain describes all the activities that are necessary to successfully implement the project and obtain the desired results. A suitable Activity Chain requires good mastery of the Industry Key Activity Ingredients and the principles of success in choosing a successful business model. This chapter emphasizes the importance of sustainable profitability, a compelling proposition to the target market, real and easily communicable Benefits, and the need for competitive advantages. The chapter also highlights the significance of making strategic trade-offs, aligning objectives with available resources, and the role of the Resource model in generating resources to satisfy Stakeholders' Aspirations.

Since ISO 56007 focuses on project selection criteria and resource investment compatibility, the content of this chapter can be used to implement ISO 56007 by providing insights into the Effort model and analyzing possible options for generating resources to satisfy Stakeholders' Aspirations.

No opportunity exists without an effort. The effort required depends on several parameters, including the Scope of the Opportunity, the Activity Chain, and the Resource Model. The Effort model consolidates these elements, encompassing the scope of the project, the necessary activities, and how resources will be generated.

Although the Effort model is a substantial component of the business model, it is important to note that the business model as defined below comprises more than just the Effort model. For instance, the value proposition, which is not included in the Effort model, is also integral to the business model.

10.1 The Business Model

One definition of a business model, proposed by Timmers (1998)[3] is:

- An architecture for the product, service, information flows, including a description of various business actors and their roles

[3]Timmers, P. (1998). Business models for electronic markets. Electronic Markets, 8(2), 3-8.

- A description of potential benefits for the various actors involved
- A description of the sources of revenue generated by the business model

The commonly accepted definition of a business model today is provided by Alexandre Osterwalder and Yves Pigneur. They define it as the rationale of how an organization creates, delivers, and captures value.[4] This definition is represented by the nine components of their business model canvas: key partners, key activities, value proposition, customer relationships, customer segments, key resources, channels, cost structure and revenue streams.

The best business model is one that satisfies the key Stakeholders' Aspirations[5] for increased wealth and/or resources (whether expressed in monetary or other terms) while consuming a minimum of resources.

The introduction of a new business model can pose a major threat to many established businesses. Very few organizations are immune to the potential challenge posed by newcomers with different business models. Examples include the airline industry facing competition from low-cost carriers, the pharmaceutical sector being challenged by generic drugs, travel agencies losing market share to online booking services, the proprietary software industry facing competition from open-source models, and more.

A notable example of a public sector activity that some time ago failed to optimize its business model is the postal service. It overlooked the changing needs of its customers and did not question its own efficiency. This flaw in the postal service's business model created a ripe opportunity for courier services. The lesson learned is quite telling: while courier services now thrive, many postal services struggle to break even. It underscores the importance of public administrations, like the postal service, periodically reassessing their business models and Mission statements in response to dynamic environments. Even workers' unions are

[4] Business Model Generation, Alexandre Osterwalder, Yves Pigneur, 2009, ISBN 978-8399-0580-0.

[5] See Chap. 13.

adapting their business models; some are even venturing into investment in commercial enterprises.

10.2 The Scope of the Opportunity

To assess the effort required, you must first define the Scope of your project. The broader the Scope or the wider the perimeter, the greater the resources necessary to manage the manage the Opportunity effectively.

It is crucial to limit the Scope of your project. Without defined boundaries, there is a risk of overextending your resources. Establishing the parameters of your project aids in maintaining focus. These parameters include:

- Geographical boundaries
- Targeted market segments
- Time frame for achieving your objectives
- Scope of needs to be addressed
- Intended technology you intend to use, etc

The Scope of a project can be a central component of both the Effort model and the business model. This is for instance the case when location is critical or in the presence of a captive audience (e.g. airport duty-free stores).

Limiting the Scope of your activities can help maintain focus, allowing you to prioritize certain Opportunities over others due to resource constraints. Essentially, it involves choosing which battles to fight and which ones to ignore.

Scope is defined by Stakeholders,[6] because they are the only ones who hold influence over your project. It is important to remember that Stakeholders, including yourself, play a crucial role in defining the boundaries and extent of your project (Fig. 10.2).

---

[6] See Chap. 13.

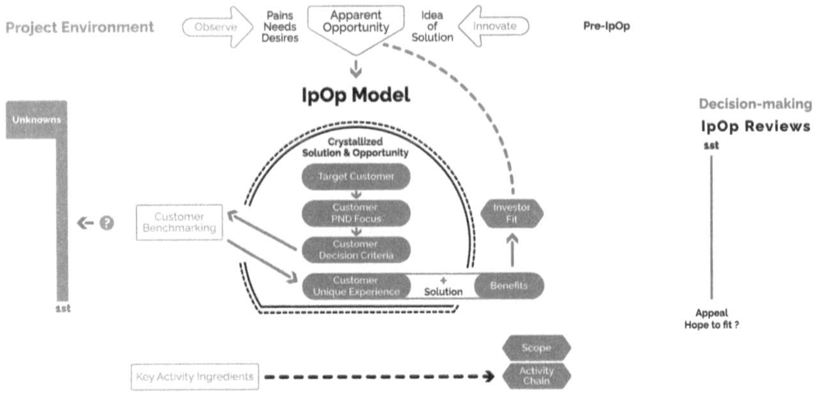

Fig. 10.2 The Scope defines the perimeter of the project

Scope of Nespresso Classic

- Geographic catchment area: Worldwide, with progressive introduction of markets
- Size of market: XXX million machines
- Target public: Households equipped with, or having the potential of being equipped with a coffee machine

10.3 Analyzing the Activity Chain

My definition of the Activity Chain is the catalog of activities required to deliver the Benefits expected by the target Customers and Stakeholders throughout the product's lifecycle. It consists of tasks performed by people, machines or subcontractors rather than individuals.

Understanding the Activity Chain fully is essential before exploiting any Opportunity. It is uncommon for an entity to fully master the entire Activity Chain. Typically, some components of the Activity chain are outsourced to subcontractors, while others are handled in-house or delegated to other players. For instance, car manufacturers don't produce and sell gasoline; that responsibility is taken up by oil companies. However, the Activity Chain for inkjet printers diverges, as the manufacturers produce and sell the consumables themselves, rather than outsourcing this to third parties, as seen with gasoline. With companies like Tesla selling energy for their own cars, it is evident that conventional Activity Chains and business models are capable of evolving.

To fully grasp the Activity chain, you must master the Industry Key Activity Ingredients. These are the fundamental ingredients required for any project to succeed within a specific industry. For example, anyone who wants to produce and sell ice-cream must have a refrigerated supply chain equipped with refrigerated trucks; without this infrastructure, distributing the products would be impossible. Similarly, luxury brands must establish service centers in key cities worldwide to facilitate successful international distribution. Low-cost airlines often use secondary, more affordable airports and maintain fleets consisting of a single type of airplane to keep costs down.[7]

Understanding these Key Activity ingredients is crucial because they shape the architecture of the project's Activity chain. This understanding demands a great familiarity with the market, the customers, and the key Stakeholders involved (Fig. 10.3).

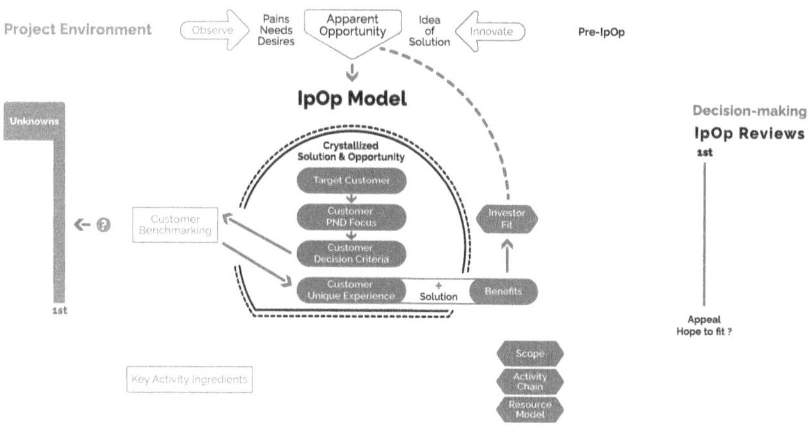

Fig. 10.3 The Activity Chain must be well understood to identify the critical components and those that can be outsourced or left to third parties

[7] Having only one model of airplane reduces the operating costs for inventory of spare parts, pilot training, etc.

It is essential to clarify which part of the Activity chain you are willing to take accountability for. Accountability doesn't preclude outsourcing; it means you have a responsibility to the client for the product or service you deliver, regardless of whether it is produced in-house or outsourced.

A clear understanding of the Activity chain should enable you to:

- Identify the resources necessary for each component of the Activity chain
- Determine which components of the Activity chain primarily enhance the perceived Benefits for the Customers
- Recognize which strategic components of the Activity chain can generate the highest profits or Benefits for you
- Decide whether you or a subcontractor is best suited to handle each part of the Activity chain
- Identify synergies between the various components of the Activity chain
- Identify components of the Activity chain that can act as barriers to competitors or could potentially do so in the future

These questions are relevant not only to private sector enterprises but also to public and nonprofit sectors, as well as government agencies.

Familiarity with the Activity chain is essential for identifying the best Resource model. Understanding where value is created clearly paves the way for capturing the maximum benefits from an opportunity.

10.4 Resource Model Vs. Business Model

I personally differentiate the Resource Model from the business model and define the Resource Model more simply as the mechanism generating (and sometimes also using) the necessary resources to satisfy the project Stakeholders. In the previous version of this book, I used the term Economic Model for a concept that is about generating resources. To avoid the frequent confusion with the business model, I now prefer to use Resource Model. This adjustment aligns with the business model canvas's notion of "revenue streams," which suggests that all projects must generate revenues. However, I choose not to use 'revenue stream' because not all projects need to produce revenues. For example, a project relying on volunteers generates 'volunteers' as a resource, which is different from 'revenues'.

While the term Resource model is clearer than Economic model, there's still potential for confusion with the Resources required to initiate the project, which are part of the Investment. It is important not to mix up the Resource model—the mechanism a project employs to generate ongoing resources—with the Investment, which supplies the initial Resources necessary for the Action Plan to reduce Unknowns and for the Action Plan aimed at achieving the Definition of Success.

The Resource model includes only some of the components of the business model. Using the terminology of the business model canvas[8] these are:

- The "revenue streams" (always)
- Sometimes the proportional part of the "cost structure" when this proportion is essential, for instance when a portion of the income is allocated to support a social cause (or to pay a commission to sales agents)

Thus, in order to survive, a project must:

- Obtain resources (money, people, equipment, subcontractors, systems, etc.)
- with a preferably recurrent mechanism (in order to be sustainable over time)
- such as to satisfy its Stakeholders

All projects, whether for profit or not, require an Resource model[9] since they always consume resources (money and/or time). For a project to be sustainable it must address the generation of the necessary resources (Fig. 10.4). This can be accomplished, for instance, through the

[8] Business Model Generation, Alexandre Osterwalder, Yves Pigneur, 2009, ISBN 978-8399-0580-0.

[9] In this book, I will primarily use the expression 'Resource model', with the understanding that it should not be confused with the concept of business model that encompasses more components than the Resource model.

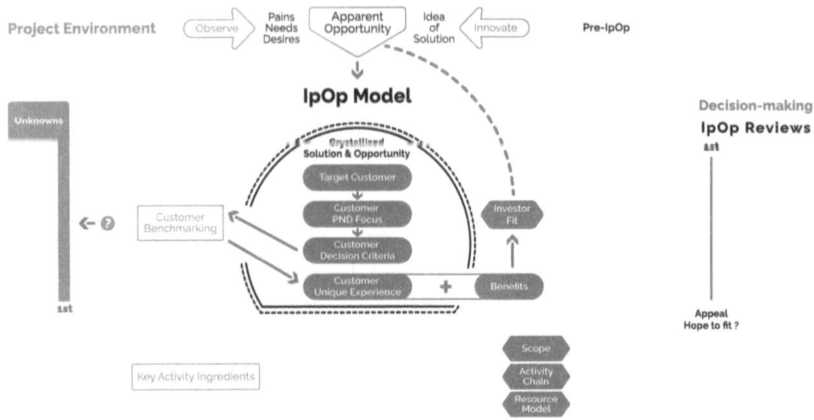

Fig. 10.4 The Resource Model is the mechanism for recurrently generating the resources to satisfy Stakeholders' Aspirations

profit margin on product sales or through ongoing funding (by investors, government bodies, donations, etc.).

In the private sector, generating income is an absolute prerequisite because it is the primary means of obtaining the necessary resources to finance growth, cover overheads, purchase equipment and pay dividends to shareholders. While net profit might appear to be an obvious and straightforward measure of Resource model efficiency, it overlooks several other dimensions, including environmental impact and Stakeholders' satisfaction levels.

Public sector and not-for-profit organizations also need to decide upon a Resource model. While this term may not sound appropriate in this context, these organizations must address similar issues, although distinct from actual profit (reminder: a no-profit objective is a profit with value of zero). All organizations, including those solely operating as cost centers, in fact operate based on an Resource model as defined above. In their Resource model, the source of income may include the State or other Stakeholders. Because (hopefully!) public-sector and not-for-profit organizations also produce some form of output, they should strive to optimize the resource/result ratio, similar to any private sector entity. This is where the Resource model becomes important. In essence, the only difference between for-profit and not-for-profit organizations lies in the *use* of the profits. Not-for-profit organizations use the profit to improve the benefits delivered to the target population rather than distributing it as dividends to investors. Not-for-profit organizations are, in fact, always willing to make a profit because it provides additional resources to further their objectives.

10.5 Choosing a Resource Model

The heart of choosing an Resource model is determining the source of your re…sources. This decision significantly impacts the project's sustainability. A striking example is seen during the dotcom bubble, where many companies failed due to choosing the wrong Resource model. Numerous defunct companies wrongly assumed that selling Internet advertising space, aiming to reach millions of users, would fund their development and marketing costs. However, this strategy only proved successful for a handful that had achieved critical mass, such as Google and Yahoo. Thus, selecting this unrealistic Resource model proved to be a fatal error for many who could not reach critical mass.

Many viable Resource models exist, and there are no one-size fits-all solution. Numerous books[10] have been written and will continue to be written, on business and/or Resource models. Here are just a few examples that illustrate different approaches to seizing opportunities. The choice of model depends on many factors, including available resources or talent:

- **Licensing:** Roland Moreno, the inventor of the smartcard, achieved massive market penetration by licensing the technology instead of manufacturing the product himself
- **Franchising**: McDonald's success demonstrates the benefits of this model. Benetton also used franchising to rapidly penetrate the market with fewer resources than proprietary retailing entities

[10] I recommend "Business Model Generation" by Alexandre Osterwalder and Yves Pigneur. The explanations and many examples it contains are an excellent source of inspiration that can help any entrepreneur or intrapreneur-to-be to explore his or her options.

- **Freebies:** The strategy of giving away certain products to generate income from other associated products. An obvious example is Google, a website that delivers free information while earning revenue by selling advertising space to advertisers
- **Captive service/supplies:** Instead of selling equipment, income is generated by selling services or supplies required by the equipment. Inkjet printers are an example: consumers get them for low prices but pay high prices for cartridges. Photocopiers are another example, where suppliers make more money servicing the units than selling them
- **Timesharing:** Long-term real estate rentals are split among many tenants, who pay for limited periods of time. This allows charging substantially more for weekly use compared to normal annual rent divided by 52

Resource models schemes include selling, renting, licensing, receiving commissions, grants or subsidies, and more. Our objective is not to detail every possible Resource model but to emphasize that selecting a suitable Resource model demands thorough analysis and sometimes even creativity to invent new ones.

Choosing the wrong Resource model is a classic cause of failure. An opportunity might succeed with one Resource model but fail with another. An interesting example is the Macromedia Flash Browser plug-in, a popular platform for interactive web content and animations initially available free of charge to end-user. This move led to Flash animation becoming an industry standard. However, Macromedia generated revenue by selling developers the programming software needed to create Flash animations. Flash was eventually supplanted by another standard (HTML/CSS), which effectively ended this Revenue Model.

Understanding your customers and the market is critical for determining a viable Resource model. While the anthropological approach mentioned earlier can certainly contribute to this understanding, it is not the only way. Experience, creativity and gut feeling also play important roles. The success of the App Store is a good example of how a creative Resource model can yield remarkable results.

When exploring Resource models, I strongly recommend seeking advice or coaching from experienced businesspeople. Given the critical importance of the Resource model to your success, such guidance can shorten the typically challenging learning curve and decrease the likelihood of failure. Genius can sometimes be the inventor or innovator's worst enemy: after making an exciting discovery, there is a tendency to believe that one has all the answers. However, it is essential to remain humble and seek qualified assistance. While talking to family and friends may offer some insight, it is not sufficient for making informed decisions in this regard.

Selecting a Resource model usually involves making several assumptions. In many cases, these assumptions cannot be fully verified until the model is implemented in real time or through a pilot study. You should test a Resource model whenever possible and be prepared to revise it or explore alternatives. The penetration of mobile phones really took off once their purchase became subsidized by operators through monthly subscriptions. This adjustment to the Resource model acted as a catalyst for wide market penetration.

Some companies simultaneously utilize multiple Resource Models. Newspapers or magazines can, for instance, generate revenue from a variety of sources: subscribers, advertising, retail sales, etc. Each of these requires certain specific conditions to be met (subscribers want high quality content while advertisers seek a wide-ranging readership, etc.). Sometimes these conditions conflict with one other, forcing the publication to perform a balancing act that would not be necessary with only a single Resource model. For instance, financial media selling advertising space to financial institutions may not have the same level of independence in their articles as financial newsletters relying solely on subscriptions.

The Resource model for the first English version of this book ("Winning Opportunities") represented a paradigm shift for both business and teaching books. In these categories, it was the first—or one of the first—books with a "set-your-own-price" Resource model. This innovative offering challenged the Resource model of traditional publishers as well as brick-and-mortar bookstores. Readers were invited to download and read "Winning Opportunities" before deciding in all fairness what value they attributed to its content. Additionally, a "print-on-demand" hardcopy version was also available at Amazon for those who wanted to own a physical version.

The choice of Resource model can "make or break" an Opportunity. Consequently, it is essential that you explore all the possible options and analyze them carefully before choosing the one most appropriate for your Opportunity. You must then test it, ideally in a pilot study, as recommended above.

Nespresso Classic's Business Model

Nespresso's classic business model was based on the following characteristics (which also contribute to its originality and market leadership):

- The integration, under a single brand name, of pre-dosed coffee capsules and machines that originally only worked with these capsules
- Mastery of the entire coffee activity chain, right from the purchase of the grains to dispatch to the consumer
- Mastery of the entire machine activity chain, apart from manufacture, which is subcontracted (but after-sales service and marketing of the machines remain in Nespresso's hands)
- Automatic membership of the Nespresso Club for everyone who buys a machine
- Direct sale of capsules through the Nespresso Club (the main source of income, part of the Resource model)
- Strong personalization of the relationship through the information obtained in the Nespresso Club, leading to customer intimacy
- Sale of derived products (a further source of income, part of the Resource model)

Nespresso Classic's Resource Model

Since I couldn't determine whether Nespresso generates a profit margin from selling the machines, I will assume here that Nespresso Classic generates resources primarily through the sale of capsules, which have a profit margin that provides recurring income for Nespresso. This approach is augmented by the sale of related products, such as cups and accessories.

10.6 Some Principles of Success

In the IpOp Model, the business model is a subset of the Action Plan designed to achieve the Definition of Success. The Action Plan covers more than just the business model; it includes all Tactical Moves, such as marketing, communication, production, logistics, supply chain management, financing, and beyond.

Several principles can significantly contribute to choosing a successful business model. Adhering to these principles will enhance your project's prospects for long-term success and satisfaction:

- **Sustainable profitability**: Make sustainable profitability your primary goal, prioritizing it over market share or volume. The dot-com bubble demonstrated the importance of this principle, as many companies focused on growth without ensuring profitability. This principle applies not only to the private sector but also to public sector and not-for-profit organizations, where profitability entails maintaining operating expenses at an optimal level. Just like private enterprises, these organizations should strive to achieve their objectives at the lowest possible cost
- **Compelling proposition**: Develop a compelling proposition tailored to an identified segment of the market (see the following chapter for more details). The more unique and irresistible your proposition is, the more compelling it will be to your target audience. To maintain the uniqueness of your Opportunity, design a model that is difficult to replicate. Creating a complex yet well-integrated Activity Chain can make it harder for competitors to copy your entire system compared to copying individual components
- **Real and Communicable Benefits**: Ensure that the Benefits of your offering are real and easily communicated. Perceived Benefits are essential for generating income and profits
- "Best practice" alone does not ensure success**:** It merely sets the minimum standard for players with the necessary resources. A competitive advantage, such as proprietary components inaccessible to others, goes beyond best practice. While following best practices is beneficial, the ultimate goal should be to attain competitive advantages
- ***Avoid "Me Too" Strategies***: "Me too" strategies may not lead to leadership positions. They are better suited for following trends or entering unsaturated markets. However, relying solely on such strategies can make you vulnerable to competitors in the long run

- **Strategic Trade-offs**: Robust strategies involve making strategic choices and trade-offs to differentiate yourself from competitors. For example, easyJet's decision to sell airline tickets exclusively online sacrificed traditional retail channels but led to a competitive advantage. When trade-offs are not possible, you may revert to a "best practice" approach
- **Resource Availability**: Ensure that financial and human resources are available when needed. If your business model requires resources beyond your reach, adapt it to align with available resources realistically. Fantasizing about miracles won't help; practical alignment of objectives and resources is crucial

Focusing on your Opportunity obliges you to forgo other opportunities because it is impossible to pursue them all simultaneously. Seizing an Opportunity involves an Opportunity cost, as opting for one Opportunity means you are unable to pursue others.

Link with ISO 56007 (Tools and Methods for Managing Opportunities and Ideas: Guidance)

ISO 56007 focuses on project selection criteria, concentrating on verifying the availability of the required resource investment and the alignment of the project's business model with the organization's business/mission model. This assessment of alignment suggests that the project possesses its own business model, inherently incorporating a 'Resource model' as defined and explained by the IpOp Model.

Furthermore, identifying the resource Investment a project demands involves understanding its Scope, Activity Chain, and Resource Model. Here, components of the IpOp Model come into play, addressing at the practical level the considerations highlighted by ISO 56007.

11

The KISsing Game

KISs Are What Define Your Success

Take-Home of This Chapter

ISO 56007 mentions the importance of the definition of success in concept selection criteria but does not explain how to state such definition of success. The IpOp Model offers a concrete definition of the 'Definition of Success': it requires to define what success means for a project and how it can be measured through Key Indicators of Success (KISs). KISs define the purpose of a project while KPIs measure the means to deliver the purpose. It also highlights the need to define measurable Objectives and milestones based on the chosen KISs to monitor progress. In the IpOp Model the Definition of Success is the table that outlines the target Objectives over time for each Key Indicators of Success. Since this table expresses the measurable end-purpose/final outcome of the project, the Definition of Success helps Decision-makers understand what is in it for them. Serving as a contract between the project team and Decision-makers, the Definition of Success should give them enough reasons to allocate the necessary Resources to the project.

The IpOp Model furthermore stresses the need to also express the Definition of Failure (the minimum objectives for the project to continue). The Key Indicators of Failure, also known as Opportunity Terminators, can lead to project termination if certain thresholds are not met within a specific time period. While the Definition of Success expresses the ambition of the project (best case scenario), the Definition of Failure expresses the minimum below which the project should be stopped. The Definition of Success

R. H Cohen, *Pre-Project Excellence*, Future of Business and Finance,
https://doi.org/10.1007/978-3-031-61774-4_11

and Failure form an explicit contract between stakeholders, and particularly Investors, expressing not only what the project will deliver but also the minimum expectations. This contributes to stakeholders' alignment at the pre-project stage.

There is no rest for the entrepreneur. If delivering a CUE Description was challenging, the next step is unfortunately likely to be even more so. Now that you can satisfy your target market, you need to translate this into measurable objectives, the only way to prove to yourself and others later that you have achieved something with your project. What we are discussing here in practical terms is your Definition of Success.

The key is to measure what you want to achieve. What can be measured can be monitored, and what can be monitored has a better chance of being delivered. Psychologically, people pay a lot more attention when something is being measured and monitored than when it is not. The first rule for making something happen is to monitor its progress. Just the act of recording the number of customer complaints in a business can lead to their reduction, and employees will focus more on customer satisfaction. Similarly, entrepreneurial behavior can often be improved by including an index that grades innovation or intrapreneurial attitudes in employees' periodical evaluations. Such improvements are less likely to occur without measurement.

Piloting a project requires monitoring instruments to help you understand how far from (or close to) your objectives you are and confirm that you are still on the right track. Jumping into a project without setting up monitoring in advance is like taking off in an airplane without cockpit instruments: no safety is possible without a constant check on speed, altitude, gasoline reserves, etc.

11.1 The Key Indicators of Success

Now you need to decide the Key Indicators of Success (KISs) that will best measure your project's success. Is it turnover? Profit? Market share? Social impact? Technological leadership? Visibility or brand recognition? Employee loyalty? The options are endless because there is no limit to such criteria. It is important to note that KISs are not limited to financial indicators alone.

Choosing KISs requires you to clarify your project's purpose. Is it for profit, enhancing reputation, enjoyment, or personal satisfaction? In simpler terms, what are the project's goals and expected outcomes? Experience suggests that project promoters may not always have clarity on this, especially when emotions are involved. Defining the project's purpose helps align everyone involved and avoids conflicts or frustrations later on. The best way to do this is to choose indicators that measure the end result, what I call Key Indicators of Success (KISs)!

The initial challenge lies in selecting KISs that can be feasibly monitored with the resources at hand. The measurement does not need to be perfectly precise but should offer enough insight to gauge your progress. The level of accuracy will depend on what is being measured. For example, measuring customer satisfaction will always involve some level of approximation. A straightforward approach to measure customer satisfaction could involve asking potential customers if they would recommend your product or service to others. It is most important to carefully interpret the results provided by each indicator.

The next challenge arises from the necessity to limit the number of KISs to a bare minimum. In fact, the fewer KISs the better. The greater the number of KISs employed, the more resources will be required to measure them, and consequently, the less attention people will pay to them. It is important to concentrate on the key issues and set aside minor aspects. Additionally, having too many KISs increases the likelihood of overlap (such as profit and return on investment being closely related). However, maintaining focus on a small number of KISs demands discipline.

While both KISs and KPIs are key indicators, KISs measure the end result, while KPIs measure the way to obtain the KIS, the 'how'. If profit is the KIS, customer satisfaction is then only a KPI, a condition to generate higher profit.

KISs can exist only after launching, because they gauge the end result, not the process of reaching it. Stakeholders are concerned with measurable outcomes, which can be effectively expressed through KISs.

The Nespresso Classic's KISs

- Profit
- Turnover
- Brand notoriety (it could alternatively also be replaced by brand valuation)

11.2 Deciding on Your Time Horizon

Deciding on which KISs to use involves envisioning the future, which requires setting a time horizon for your project—an intriguing exercise in itself. If your horizon is too short, the Opportunity may not have a fair chance to demonstrate its potential. Conversely, if you look too far ahead, your plans plans may become unrealistic, given the likelihood of evolving circumstances.

Therefore, you need to set meaningful milestones for your Opportunity. The time frame—whether it is weeks, months, or years—will depend on the nature of the project. This essentially involves projecting yourself into the future, and determining when a checkpoint is necessary. In the case of a start-up, for instance, the milestones might include:

- 6 months after launch
- 1 year after launch
- 3 or 4 years after launch (although in some fast-moving industries today, 4 years might be too distant to plan for)

Consider your Stakeholders' time horizon carefully. Since you are dedicated to meeting the needs of key Stakeholders, it is important to align your time frame with theirs. For example, if your investors expect a 3-year payback, presenting them with a 7-year plan may not be beneficial. Therefore, it is highly recommended to understand your Stakeholders' time horizon beforehand.

11.3 Setting Objectives

Your Definition of Success will encompass all the KISs Objectives at each milestone. Once the KISs are selected and the time horizon is defined, the next step is to establish measurable values for each indicator.

Setting Objectives involves assigning future time-stamped value to each KISs. These Objectives are not necessarily based on financial projections, but rather express what can be realistically achieved without considering the quantity or current availability of resources. They represent what you are aiming for.

Later you will be able to verify the feasibility of your initial Definition of Success. Once you adopt an Action Plan, which will in turn determine the necessary Resources, you will likely need to adjust your initial Objectives to align with this more realistic plan. Until then, you are considering only the ideal potential, without factoring in Resources. Coordinating Resources and Objectives will occur at a later stage. This early estimation of target Objectives enables you to assess the overall potential without the distortion that may result from considering possibly limited resources.

Establishing a Definition of Success demands careful consideration. If your Definition of Success (and its corresponding Objectives) is set too low, the Opportunity will not be worth pursuing. Whereas if it is aimed too high, you will inevitably lose credibility as soon as someone (usually the Decision-makers or the Investors, or both!) wakes up and realizes that you have overstated the case. This could happen early on or once you have failed to live up to your optimistic promise. So between the pessimistic and the optimistic scenarios, there is only one path: realistic Objectives!

The Definition of Success determines a project's appeal. Those tasked with evaluating proposals—Investors, review boards, fund providers, management, board of directors, incubators, grant providers, and more—scrutinize the Definition of Success closely. Their objective is to ensure that sponsored projects are worthwhile, realistic, and capable of delivering on their promise. The Definition of Success encapsulates a substantial portion of that promise. While other factors like market entry challenges, exploring new markets, or diverting Stakeholders' attention from other matters may influence decision-making, the Definition of Success remains paramount. The Definition of Success is the contract between your Decision-makers and you: it expresses what you will deliver in exchange of their support.

Many Opportunities never progress beyond this stage, because when promoters start playing with numbers, they often realize that the Opportunity is not worth their time. Setting overly ambitious Objectives has frightened off more than one intrapreneur-to-be. Finding the right balance is challenging and typically a major hurdle for the project team.

Establishing a Definition of Success acts as an important filter for the process. This happens at least twice: first when the promoters choose the Objectives and second when Stakeholders evaluate the Opportunity's potential.

A clear Definition of Success guides Tactical Moves. Once you establish your goals, you naturally begin considering the actions necessary to achieve them. For instance, hitting the targeted sales volume requires strategic maneuvers like deploying a sales force or launching a PR campaign to effectively reach Customers.

Nespresso Classic's Definition of Success (This table is based on fictitious data, as the actual information is confidential)

			Milestones			
N°	Key Indicators of Success (KISs)	Unit of measure	1 year	2 years	4 years	7 years
1	Profit	Million dollars	40	53	75	100
2	Sales	Million dollars	400	500	700	900
3	Brand notoriety	%	40%	60%	75%	90%

11.4 Defining Failure

Some indicators are so critical they are considered Opportunity Terminators or Key Indicators of Failure (KIFs). If a specific threshold is not met within a set timeframe for any of these Opportunity Terminators, the project must be halted.

Opportunity Terminators establish clear Stop/No Stop criteria. Setting a rule that the project will be abandoned if it fails to meet at least one minimum Objective (related to any of the Terminators or Key Indicators of Failure) is a powerful declaration. It shows exceptional discipline and a belief that all set thresholds can be achieved. Any seasoned stock market investor knows that the discipline to predefine the point at which to exit a losing investment is a key strategy for success.

People can easily become swayed by their emotions and struggle to accept cutting their losses early or capping their profits. This applies equally to Opportunities: making the decision in advance to quit, and having the discipline to follow through, both require significant maturity. Demonstrating that you can control your emotions will enhance your credibility.

Choosing Opportunity Terminators is not only for Investors but primarily for yourself. It can be advantageous to exit early before too much damage is incurred. It is so much healthier to throw in the towel before wasting excessive resources and energy on a hopeless proposal. Therefore, you must first decide which indicators should serve as killjoys and then establish the threshold for each of them that will trigger the decision to pull out.

Terminators act like a "sword of Damocles" that you voluntarily hang over your own head. Being aware that the project will stop if you do fail to meet the minimum Objectives set by the Terminators serves as powerful source of motivation for you and your team, the driving force behind the project. Understanding the consequences of insufficient performance will compel you to do everything necessary to avoid it. Terminators reduce the temptation to be too forgiving or complacent.

11.5 The Consequences of Failure

Acknowledging the possibility of failure also entails addressing its consequences, as aborting a project typically incurs costs. One significant consequence is accepting that all the money and other Resources invested in the project thus far have essentially been wasted. This realization can be difficult to accept on both a psychological and ego level. Consequently, many projects that should be stopped persist simply because Decision-makers struggle to admit they made the wrong decision.

Putting one's head in the sand becomes even more detrimental when Decision-makers believe that any negative consequences will only become apparent after they have moved on to different roles or been promoted. In such cases, they may feel no personal incentive to halt the project, as the "problem" will then become the responsibility of their successors. This phenomenon is particularly pronounced in politics, where politicians may initiate or fail to act on policies knowing that the repercussions, whether positive or negative, will manifest after their term in office has ended. A prime example of this short-term thinking is evident in the neglect of implementing a well-conceived immigration policy in France. The failure to facilitate the integration of immigrants has resulted, several years later, in the emergence of immigrant-dominated areas where even law enforcement officers are hesitant to enter.

Evaluating the consequences of curtailing the project is crucial because the likelihood of such action is never zero. Given that unforeseen events can, and often do, occur, it is imperative to assess potential outcomes to avoid being caught off guard. A prime example of this is evident in the experiences of numerous companies that introduced sophisticated enterprise resource planning systems (ERP) without considering this issue. Their objective was to achieve control, but instead, it resulted in the need to adapt processes to fit the software, rather than the other way around. Despite the frustration and decreased efficiency experienced by employees due to the new ERP, there was no feasible way to halt the implementation, as reversing the process would have incurred exorbitant costs.

Being responsible at the pre-project level requires not only defining the threshold of failure but also evaluating the consequences of curtailing the project. It is essential to ensure that you can afford those consequences; otherwise, you are in a difficult situation.

11.6 The Definitions of Success and Failure Are Tantamount to a Contract

The Definition of Failure is structured similarly to the Definition of Success but replaces Key Indicators of Success (KISs) with Key Indicators of Failure (KIFs) and objectives with minimum thresholds. Without these corresponding minimum thresholds, KIFs are not effective. The example below for Nespresso serves as a clear illustration of a Definition of Failure table.

The Definition of Success specifies your goals, while the Definition of Failure outlines the commitment to minimum standards below which the project should be discontinued. This approach, though straightforward, provides a more meaningful framework to Decision-makers. Simple perhaps, but far more compelling for Investors!

Since KISs and KIFs typically differ, the Definition of Failure often features different indicators than the Definition of Success. Customer satisfaction, for instance, might not always be a Key Indicator of Success because it is not an ultimate goal. However, it can be a critical indicator of failure: failing to achieve sufficient customer satisfaction could jeopardize success, suggesting the project should be terminated if it becomes clear that the required level of customer satisfaction to meet sales targets (often a KIS) is unattainable.

This pairing of the Definition of Success and the Definition of Failure is more useful than the usual optimistic-pessimistic-realistic (OPR) scenarios frequently included in business plans. OPR scenarios are often seen as speculative and fail to demonstrate true commitment or convince stakeholders. As such, the Definition of Failure is an essential complement to your Definition of Success.

The Definition of Success and the Definition of Failure constitute an explicit contract between Stakeholders (you included) because together they express what you commit to deliver. It is a straightforward agreement: you propose to achieve the Definition of Success (or at least avoid the Definition of Failure), and your Stakeholders agree to provide the necessary Resources—money, authorizations, and so on—because the end result (somewhere between the Definition of Success and the Definition of Failure) is appealing enough to them.

Allocating resources or authorizing projects without Definitions of Success and Failure would be like making an investment without knowing the potential return or the exit strategy. In theory, only foolish Decision-makers fall into such a trap. However, in practice, Decision-makers often support projects with a vague objectives and unclear deliverables. This might explain why many projects come to a halt before completion; by the time the Decision-makers realize the project is not progressing, a significant number of Resources has already been wasted.

Ratification of your Definitions of Success and Failure by Stakeholders, to whom you are accountable, by definition, is the simplest way to ensure that their Aspirations are met. Lack of such ratification must be interpreted as a clear sign that you should review your Objectives and possibly negotiate the content of the Definitions of Success and Failure. The benefit of this validation process is that it aligns your concept with the Aspirations of the main Stakeholders. The Definition of Success and Failure can also be considered as expressing the Stakeholders' WiiifT ("What's in it for Them").

This approach eliminates any unclear understandings and assumptions because the Definitions of Success and Failure are clearly stated. By making Objectives clear, you ensure that you and your Stakeholders agree on the ultimate deliverables. If you succeed, everyone will be pleased. However, if you do not meet the level of the Definition of Failure, some or all of your Stakeholders will be very disappointed.

The Definitions of Success and Failure instill discipline and focus. Stating Objectives explicitly creates liabilities, so this is a compelling driver to make things happen. They are crucial for any venture or project's success because once the Objectives are set, everyone, including yourself, can use them to track progress. If some Objectives are not met, you must provide a valid justification or face consequences. This forces an entrepreneur to focus on meeting the Definition of Success or at least the Definition of Failure.

Many investors are tempted to link the reward to the ability to deliver the promise. This could translate into founders' ownership dilution[1] if certain milestones such as the Definition of Failure are not reached. In some cases, founders lost everything because their plans did not unfold as expected, despite their initial promises to Investors.

Nespresso Classic Definition of Failure (the terminators below are fictitious, as this information is confidential)

		Milestones	
Indicators	Unit of measure	1 year	2 years
Profit	Million dollars	<5	<10
Sales	Million dollars	<100	<150
Taste preference	%	<40%	<50%

11.7 Your Credibility Will Depend on How You Define Success and Failure

Your Definition of Success helps to establish your credibility. At some point, Decision-makers and Investors will want to know where you are headed and the potential of the project. So, it is wise to be proactive and have a Definition of Success ready to address these concerns.

Having a Definition of Success proves that you have done your homework. It demonstrates that the promoters have thought ahead and are not rushing into the project without proper analysis. Only present your Definition of Success and Failure when you are ready to support your claims with solid justification.

[1] Mechanism reducing the percentage of the company owned by the founders with a corresponding increase of the percentage owned by Investor(s).

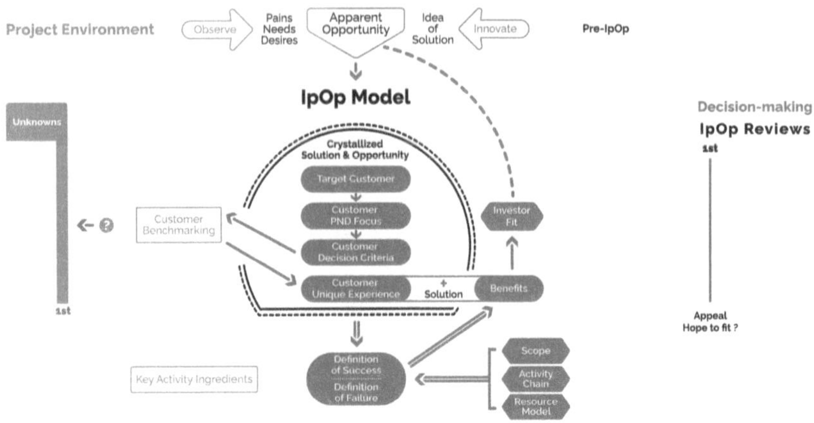

Fig. 11.1 The Definition of Success and Failure states the target and minimum Objectives

A project presented with a credible Definition of Success has a better chance of receiving a positive evaluation. It enables Decision-makers to easily verify that the proposal is compatible with their objectives and perception of its potential. Remember, a project with an unrealistic Definition of Success and Failure will damage your credibility (Fig. 11.1).

Link with ISO 56007 (Tools and Methods for Managing Opportunities and Ideas: Guidance)

ISO 56007 mentions the concept of the Definition of Success as one of the criteria for selecting the concept which is aligned with the organization. However, it does not provide a specific definition for this concept. This is typical of ISO standards, as they are not intended to serve as textbooks.

For those seeking a concrete definition of the 'Definition of Success' mentioned in ISO 56007, the IpOp Model offers a view on this aspect.

Although the Definition of Failure is not highlighted in the main text of the standard, it is featured as an essential part of the 'innovation concept case' template in the annex of ISO 56007.[2] This template advises specifying the minimum objectives that a project must meet, underscoring the role of the Definition of Failure as a complement to the Definition of Success.

[2] ISO 56007, annex C5.2.2.

12

Factoring in the Factors

Or More Bluntly: The Difference Between Success and… Failure

Recap of IpOp Review 2

Reminder: the objective of IpOp Review 2 is to confirm that the opportunity is worth pursuing. This is verified by comparing the effort[1] required to deliver the Definition of Success & Failure described in this chapter. Additional Unknowns will be catalogued during IpOp Review 2.

Once IpOp Review 2 has confirmed that the opportunity is worth pursuing, you can proceed to IpOp Review 3 (Fig. 12.1).

[1] (Chap. 10).

R. H Cohen, *Pre-Project Excellence*, Future of Business and Finance,
https://doi.org/10.1007/978-3-031-61774-4_12

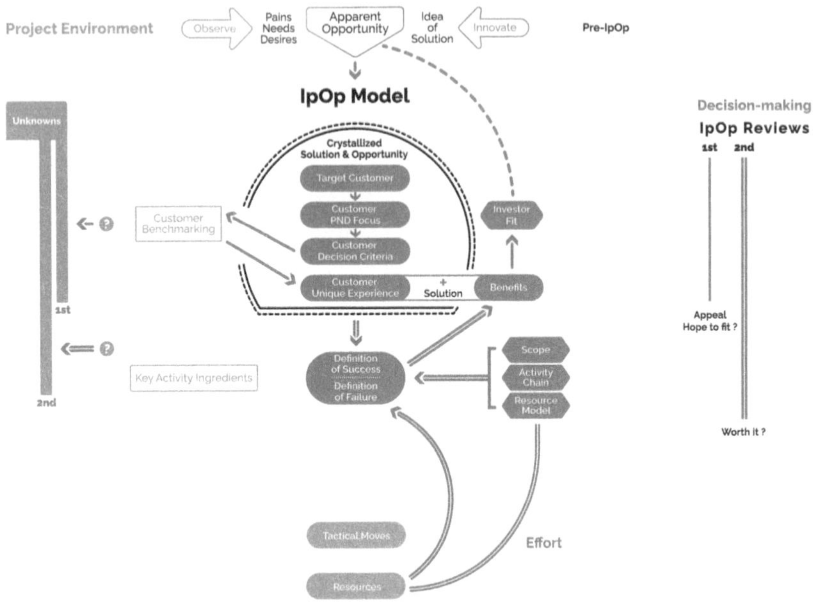

Fig. 12.1 IpOp Review 2 ("Is it worth it?) shows which effort is necessary to deliver the Definition of Success

IpOp Review 3

Chapters 12 and 13 will guide you on how to respond to the IpOp Review 3 question: **Are the Influencers acceptable?**

Reminder: IpOp Review 3 requires that you check whether you can live with all the parameters that can positively or negatively influence your ability to obtain the "prize". If the project is too risky or faces too many obstacles it might be preferable to give up. If you feel comfortable with those Influencers you can move on to the next Review.

Take-Home of This Chapter

This chapter discusses the importance of analyzing Factors in order to identify relevant Tactical Moves for a given Opportunity. It explains that Factors are parameters that have a positive or negative impact on the success of a project, both internal and external to the company. The IpOp Model is presented as a bottom-up approach that focuses on Factors that directly affect the Opportunity itself, rather than factors—like the SWOT—that impact the organization as a whole.

ISO 56007 addresses the acceptability of factors that hinder or boost implementation, but it does not provide specific guidance on how to handle these project selection criteria. This chapter provides insights on how to identify such Factors and emphasizes the need for a systematic assessment with a scale for rating their importance and probability of occurrence.

Factors are all the facts, issues, conditions, etc., that can have an impact on your ability to deliver what you have promised in your Definition of Success. You usually have little control over Factors. They are something you must live with and manage as best you can.

Integrating the Factors into your Opportunity analysis is indispensable. Once you know what you want to do (the Solution) and what you want to deliver (Definition of Success and Failure), you need to identify the Factors that can influence the success of your Opportunity.

12.1 SWOT Analysis

SWOT[2] analysis is the classic and best-known method for considering factors. A cornerstone of strategic analysis, SWOT is traditionally divided into:

- Strengths and Weaknesses, the internal factors
- Opportunities and Threats, the external factors

In strategic analysis, four key factors are examined to devise the optimal strategy that enables a company to leverage its *strengths* to capitalize on *opportunities*, overcome its *weaknesses*, and navigate around

[2] SWOT (Strengths, Weakness, Opportunities, and Threats).

threats. Because the starting point is the environment (identifying *opportunities*), this is typically a top-down approach, which is very useful and effective for optimizing resource allocation. SWOT analysis is especially pertinent for companies already in operation that need to develop or review a strategy, which defines future directions and outcomes.

Limits to the effectiveness of the SWOT top-down approach:

- The SWOT approach aims to integrate all the factors into a comprehensive strategy, starting from an analysis of the environment and including the Strengths and Weaknesses of the organization
- This top-down bird's-eye view requires a very broad analysis of the overall picture, and as such, it is likely to reveal many factors that are not relevant to the Opportunity under analysis
- Strategists at the top tend to be too distant from the action to discern all the parameters to be considered. Additionally, the information received by top-level individuals is often filtered as it moves up the hierarchy

12.2 The Bottom-Up Approach

Working on an Opportunity requires a bottom-up line of attack. The IpOp Model embodies such an approach. You only need to consider those SWOT factors that directly impact your own Opportunity, ignoring any that impact the organization without influencing the Opportunity itself.

Strengths and Weaknesses are not typically part of the intrapreneur's vocabulary. Moreover, at the pre-project stage, they are not yet relevant. For example, limited resources might be considered a Weakness, but the IpOp Model assumes that you are not yet concerned with resources and competences, which will be addressed later on. At this stage, the assumption is that if the Opportunity is worthwhile, the necessary Resources will be found when the time comes.[3]

In the IpOp Model Factors are parameters that you have very little or no control over, yet they significantly influence your likelihood of

[3] See Chap. 16.

success. They represent the environment in which your Opportunity operates, influenced by both internal and external elements of the organization and its surroundings.

Unlike SWOT, the distinction between internal and external factors is not relevant here. Both internal and external factors equally affect your ability to deliver your Definition of Success and Failure. For instance, internal factors defined by SWOT, such as a corporate culture focused solely on in-house technological excellence, can pose a major obstacle to introducing external innovations. In such cases, labeling this internal factor as a weakness may not be appropriate. This highlights the unsuitability of SWOT analysis for innovative projects, leading some to dismiss SWOT as "*so-what?*" or even "*such a waste of time*".

12.3 How to Identify Factors

Brainstorming serves as an effective starting point for listing all the Factors that directly or indirectly impact your Opportunity. It encourages lateral thinking, allowing for the exploration of connections between unrelated factors, which can unveil interesting Opportunities, as seen in the example of laser vision correction technology.

PESTEL analysis also proves valuable in identifying Factors. PESTEL, a trend analysis, encompasses six dimensions: Political, Economic, Social/Sociological, Technological, Environmental, and Legal/regulatory issues. Understanding trends and societal shifts can significantly influence your chances of success. For instance, the rise in Muslim fundamentalist terrorism exemplified by the September 11 attacks has created opportunities for security-related companies, posed risks for the travel industry, and presented temporary setbacks (Obstacles) for Arab companies conducting business abroad.

Corporate and cultural factors hold considerable sway over the trajectory of an intrapreneurial project. For example, within one company, a new product with the potential to compete with an existing offering might provoke hostility from other teams feeling threatened. In contrast, in a different corporate culture, such innovation could be embraced and endorsed.

Additionally, territorial and personal concerns can have a significant impact on your ability to obtain buy-in from some of your colleagues.

The list of Factors can never be exhaustive since it is impossible to anticipate every potential influence. Initially, a brainstorming session generates a list, with additional Factors continually added as preparation advances. It is important to maintain discipline in documenting these Factors to ensure they are systematically evaluated.

Factors are subject to change, amplifying their impact on your Opportunity. For example, the substantial decrease in long-distance telephone call prices due to the rise of VoIP has altered the Resource model for many telephone operators, impacting their revenue streams. A comprehensive approach involves considering how Factors may evolve over time and evaluating their potential impact on your Opportunity. This process also demands discipline.

12.4 Types of Factors

Essentially, in the IpOp Model Factors can be categorized into two groups:

- **Boosters,** which positively impact your project
- **Hurdles,** which must be overcome or dealt with for your project to succeed

Each of these categories can further be subdivided based on the degree of probability:

- **Certain:** Events that will happen for sure
- **Uncertain:** Events that may or may not occur

Risks are Hurdles that may or may not happen. Obstacles are also Hurdles. The distinction between a Risk and an Obstacle lies in their probability: a Risk falls into the uncertain category and may never materialize, whereas an Obstacle is certain to have a negative impact. Additionally, it is worth noting that some Boosters may also belong in the uncertain category (Fig 12.2).

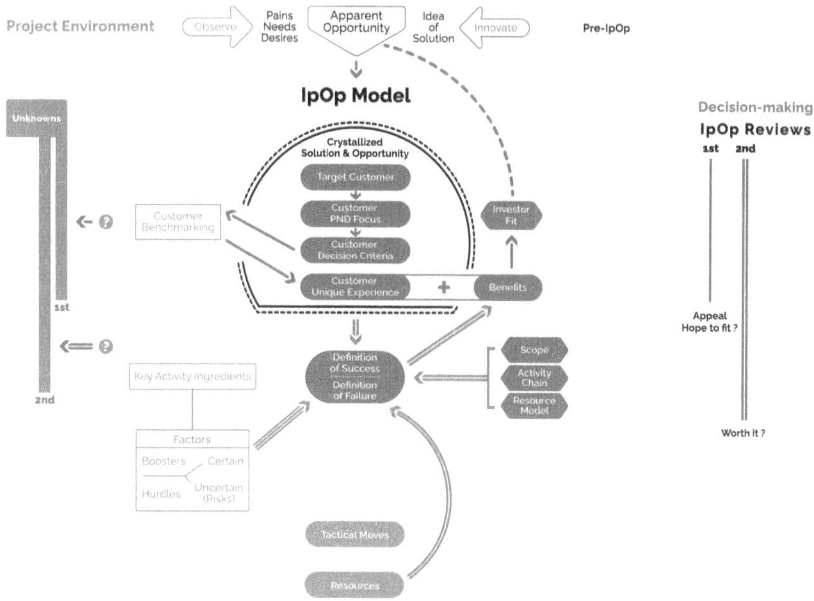

Fig. 12.2 Factors can positively or negatively influence the fate of the Project

Subcategories that need to be identified to complete the picture are:

- **Barriers to Entry**: These are specific obstacles (a major Hurdle) in your path. The key aspect about them is that they are usually unavoidable and particularly difficult to overcome. Their primary objective is often to prevent competitors, like yourself, from entering the market
- **Opportunity Killers**: These are Factors that can have a lethal impact on your project

12.5 Getting Factors Sorted

Analyzing Factors is an obvious necessity, for they may come under several categories. The imposition of email signature authentication standards—or the decision not to introduce them—is an interesting example.

Big players like Verisign doubtless have a different perception from smaller players such as WISeKey in its early days, as such a Factor could make or break a smaller company. For certain providers, such government regulations (before adopted) may represent either:

- **A Risk**: Regulatory requirements can introduce uncertain Hurdles when new regulations come into effect, such as the need to comply with a specific norm currently incompatible with your proposed Solution. Whether this Hurdle needs to be overcome depends on the final details of the regulation
- **A Booster**: Demand for your Solution will significantly increase, provided it meets the requirements once the regulation is enforced
- **A Barrier to Entry:** Some aspects of the regulator's standards may impose conditions that restrict access to certain providers
- **An Opportunity Killer**: Compliance with the new regulation is too onerous

12.6 Analyzing Factors

Understanding the impact that all Factors have on your Opportunity is crucial. Since you will be focusing on a specific Opportunity, you must assess their impact on:

- **Your Definitions of Success and Failure**. Because the KISs will determine your fate, all Factors affecting them deserve your full attention
- **Possibly the Customer Decision Criteria**: Given the significance of CDCs for your success, you must pay particular attention to all Factors affecting them[4]

If you are unaware of the Definition of Success and Failure, you are poorly prepared to grasp the role and significance of each Factor. This underscores the interconnected nature of all components within the

[4] Since CDCs are critical to achieving the Definitions of Success and Failure they are de facto included in assessing the impact of Factors on the Definitions of Success and Failure. Because this is an indirect impact I recommend that the impact on CDCs be evaluated separately as a safety measure.

IpOp Model. Likewise, should the Definition of Success and Failure evolve, it is crucial to reevaluate the impact of each Factor on your capacity to achieve the Definition of Success. A shift in the Definition of Success can alter the perceived importance of each Factor.

A systematic assessment of Factors is necessary to provide you as complete an understanding as possible of their influence on your project. You must screen each of them individually and define it as a Booster and/or a Hurdle, while also assessing its impact on both your Definition of Success and your CDCs. While some individuals may have instinctive talent in this regard, nothing beats a systematic approach. A combination of talent, intuition, and methodology forms a compelling recipe for success.

Once you have determined which Factors are critical, you can focus on those that have the greatest impact on your Definition of Success. Each Factor should be rated on the following scale:

- **Critical**: Its outcome could make or break the project
- **Important:** It could have a major impact on the project but probably not a critical one
- **Unimportant**: Its impact on the project will be only negligible

Cataloging Factors helps identify Tactical Moves. When a Hurdle emerges, it is natural to consider how to prevent it or address it. Similarly, there is a natural temptation to leverage a Booster. Any Tactical Moves identified should be recorded for later use.[5] The main purpose of analyzing Factors is not just to show that you have done your homework, as often the case with SWOT analysis, but to identify and record highly relevant Tactical Moves.

The Nespresso table provided below merely demonstrates how Factors are categorized, but this alone is not sufficient. It should also include additional columns for each Factor, detailing:[6]

[5] See Chap. 14.

[6] See Table 15.1 in Chap. 15

Factors for Nespresso Classic

		Nature				
Nº	Factor	Hurdle	Booster	Uncertain probability	Barrier to entry	Opportunity killer
1	Support from head office	X	X	X	X	X
2	Reaction by the competition	X	X	X		X
3	Technological evolution		X	X		X
4	Media reaction		X	X		
5	Raw material price fluctuations	X	X	X		
6	Economic trends and purchasing power evolution	X	X	X		
7	Cocooning		X			
8	Perception of coffee's impact on health	X	X	X		
9	Retailers' reaction	X				
10	Machine partners' reaction	X	X	X	X	
11	Quality problems	X		X		X
12	New way to make espresso	X	X		X	
13	Unknown brand	X			X	X
14	Absence of distribution network		X		X	
15	Sustainable development trend	X	X			

- **The level of importance** based on its impact on achieving the Definition of Success (e.g., critical, important, moderate, not important)
- **The probability of occurrence** (e.g., 100%, high, medium, low)
- **For Hurdles, the Tactical Move that can be applied to prevent the Factor from materializing** ("preventive" Tactical Move)
- **The Tactical Move required to address the Factor if it does occur** ("contingency" Tactical Move)

Link with ISO 56007 (Tools and Methods for Managing Opportunities and Ideas—Guidance)

ISO 56007 introduces the "acceptability of other factors that hinder or boost implementation" as a concept decision criterion for assessing the feasibility of implementation, though it lacks detailed elaboration. The IpOp Model, however, advocates for a more nuanced analysis of these Factors, suggesting they be evaluated and ranked based on their probability and level of impact on achieving the Definition of Success. Within the IpOp Model, Factors are pivotal for pinpointing relevant "preventive" or "contingency" Tactical Moves, which are integral to the Action Plan.

Moreover, ISO 56007 discusses "risk exposure" as a criterion for determining alignment with the organization. "Risk exposure" pertains to the potential risks a project may pose to the organization, viewed in the IpOp Model as possible Collateral damage and/or a critical aspect to assess in determining the "Investor or strategic fit."

Given that Risks influencing the project's outcome are not explicitly covered by ISO 56007, they fall under "other factors that hinder or boost implementation." In the IpOp Model, Risks are categorized under Hurdles, which can significantly impact the project's success. Therefore, the IpOp Model emphasizes the importance of thoroughly examining these Risks and their effects to devise appropriate preventive or contingency Tactical Moves.

13

Your Stakeholders Control You

Neglecting Stakeholders' Expectations Can Be Fatal

Take-Home of This Chapter

ISO 56007 recognizes the critical role of interested parties by including the "interested parties alignment" as one of the "key decision areas" for selecting concepts. Since ISO 56007 only mentions three concerns for this alignment (overall acceptance, Collateral effects, and sustainability & durability), this chapter provides clues for a more comprehensive analysis. Instead of "interested parties" the IpOp Model focuses on Stakeholders, a limited group of interested parties to whom the project team is accountable, as they play a crucial role in the success of a project. This nuance means that the IpOp Model ignores "interested parties" to whom the team in not accountable.

As ignoring the Stakeholders' concerns and preoccupations can have very significant consequences for the project's success, this chapter discusses the importance of considering the Aspirations, Resistances, and Constraints of Stakeholders, particularly Investors, when evaluating and implementing a project. Proper mapping of Stakeholders' Aspirations and Resistances helps in identifying Tactical Moves and Developing systematic Action Plans. This chapter furthermore emphasizes the need to understand Investors' Decision Criteria, which are derived from their Resistances, Aspirations, and Constraints and align the project with their goals and objectives. The chapter also introduces the concept of Investor Benchmarking based on the Investor Decision Criteria, which involves comparing the proposed project with other opportunities competing for the Investors' resources. The Investor Benchmarking is a powerful and efficient way to verify the fit with

R. H Cohen, *Pre-Project Excellence*, Future of Business and Finance,
https://doi.org/10.1007/978-3-031-61774-4_13

the Investor's guiding principles. Since it is based on the Investor Decision Criteria it also helps in presenting the project in a more compelling manner. Overall, this chapter provides valuable insights for entrepreneurs and intrapreneurs in effectively navigating the complexities of project implementation.

Because you rarely stand alone in a project, you must beware of the common temptation to believe that others have the same aspirations as yourself. While this may occasionally be the case, it is not common, and you then have to consider the expectations of all the Stakeholders in your project.

13.1 Stakeholders

In the IpOp Model, Stakeholders are all the individuals to whom you are accountable. Failing to consider their Aspirations could lead to dissatisfaction among them. Being accountable to Stakeholders gives them a certain level of power over you. Suppliers may cease deliveries if payments are not made, customers may stop buying, employees may become less committed, and authorities may impose restrictions if taxes are unpaid (Fig. 13.1).

Competitors are not Stakeholders. While competitors can significantly affect your success, you are not accountable to them. This is why in the IpOp Model they are Factors and not Stakeholders.[1]

Because they have power over you, Stakeholders deserve your utmost attention. Consequently, you need to know who the Stakeholders are and be familiar with their individual Aspirations.

In the context of an Opportunity, Stakeholders might include different individuals, as shown in Table 13.1:

Stakeholders can be categorized as shown in Table 13.2:

Effective "turf management" involves placating Stakeholders who might resist the changes brought about by the Opportunity. One strategy would be to partner with them or possibly offer them a share in the Benefits (Fig. 13.1).

[1] See Chap. 12.

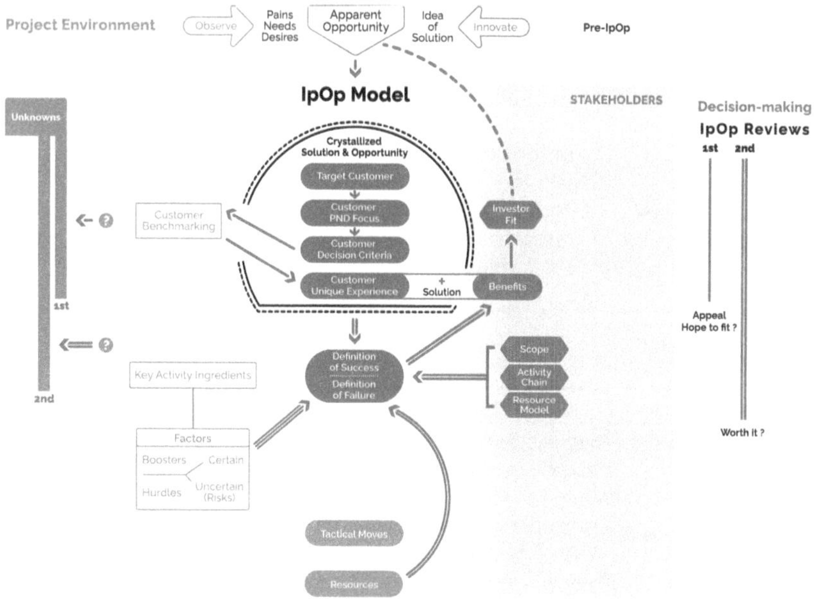

Fig. 13.1 Stakeholders include Investors, decision-makers who can influence the Scope as well as anyone involved in the Activity Chain or the Resource Model

Table 13.1 Example of stakeholders

For entrepreneurs	For intrapreneurs	Comments
Start-up founder(s)	Opportunity initiator(s)	
Decision-makers or investors	Senior management	
Executive team	Executive team	
Staff	Staff	
	Other departments or business units	Any internal entity with different Aspirations must be treated as a separate Stakeholder if it has the power to stop the project
Customers or clients	Customers or clients	Internal or external
Suppliers	Suppliers	Internal or external
Media	Media	
Related shareholders		Family and friends
Unrelated shareholders	Shareholders	

(continued)

Table 13.1 (continued)

For entrepreneurs	For intrapreneurs	Comments
The public in general	The public in general	This can be expanded to civil society
Authorities	Authorities	
Specifiers	Specifiers	
Research centers/ academia	Internal or external research centers/ academia	
Etc.	Etc.	

Table 13.2 Categories of stakeholders

Stakeholder type	Project consequences for them
The Winners	They are benefiting and they will love you. They need to be turned into allies
The Neutrals	While the Opportunity may not significantly impact them, it is prudent to take measures to prevent them from allying with "frustrated" or "losers."
The Frustrated	They will suffer but there is still room for you to negotiate acceptable terms with them
The Losers	They feel that they will lose too much; whatever you do represents a declaration of war. You are their enemy, and you must be ready to deal with their wrath!

13.2 Stakeholders' Aspirations

Not all Stakeholders will share the same Aspirations regarding the Opportunity, so it is important to list the specific Aspirations or expectations of each one. Mapping out these aspirations can help create a comprehensive overview.

Aspirations may vary in terms of their reality or perception. They can be short- or long-term and may evolve over time or in different circumstances. Table 13.3 provides a short list of possible Aspirations, highlighting some distinctions between entrepreneurs and intrapreneurs.

To identify Stakeholders' Aspirations, it is useful to remember that most people are conditioned by:

- Their "stakes," in other words their personal interests, desires, or investments (in their own perspective)
- Their goals and aspirations

Table 13.3 Examples of aspirations for entrepreneurs and intrapreneurs

For entrepreneurs	For intrapreneurs	Comments
Profit	Profit	In the case of public, philanthropic, and non-profit sectors, profit may be zero. The Aspiration is then to avoid a deficit.
Growth	Growth	
Personal recognition	Personal recognition	
Corporate image	Corporate image	
Long-term independence	Long-term independence	
Technical leadership	Technical leadership	
Commercial leadership	Commercial leadership	
Founder's ego	Promoter's and/or management's ego	
Job creation	Professional development	
Social contribution	Social contribution	
Personal independence	Recognition	
Drive for success	Drive for success	
Fun	Fun	
Founder's financial reward	Team reward	
Etc.	Etc.	

- Their constraints: those that they face and those they impose on you
- Their past experiences and educational background
- Their cognitive abilities and intelligence
- Their fears
- Their emotional state at any given time

Considering these parameters can lead to a more precise understanding of each individual Stakeholder's Aspirations. Personal Aspirations are particularly significant for emotionally driven decision-makers. Identifying these Aspirations can be difficult, and whenever feasible, engaging each Stakeholder individually to clarify their Aspirations can prove more effective than relying on assumptions. Another approach is to gather information about each Stakeholder by querying individuals who are familiar with them or have worked alongside them.

Every Opportunity must take Stakeholders' Aspirations into account. Familiarity with all Stakeholders reduces the risk of overlooking any of their Aspirations. For example, if the CEO of a large corporation has a large ego, ignoring his need for recognition could upset him and potentially lead him to kill your initiative. This scenario is a classic case of the NIH ("Not Invented Here") syndrome, where ideas are dismissed simply because they come from individuals other than key stakeholders. Identifying such ego-driven individuals early on allows the project team to address their Aspirations, highlighting the importance of being familiar with all Stakeholders.

Failure to fully consider Stakeholders' Aspirations can lead to costly outcomes. Take Napster,[2] for example. Its business model significantly harmed the music industry, prompting decisive action to shut it down. While some Napster imitators may have so far evaded consequences, this business model is not a viable long-term approach. It highlights the importance of identifying all Stakeholders involved in an Opportunity and considering their Aspirations. While this task may present difficulties, it is invariably beneficial to undertake.

13.3 Drivers and Satisfiers

There are two types of Aspirations: Drivers and Satisfiers. Satisfiers have an upper threshold, while Drivers do not. In simple terms:

- Driver: The more satisfaction, the better
- Satisfier: Going beyond the expected level of satisfaction is unnecessary

Since Drivers have no limit, it is crucial to prioritize them and ensure that the Opportunity satisfies them. Also you must give priority to the Aspirations of the more important/powerful Stakeholders.

This does not mean that Satisfiers should be neglected, for they are vital, especially in the stages before reaching their threshold. Afterward, your focus can shift toward satisfying Drivers.

Distinguishing between Drivers and Satisfiers helps prioritize mission-critical Aspirations effectively. See the example of application in the Nespresso case study.

[2] https://en.wikipedia.org/wiki/Napster

Nespresso Classic Stakeholders and their Aspirations

	Stakeholders					
Aspirations	Consumers	Retailers	Nestlé management	Machine partners	Nestlé shareholders	Project promoters
Profit		D	D	D	D	D
Image	S	S	D	D		D or S
Recognition			D			D
Ego			S			S
Growth		D	D	D	D	
Fun	S					D
Sustainability	S	S	S	S	S	
Health	S		S		S	D

S satisfier, *D* driver

13.4 Stakeholders' Resistances

Some Stakeholders will oppose certain aspects. Conceptually, these Resistances are considered as "negative Aspirations" and should be mapped out similarly to Aspirations.

Ignoring Stakeholders' Resistances can be deadlier than neglecting their Aspirations. Resistances often stem from fear, which can be irrational. When people perceive something as a threat, they may react emotionally, making it crucial to handle Resistances carefully.

Resistances for Nespresso

- Consumers do not like being captive
- Consumers are concerned about the environmental impact
- Nestlé's upper management does not want the Nespresso brand or image to be spoiled
- Consumers do not like to wait to receive capsules

The Tactical Move(s) designed to minimize each Resistance should be indicated alongside the Resistance. Given that many of these Tactical Moves have been discussed elsewhere in this book, and to avoid redundancy, they are not reiterated here.

13.5 The Benefit of Analyzing Aspirations

When analyzing Aspirations and Resistances, spontaneous strategies for addressing them often arise. These ideas are referred to as "Tactical Moves." It is important to document all these Tactical Moves as soon as they are identified, whether on a sheet of paper, a spreadsheet, a Post-it™ notes, or any other method. This repository of Tactical Moves will prove invaluable later.[3]

Identifying Tactical Moves is a major advantage of analyzing Aspirations and Resistances. Various steps in the IpOp Model often trigger ideas for these Moves, enriching your understanding of the

[3] See Chap. 14.

project and aiding in the development of a systematic Action Plan. Properly mapping Stakeholders' Aspirations and Resistances is not just an academic exercise; it is a valuable tool for identifying important Tactical Moves that must not be overlooked.

Understanding Decision-makers' Aspirations and Resistances is critical for comprehending their decision-making criteria. Their support for your project hinges on THEIR criteria, not yours. Knowing these criteria enables you to present your project in the most appealing way, highlighting the benefits they stand to gain. Disregarding even one Decision-maker's Resistance could be disastrous. Neglecting an Aspiration might mean missing out on something that could significantly enhance your project's appeal to a specific Decision-maker. For instance, a business angel might be inclined to invest in a fashion company because he sees an opportunity for his daughter, who is graduating from a fashion design school, to be involved.

13.6 Constraints

Stakeholders also enforce Constraints, which are unyielding rules. A rule that can be broken or bent is not a true Constraint. A genuine Constraint is fundamentally non-negotiable.

Only Stakeholders, to whom you are accountable due to their power over you or your project, can impose Constraints. Verifying people's authority to impose demands is key in identifying if they are Stakeholders. Since competitors lack direct power over you, they cannot impose Constraints; it is Customers, other Stakeholders, or the market at large that hold this power (Fig. 13.2).

Constraints limit your freedom to do certain things. Examples include banning bribery payments or transactions with specific organizations. Selling ground-to-air missiles to terrorist groups or to countries that sponsor terrorism, such as Iran, is not as acceptable as selling them to a democratic government like Switzerland.

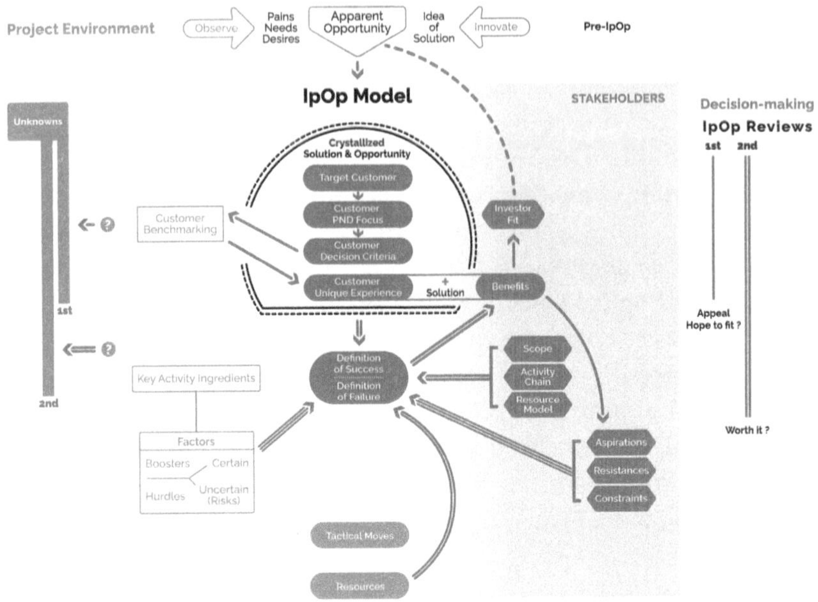

Fig. 13.2 Stakeholders' Constraints, Aspirations, and Resistances all have to be identified and taken into account

Constraints can be either self-imposed or imposed by others such as an organization or the law. Self-imposed constraints might be:

- Restricting activities within a certain geographical area
- Limiting business to environmentally friendly activities
- Prohibiting the use of child labor
- Implementing a cap on dividends that may be distributed (for example, the Migros supermarket chain in Switzerland), etc
- Demanding a certain level of return on investment

Some Constraints are imposed by clients or other partners. For example, large retailers increasingly require their suppliers to be EDI (Electronic Data Interface) compliant for sending/receiving digital order confirmations, invoices, etc. Similarly, corporate clients also often avoid depending on a single source for critical processes or components, steering clear of new technologies to prevent reliance on a single provider. This dependence avoidance is crucial for start-ups, which are vulnerable to closure at any time. Ignoring this Constraint has proven to be a costly and painful mistake for many start-ups unable to sell to Customers who doubted their sustainability.

Some Constraints are shaped by corporate values and culture. Until recently, some Swiss private bankers refrained from advertising or promoting their image, as the prevailing culture mandated a low profile. Consequently, any initiative or innovation requiring visibility was likely to be rejected by senior management. However, the climate has shifted, and this particular Constraint is gradually disappearing: Swiss private bankers now feel free to advertise.

Acknowledging that some Constraints are not real Constraints can lead to new Opportunities. Richard Branson's concept of providing first-class service to business-class passengers on Virgin Atlantic challenged the notion of needing a separate first-class section on airplanes. While other airlines viewed first class as a constraint, Branson did not. Many of IATA's regulations restricted traditional airlines but did not apply to low-cost carriers, as they were not members of IATA. This absence of constraints gave low-cost carriers the flexibility to innovate and transform the air transportation business model.

Creating a catalog of Constraints is useful because overlooking any of them could be fatal. Documenting Constraints not only provides a better understanding of the situation but also sparks ideas for Tactical Moves (as mentioned earlier) to add to the Action Plan.

Constraints for Nespresso Classic

- Constant assurance of high quality
- Adherence to Nestlé's management and development principles
- Generation of a level of profitability equal to or greater than the Nestlé group average

13.7 Investors Benchmarking

One very important Stakeholder is your Investor.[4] As mentioned earlier, the Investor could be yourself, your family, your friends, or any funding provider. As an intrapreneur, your Investor will be your management or any company Decision-maker. Because Stakeholders like this are vital to your success, you cannot disregard their decision criteria.

In addition to assessing the merits of the Opportunity, Investors will also apply their own criteria to ensure it aligns with their Aspirations and strategic objectives. These Investor Decision Criteria (IDC) may include parameters unrelated to Customer satisfaction or the Opportunity itself, such as:

- Synergies with other projects managed by the Investor
- The amount of time the project will require from the Investor
- The current availability of company resources, including employees, skills, or cash
- A hiring freeze
- A minimum RoI (Return on Investment) for new projects
- The Investor's risk aversion
- Etc

Understanding your Investor's Aspirations, Resistances, and Constraints can help identify most of the Investor Decision Criteria. If you lack this knowledge, it indicates a gap in understanding one of your most important Stakeholders. This lack of insight introduces additional Unknowns. To fill this gap, you can directly ask the Investor about their decision criteria. Alternatively, you can seek input from individuals who are familiar with the Investor.

Understanding your Investor decision criteria is essential for benchmarking your Opportunity against others that the same Investor may consider. These decision criteria might include various parameters such as the geographical location of your project, the project time to

[4] See Chap. 16.

market, capital expenditure (capex), risk level, availability of in-house key competencies, and more.

Be cautious of unexpected investor criteria, especially those tied to the personal concerns of decision-makers. For example, a decision-maker might be very receptive to a proposal that provides a collateral benefit to another venture he is involved in. While this benefit may not be part of your Project's Definition of Success and Failure, it could significantly influence the decision-maker's choice. Conversely, the total investment required might deter an investor or business angel from proceeding if it exceeds his investment capacity.

Once convinced that the Customer Unique Experience is satisfactory, most Decision-makers seek to understand why the proposed Solution surpasses other potential methods for delivering the same Customer Unique Experience or for addressing the Customers' Pain/Need/Desire(s): the Variants. Their goal, whether conscious or unconscious, is to eliminate doubt and confirm that the selected Variant represents the optimal choice. To achieve this, they need to:

- Comprehend the alternative ways available for delivering similar Solutions: the Variants
- Compare their performance against each other (evaluating their relative strengths and weaknesses)

Warning: Variants available to Decision-makers are not necessarily the same as the Alternatives available to Customers.

Benchmarking your proposal against other Variants available to decision-makers is the most effective way to demonstrate why your overall Solution outperforms other potential ways of providing a similar Solution. This can be achieved through an Investor Benchmarking table, similar to the Customer Benchmarking shown in Table 8.3, but tailored to include the Decision-makers' criteria instead. For instance, if you are evaluating the acquisition of new software to manage a specific process in your company, you should benchmark against Variants like maintaining the current system, developing software in-house, or outsourcing software development. Additional Investor Decision Criteria to consider could include the time needed to become operational, software compatibility with existing systems, effects on full-time employee (FTE) count, impacts on customer and/or employee satisfaction, and alignment with core business activities, among others.

This Decision-maker Benchmarking is indispensable not only to showcase to Decision-makers that the chosen Variant is optimal for the project but also to verify the Investor fit, which is a component of IpOp Review 1 ("Is there hope?"). IpOp Review 1 evaluates the overall Investor fit, while Investor Benchmarking, based on Investor Decision Criteria, verifies alignment with the Decision-maker's concerns—specifically, those of the Investor providing resources or granting permission. This implies that the Investor Decision Criteria must encompass all the selection criteria of the Decision-makers. If even one criterion is absent, it becomes impossible to make a decision that fully addresses all concerns (Fig. 13.3).

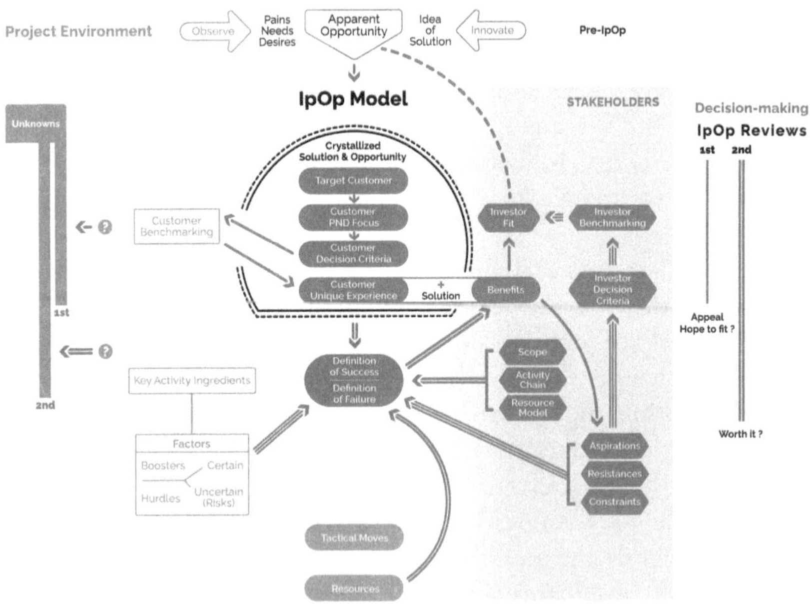

Fig. 13.3 Investor Benchmarking using Investor Decision Criteria shows whether the proposed Solution is best for the Investor and/or how it compares with other possible opportunities for this Investor

Comparison of Investment and Benefits (the Definition of Success and Failure) as a critical and universal decision criterion always included in the Investor Decision Criteria. For-profit organizations will compare the financial reward (net profit) of a project against the funds required for it. This Return on Investment (ROI)[5] indicates whether the allocation of Resources is justified. Non-profit and public sector organizations measure the ROI based on Benefits other than profit, such as financial savings, improved performance, better working conditions, better service, greater user satisfaction, less negative impact on the environment, etc. Fortunately, the distinction between for-profit and non-profit ROI is gradually narrowing as more for-profit entities adopt a holistic approach that considers societal Benefits alongside financial ones. This holistic perspective also encourages non-profit organizations to focus on maximizing Benefits per dollar spent on their target beneficiaries.

When seeking to obtain the Investment,[6] **it is important to ensure that the Benefits justify it** (and/or the necessary authorizations) in the eyes of those providing it. The key is to maximize the WiiifT factor[7] for the provider(s) of the Resources. To obtain something from people, it is essential to understand what drives them. However, many project initiators become so focused on their own needs that they struggle to empathize with other Stakeholders and present a compelling argument to justify their requests for Resources. In other words, they fail to leverage the Investor Decision Criteria to obtain what they want (Resources, permissions, etc.).

The necessary qualities of an attractive entrepreneurial or intrapreneurial project are:

- The ability to deliver a convincing Definition of Success (along with possible additional Benefits) in comparison to the required Resources (Return on Investment)
- A realistic likelihood of success, considering the project team's critical expertise and other critical Influencers and Unknowns

[5] Conceptually, Return means the Benefits and Investment means the Resources.

[6] See Chap. 16.

[7] "What is in it for Them?"

For intrapreneurs, an attractive project must also:

- Align with the corporate strategy and genuinely contribute to achieving the company's objectives (the Investor or strategic fit)
- Adhere to corporate Constraints and avoid triggering "political reactions"
- Provide the company with Market advantages

If these conditions are met and the corporation is not hampered by a cash shortage or adverse circumstances, chances are that the resources necessary to support the project will be made available.

For start-ups or entrepreneurs, an attractive project must also allow both Investor(s) and project champion(s) to reach their own goals and objectives. Entrepreneurial projects with this quality usually secure the Investment they need.

Many entrepreneurs struggle to objectively evaluate how appealing their project is to Stakeholders, especially Investors. They frequently assume that what attracts them will naturally attract others as well. Utilizing Investor Benchmarking can aid them in doing this in a more systematic way.

Link with ISO 56007 (Tools and Methods for Managing Opportunities and Ideas—Guidance)

ISO 56007 addresses "interested parties' acceptance" among its decision criteria but does not detail how to measure this acceptance. The IpOp Model fills this gap by offering tools to assess acceptance levels, focusing on the project's alignment with Stakeholders' Aspirations, Resistances, and Constraints.

Despite frequent references to "interested parties" in ISO 56007, the standard does not provide a formal definition of the term. This absence is notable since ISO 56000, the foundational standard for innovation management, aims to establish terminology for the ISO 56000 family of standards. In practice, "interested parties" are understood within ISO standards as "stakeholders, individuals, or organizations that may be affected by or see themselves as impacted by a decision or activity."

According to this interpretation, competitors would be considered interested parties as their interests are impacted by an organization's activities, particularly when it involves targeting their customers. However, the IpOp Model differentiates by importance, considering only those to whom accountability is due as "stakeholders." In certain contexts, such as "coopetition" where cooperation and competition coexist, this accountability might extend to selected competitors.

The IpOp Model essentially categorizes "Stakeholders" as a subset of "interested parties" to whom accountability is due. These stakeholders have a direct influence on decisions and actions, necessitating careful attention. Remaining interested parties are seen as "Factors," as there is no direct accountability to them. This distinction emphasizes the importance of accurately identifying true Stakeholders to prevent potential negative impacts of misclassification.

The IpOp Model's approach to Stakeholder engagement is predicated on understanding what motivates their buy-in, by delving into their Aspirations and addressing any Resistances. Recognizing the criticality of internal Stakeholder support is vital, as its absence often leads to project delays or budget overruns. Organizations sometimes erroneously assume internal Stakeholders will naturally align with organizational goals, overlooking their potential to impede progress. Accurately gauging Stakeholder challenges is essential for securing the support crucial for project success.

14

The Time to Move Has Come

The Path to the Definition of Success Is Paved with Tactical Moves

Recap of IpOp Review 3

Reminder: The objective of IpOp Review 3 is to verify whether you and your opportunity can accommodate the Influencers. These include Factors.[1] and Stakeholders.[2] Their analysis will point to Risks and Resistances, indicating how vulnerable the project is. Additional Unknowns will also be cataloged.

Once IpOp Review 3 has shown that you can live with the Influencers you can proceed to IpOp Review 4 (Fig. 14.1).

[1] See Chap. 12.

[2] See Chap. 13.

R. H Cohen, *Pre-Project Excellence*, Future of Business and Finance,
https://doi.org/10.1007/978-3-031-61774-4_14

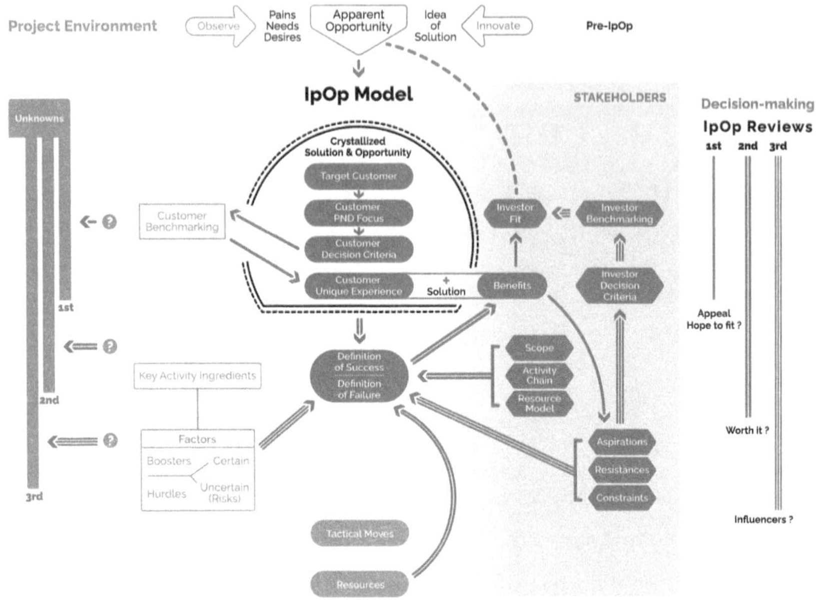

Fig. 14.1 IpOp Review 3 ("Are the Influencers acceptable?")

IpOp Review 4

Chapters 14 to 16 will guide you on how to respond to the IpOp Review 4 question: **How, who, and how much?**

Reminder: To evaluate the feasibility of implementation, it is crucial to have two effective Action Plans and their associated Investment. One Action Plan allows you to reduce the critical Unknowns (how, who and at what cost). The second Action Plan allows you to understand "how" you will leverage the Opportunity, "who" will carry it out, and "how much" needs to be invested. Remember, the Investment encompasses not just financial resources but can also include time or other resources.

Take-Home of This Chapter

This chapter discusses the importance of selecting the right Tactical Moves to implement an Action Plan that achieves the Definition of Success. Tactical Moves are the actions that bridge the gap between the current situation and the desired outcome. It emphasizes the need for a structured selection methodology to evaluate the benefits, drawbacks, and impact of each Tactical Move. The IpOp Model provides indeed a rational process for qualifying Tactical Moves based on their ability to ultimately achieve the Definition of Success. The chapter also highlights the various advantages gained from specific Tactical Moves, such as Customer intimacy, brand value enhancement, and development of partnerships. Additionally, it mentions the importance of building Barriers to Entry to protect against competition. It also stresses the need to consider Collateral Damages that are triggered by Tactical Moves and which adversaly affect key Stakeholders. The content of this chapter can be used to implement ISO 56007 by providing guidance on managing opportunities and ideas, specifically in the context of Action Plans and Tactical Moves.

The excitement often lies in taking action. This eagerness explains why many people quickly jump to brainstorming Tactical Moves immediately after spotting an Opportunity, diving into action with little to no prior planning. Particularly creative individuals, who tend to be action-oriented, may neglect the strategic analysis emphasized in earlier chapters. While tasks such as analyzing, understanding, thinking, and learning are intellectually engaging, they do not directly involve action, which is what these individuals crave. My goal here is to illustrate that a lack of strategic analysis can lessen the impact of Tactical Moves.

Tactical Moves encompass all actions required to acquire the information needed to reduce Unknowns and to transition from your current state to the one described in your Definition of Success.

14.1 Barriers to Entry

Most Tactical Moves are geared toward achieving your Definition of Success, but one category specifically aims to ensure that you reach that goal ahead of others, ideally without facing competitors. Its primary objective is to safeguard your position by erecting Barriers to Entry, thereby preventing competitors from entering your market and sharing in your success.

Barriers to entry that protect Nespresso Classic

Barriers	Comments
The Nespresso brand name	Perception of a top-quality product Sensual and emotional associations
Customer service through the Nespresso Club	24/7 availability Personalized service Customer intimacy
Vertical control of the production chain	From purchasing the raw coffee to the final cup of coffee
A plethora of channels for distribution and consumer access	Internet including social media Call center Email, SMS, fax Boutiques Bars, hotels, restaurants Equipped businesses
A very small number of machine manufacturers	No leakage of confidential information in regard to machine manufacture
Exclusive relationship with machine partners	Machine partners worldwide covering a vast part of the market
Capsule production	Expense of a factory costing tens of millions of Euros Specific know-how
Machine design	Experience with the technology ensuring reliability
Patents	Exclusive technology and sufficient clout to combat fraudulent imitations

Barriers to Entry are usually necessary if you want to become (and/or remain) a market leader. The idea is to keep potential challengers at bay because increased competition leads to lower profit margins. This approach could also be referred to as the "leave me alone" strategy. While some individuals in the non-profit or public sector may perceive this issue as relevant only to the private sector, the reality can be different, as evidenced by the emergence of private business schools in Europe challenging public universities.

Some of the many types of Barriers to Entry are:

- Patents (e.g., patented drugs)
- Brand recognition (e.g., Amazon or Google)

- Exclusive rights (e.g., oil drilling in certain countries)
- Government regulations (e.g., banking license)
- Proprietary systems (e.g., Apple computer operating system)
- Capital-intensive activities (e.g., manufacturing of chips for artificial intelligence)
- Distribution network (e.g., ice cream distribution)
- Strategic partnerships (e.g., OpenAI and Microsoft)
- Access to customers (e.g., TikTok or PADI's access to scuba divers worldwide)
- Support of powerful influencers and specifiers (e.g., the Kardashians, or even medical doctors for treatments)
- Secret knowledge (e.g., Coca-Cola recipe)
- Etc

14.2 Brainstorming to Find the Moves

Generating Tactical Moves is a highly creative process. While people often come up with spontaneous ideas, they may lack originality or fail to meaningfully advance toward the Definition of Success. This is why brainstorming techniques, which encourage lateral thinking, are highly recommended for producing innovative Tactical Moves.

Tactical Moves contribute to building the Activity Chain. For example, eBay's vendor rating system significantly enhanced trust—a critical success factor—by allowing buyers to rate their purchase experience. Other Tactical Moves by eBay include introducing an escrow payment system to boost buyer confidence, implementing a neutral dispute resolution mechanism, offering online tutorials, and creating a user-friendly interface for buyers and sellers.

The purpose of Tactical Moves is to contribute to (Fig. 14.2):

- **Reducing the level of Unknowns** by obtaining missing information or knowledge
- **Satisfying Pains Needs and Desires (PNDs),** especially those outlined in the Customer PND Focus Statement
- **Fulfilling Stakeholders' Aspirations**

- **Addressing and mitigating Stakeholders' Resistances**
- **Adhering to the Constraints** that must be respected to avoid antagonizing key stakeholders
- **Improving the product CDCs** to secure customers' buy-in, indispensable for achieving the Definition of Success; this involves improving the Solution by refining its features
- **Delivering the Definition of Success** (for example, implementing a distribution channel to reach the target customers)
- **Leveraging Boosters** that facilitate reaching the Definition of Success
- **Overcoming existing Hurdles** on your road to the Definition of Success
- **Mitigating Risks** (uncertain Hurdles) by preventing them or minimizing their impact
- **Safeguarding your territory**, mainly through constructing Barriers to Entry to block competitors

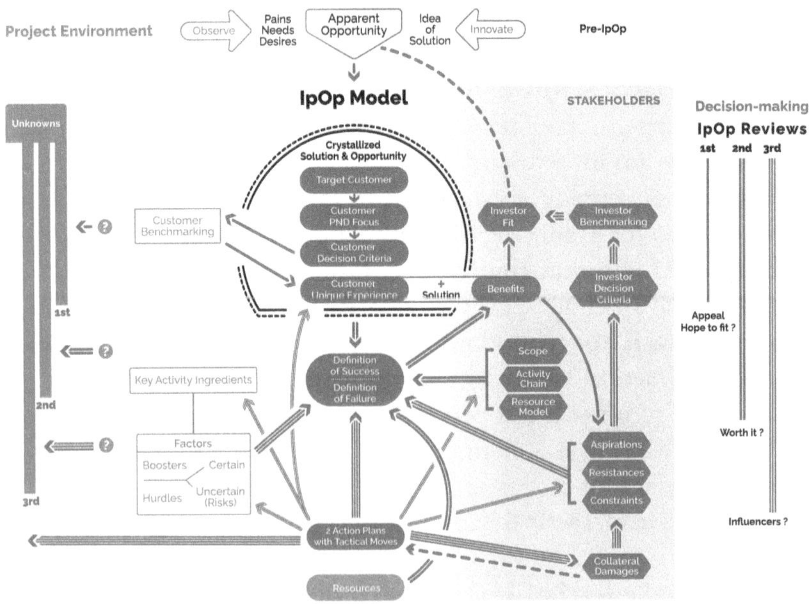

Fig. 14.2 Tactical Moves that will eventually be integrated in two Action Plans are the required actions to reduce Unknowns, deliver the Definition of Success and address all other parameters

The ability to execute certain Tactical Moves cannot be taken for granted. Some Moves may require the assistance or cooperation of others. For example, selling through the Internet requires the use of a credit card or another payment system. To prevent setbacks, it is important to understand clearly what the dependences are. These "pre-conditions" can be considered as Hurdles to overcome.

14.3 The Nature of Tactical Moves

Tactical Moves can cover a wide variety of dimensions and issues, restricted only by the limits of our imagination. The following examples illustrate what some companies have undertaken, demonstrating how each of these sub-strategies is bolstered by a range of Moves:

Sub-strategy	Examples of implementation	Examples of Tactical Moves
Brand identification	Intel	"Intel Inside" sticker on each PC, serving as branding
Choice of distribution channel	Dell	Direct selling to consumers instead of going through retailers
Pricing	easyJet or Southwest Airlines	Dynamic pricing
Technical leadership	Cisco	Acquiring most of the new competing technologies (except Juniper)
Delocalization	Accenture	Software development in India
Differentiation	Alessi kitchenware	Superior design
Vertical integration	Migros, Switzerland	Retail outlet with own food production facilities
Packaging	Voss	Elegant, designer-like bottles of water
Logistics	DHL/FedEx	Package tracking system
Working conditions	Google	Excellent work environment
Empowerment	Google	Encouragement of employees to innovate
Remuneration	World Wrestling Entertainment	Linking wrestlers' income to the turnover they generate

(continued)

Sub-strategy	Examples of implementation	Examples of Tactical Moves
Executive development	LinkedIn	Training webinars
Financing	Car suppliers	Offering leasing schemes to customers
Try and buy	Shareware	Downloadable freemium software with restricted features or limited use
Open source	Linux	Licensing, commitment to allow others to benefit from any improvements free of charge
Specialization	CNBC	Continuous business information ticker on screen
Procurement	Nestlé	Centralized global raw material purchasing
Bundling	Microsoft	Preinstalled Windows operating system and browser on new PCs
Standardization	Wireless 802.11ax	WIFI label, certification
Extension of product range	Mercedes	"A" series and Smart to open up new markets
Diversification	Honda	Producing engines for many purposes (cars, boats, lawn mowers, construction equipment, etc.)
Subcontracting	Apple	Subcontracting manufacturing to Foxconn
Partnering	Nike and Apple	Creating the Apple watch
Patenting	Amazon	"One click"
Secrecy	Coca Cola	Secret recipe

14.4 Collateral Damages

Not all Moves are innocuous. In addition to their impact on the project, some of your Moves may also negatively impact Stakeholders. This is a Collateral Damage. When the impact is positive, it is a Benefit, and nobody will complain. But when a Move has a negative impact on someone like a Stakeholder, you are in danger.

Since you are accountable to Stakeholders, ignoring Collateral Damages can be risky, unless you like living dangerously. Bear in mind that Stakeholders hold power over you, so you must evaluate the Collateral Damages of your Tactical Moves (or combinations of Moves) if you want to avoid their wrath.

There are many types of Collateral Damages. Here are some of them:

- Damaging the company's reputation
- Altering the essence or image of an existing brand
- Upsetting distributors or other partners
- Reducing the market share of other company products (cannibalization)
- Irritating management
- Disclosing critical information
- Polluting the environment or damaging the climate

It is suicidal to ignore the possibility of Collateral Damages. Therefore, they should be integrated in your risk management efforts.[3] Just like any other Risk, a contingency plan must be on hand in case a Collateral Damage materializes. Collateral Damages resulting from Tactical Moves may require other Moves to mitigate their consequences or prevent them from happening (Fig. 14.3).

Possible Collateral Damages for Nespresso

- Reduction of Nestlé profit
- Damaging the reputation of Nestlé
- Damaging the Nespresso brand
- Cannibalizing other Nestlé products
- Hurting machine partners' interests
- Negative impact on the environment

[3] See Chap. 12.

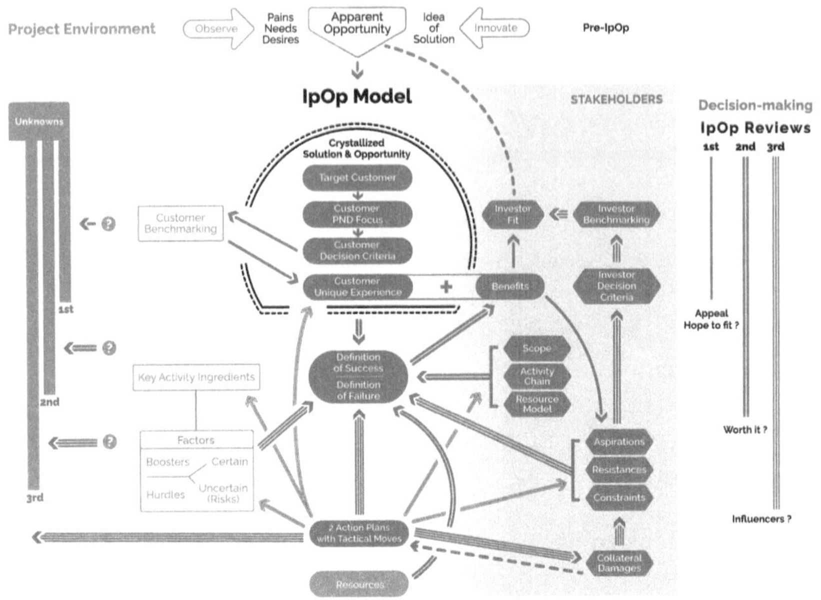

Fig. 14.3 Tactical Moves can produce Collateral Damages that might upset Stakeholders

> To reassure Investors, similar to the approach for Resistances, the corresponding Tactical Move(s) aimed at mitigating each Collateral Damage should be listed alongside the damage. Given that these Tactical Moves may involve internal or confidential information, they are not specified here.
>
> Regarding environmental impact, details on Tactical Moves for environmental protection are discussed in the Nespresso profile found in Chap. 3.

14.5 Suicidal Moves

Certain Moves are ineffective or even counterproductive, often stemming from a poor understanding of people's behavior. They prevent the adoption of new products or the sustainability of the project.

Ignoring people's Resistance to certain things can lead to failure. Classical examples of Resistance are listed in Table 14.1:

Table 14.1 Example of resistances

Resistance to	Examples	Result
Learning something new	QWERTY keyboard	Faster and more effective ways to enter text have not managed to dethrone the QWERTY keyboard (or its equivalent in other countries)
Writing off capital or infrastructure	TGV (French fast train network)	Only a limited number of countries have adopted the TGV because it requires new railroad tracks.
Relying on a sole resource or supplier	Linux vs. Microsoft	Linux' success can be partially attributed to the fact that some users do not want to be in the exclusive hands of Microsoft
Using something imposed on them	New Coke	In 1985 Coca-Cola consumers managed to reverse the replacement of Classic Coke by the New Coke recipe
Paying for something that is expected to be free	Internet subscriptions	Very few information providers have managed to convince Internet users to subscribe to paying services
Sacrificing comfort	Using multiple garbage disposal bins to recycle waste	Only a small percentage of consumers make the effort to separate the various components of garbage
Not getting what has been promised	Dell	Users not buying Dell anymore because of the poor quality of telephone support (e.g., 15 h arguing on the phone to obtain replacement of a US$100 hard disk that is still under warranty)

Nespresso Classic's Tactical Moves

The following list is not exhaustive:

Tactical Moves	Advantages gained
Separate trade mark and entity from Nestlé's	Increase in Nespresso's freedom of movement by limiting the organizational constraints characteristic of multinational companies "Luxury" positioning Limitation of impact on Nestlé's image in the event of failure Avoidance of a negative impact of Nespresso's business strategy on that of Nestlé
Technical design of machines by Nespresso	Perfect correlation of capsules and machines Mastery of production chain and quality
Uniform design for all machines managed by Nespresso	Influence the consumer's experience Uniformity of image Optimal integration of machine design and functions
Wide choice of machines (six basic models available in tens of versions)	Possibility for consumers and machine partners to personalize their machines Variety of systems without compromising the coffee quality
Use of a sole producer for manufacturing all machines commercialized by machine partners	Control of machine quality Avoidance of dependence on machine partners Safeguarding of machine-production know-how
Centralization of capsule production	Safeguarding of capsule-production know-how Control of capsule quality Savings thanks to large-scale production
Purchase and control of raw materials in producer countries	Promotion of fair trade Mastery of entire production chain Freedom to select the most appropriate products
"Luxury" positioning and status symbol	Remove resistance to price and achieve greater profit margin Stand out from the competition and its "household product" positioning
Rapid international deployment	Maintenance of international leadership Satisfaction of Nestlé's growth ambitions
Highly dynamic website	Development of customer/client intimacy Supply of completely new markets Sale of derivative products

Tactical Moves	Advantages gained
Launching of Nespresso magazine	Development of customer/client intimacy Development of partnership with advertisers Enhancement of brand value Ability to educate consumers
Retail boutiques	Additional sales outlets Full-time visibility Strengthening of "luxury" positioning by choice of location and decor
Sale of derivative products	Enhancement of brand value Mastery of more dimensions underlying the consumer's experience
Highly motivated, proactive team	Exploit all opportunities without being subject to the constraints of a large company (while culling the benefits it brings)

14.6 Evaluating and Choosing Moves

The most critical issue is choosing the right Tactical Moves because no entity can afford to make all the Moves that may come to mind. Their implementation is limited for various reasons: lack of resources; incompatibility of some Moves with others; counterproductive effects, and so on. A selective approach is thus indispensable. Selection is often done by gut feeling, not to mention other esoteric or random methods that are used more frequently than people think (e.g., astrology, blood groups, flipping a coin, etc.)!

A structured selection methodology provides coherence and security, complementing intuition and gut feelings (not that these should be discounted!), while alleviating the impact of emotional factors. The IpOp Model provides a process for qualifying Tactical Moves in a rational manner.

The benefits, drawbacks, and impact of each Tactical Move considered must be evaluated in respect of its ability to ultimately achieve the Definition of Success and Failure. This involves addressing the following contributions:

- **Definition of Success:** Each Tactical Move should be assessed based on its potential to improve the measured value of Key Indicators of Success (KISs). Priority should be given to Moves that have the most positive impact on achieving the objectives stated in the Definition of Success
- **Customer Decision Criteria:** Evaluate whether each Tactical Move contributes to improving the features corresponding to the CDCs. Moves that enhance the performance of Customer Decision Criteria can translate into significant market advantages
- **Unknowns:** Consider whether the Tactical Move helps reduce the degree of ignorance about critical Unknowns. Some Moves may be necessary to increase knowledge and reduce uncertainty
- **Boosters:** Assess whether the Tactical Move capitalizes on Factors that can boost the chances of reaching the Definition of Success. It would be a pity to miss opportunities that can enhance success
- **Activity Chain**: Analyze how each Tactical Move contributes to building a robust and efficient Activity Chain
- **Hurdles:** Evaluate whether the Tactical Move helps overcome or avoid Hurdles, including preexisting Barriers to entry. Implementing Tactical Moves that address difficulties can facilitate the achievement of the Definition of Success
- **Risks:** Consider whether the Tactical Move helps reduce the impact of Risks. Moves that contribute to mitigating Hurdles are crucial for ensuring project success and minimizing potential negative consequences
- **Protection:** Assess whether the Tactical Move helps build Barriers to entry that protect the project from competitors. Moves that establish Barriers to entry can safeguard the project's position and prevent competitors from impeding success

By carefully evaluating Tactical Moves against these criteria, you can prioritize actions that align with the overarching goals of the project and maximize the likelihood of achieving success while minimizing Risks and Obstacles.

To be even more comprehensive, you might also consider the following implications:

- **Constraints:** Evaluate whether each Tactical Move adheres to the Constraints imposed by internal or external Stakeholders, such as legal regulations, organizational policies, or ethical considerations
- **Resources:** Assess the availability and allocation of Resources required to implement each Tactical Move. Evaluate whether the Move is feasible within the constraints of available Resources, including financial, human, and technological Resources
- **Collateral Damages:** Consider the potential unintended consequences or Collateral Damages of each Tactical Moves. Evaluate whether the Move could have negative impacts on Stakeholders, the organization's reputation, or other aspects of the project

The evaluation process could include assigning a value to the level of benefits provided by each Tactical Move. One way to do this is by using a scale to quantify the impact of each Move. Here is an example of a scale that can be used for evaluation:

- **3** = Essential/critical: must be done
- **2** = Valuable: should be done
- **1** = Useful: nice to do
- **0** = Not worth it

By using such a scale, project Stakeholders can rationally evaluate and prioritize Tactical Moves based on their perceived contribution. This helps in making informed decisions and allocating Resources effectively to maximize project outcomes.

Your "final decision" consists in choosing to make or not make each Tactical Move, based on your overall assessment of the impact of each Move on the various parameters. It reflects an arbitration process evaluating the contribution each Tactical Move can make toward your delivering your Definition of Success with the lowest possible consumption of resources.

This "final decision" is not yet final, because you will later need to verify that the combination of Moves is coherent and that you have the necessary Resources to implement them. If adjustments are needed based on Resource constraints or other parameters, you may need to revisit the decision-making process and refine your selection of Tactical Moves accordingly.

Link with ISO 56007 (Tools and Methods for Managing Opportunities and Ideas—Guidance)

In ISO 56007, the emphasis is placed on Action Plans without delving into the specifics of Tactical Moves, which are essential elements of these plans. The IpOp Model, however, offers a comprehensive perspective on the role and considerations involved in identifying and choosing Tactical Moves.

The standard's decision criteria make a distinction between "sustainability and durability" and "collateral effects." On the other hand, the IpOp Model considers that "Collateral Damages" refer to any outcomes of the project that adversely affect "Stakeholders," covering all types of externalities, including those affecting the climate, the environment or even the project itself.

15

Moving According to Plan!

Moves Do Not Mean Much Until They Are Integrated into a Coherent Plan

Take-Home of This Chapter

This chapter discusses the importance of having two Action Plans in managing projects, concepts, and opportunities. It emphasizes the need to reduce Unknowns before launching any project while highlighting the critical role of the IpOp Model in identifying Unknowns/uncertainties as early as possible, as recommended by ISO 56007.

The content of this chapter can be used to understand the selection criteria mentioned in ISO 56007, such as reducing uncertainties and feasibility of the Action Plan. It also highlights the importance of risk analysis, which aligns partially with ISO 56007's consideration of risk exposure. This chapter also mentions the significance of having a champion and a driven team that has the required skills to deliver the Definition of Success. Additionally, it emphasizes the need for senior management support and alignment with corporate procedures, which are crucial aspects of ISO 56007. By applying the concepts and principles discussed in this chapter, organizations can effectively implement ISO 56007 and improve their management of projects, concepts, opportunities, and ideas.

Your Action Plan will then integrate and organize all the Moves you have selected to achieve your Definition of Success, defining the path to it. Since you have a commitment to your Stakeholders—yourself included—to deliver the Definition of Success, or at the very least the

R. H Cohen, *Pre-Project Excellence*, Future of Business and Finance,
https://doi.org/10.1007/978-3-031-61774-4_15

Definition of Failure, selecting the most appropriate and resource-effective combination of Moves is critical.

15.1 A Coherent Plan

Aim to avoid the YTYTBYNS syndrome. "YTYTBYNS" stands for "You Try, You Try, But You Never Succeed."[1] In clear terms, the name of the game is to deliver the maximum output (corresponding to your Definition of Success) using a minimum of resources and experiencing a minimum of problems.

It is critical to have a coherent Action Plan to maximize the benefits generated by the potential synergies of combined Tactical Moves. Lack of coherence leads to a waste of resources (including money and time). The Moves selected must therefore not only be compatible with each other but must also be put into effect at the right time. It is useful to position the Moves on a timeline (for example, a Gantt chart) visualizing what should happen and when.

Understanding the interrelationships between Moves is necessary to maximize the "return on Moves." It might, for instance, be counterproductive to advertise heavily before the product has become readily available in the stores. Other Moves can be made only after certain milestones have been reached or certain Factors have materialized. The use of traditional project management tools—of which Critical Path Analysis (CPA) or Program Evaluation and Review Techniques (PERT) are classic examples—can be useful in managing these interrelationships.

Compatibility with the corporate mission and the organization's strategy needs to be verified at this stage. It may, for example, transpire that the Opportunity is compatible with the mission but that the Action Plan no longer fits in with the current strategic options. Selling advertising space is compatible with the mission of a newspaper whereas the sale of that space to advertise pornographic material may be out of synch with the company's strategy.

[1] Another easier to remember version is the TAHALBUNS syndrome (Try As Hard As you Like, But You'll Never Succeed).

The risk of cannibalizing existing company offerings must also be weighed, for this could trigger a war between departments or other group entities. For instance, EDF (the French Electricity Company) could consider providing Internet services via its electricity network. Although compatible with its mission, this might put the company in competition with its sister company French Telecom. Since both companies belong to the French government, this kind of competition could open up a can of worms.

The impact on other departments must also be considered. In addition to cannibalization within the company, it is important to ensure that territorial issues are properly factored in. If the distribution of the new product involves the sales department, for example, you need to be aware of this parameter and think about how you can get that department to cooperate. Here of course we are talking about a Collateral Damage, as defined above.[2]

15.2 Handling Risks

Large, deep-pocketed organizations are notoriously averse to taking risks. But actually, we should all be averse to taking risks! Contrary to common belief, entrepreneurs do not like to take risks. What they like is success, and they are willing to take certain risks to achieve it. Only gamblers like taking risks. Entrepreneurs would do well to know how to cope with risks (i.e., manage them), but not to seek them.

Showing that the Risks have been thoroughly analyzed is particularly important in large organizations because of this natural aversion to risk. They will usually prefer to miss an opportunity than run excessive risks. Risks can of course also be deadly for smaller organizations, but the more vulnerable among them sometimes feel compelled to take the gamble. It is very important to clearly identify and monitor the Risks that you absolutely cannot afford to take if failure would be fatal or at the very least too painful.

Not only the Risk itself must be monitored, but just as important is monitoring its triggering Factor. Monitoring the triggering Factor

[2] See Chap. 14.

provides an earlier warning and offers more time to react. For example, if the exchange rate is a critical Factor, you would do well to identify the elements that can cause it to fluctuate. Once a new situation (Risks included) has arisen, there is usually no time for a thorough analysis. To keep improvisation to a minimum it is healthier to anticipate the most suitable (clearly defined) reaction as far as is possible.

There are four categories of Risks. Each must be addressed to avoid a painful landing:

Risks that can affect the project are the most obvious. Any business plan that does not include them (and this is rarely the case) would end up in the garbage can. These Risks are most accurately defined as Factors (more precisely uncertain Hurdles) that would detract from delivering the Definition of Success if they were to materialize.

The global risk that the project runs, because it is vital to know how far you can go and what the consequences are if the whole thing turns sour. Looking at the individual Risks is not enough: you must evaluate the overall picture of the Risks associated with your project, including their combinations. The fate of subprime loans[3] exemplifies how failure to take combinations of risks into account could create unbearable exposure or even a serious crisis.

The cost associated with the premature termination or suspension of a project is not always properly factored in. Getting rid of subprime loans or closing a nuclear plant are obvious examples of how difficult it can be to quit the game. Getting rid of an oil-drilling platform can also turn out to be a very costly exercise. For instance, Shell came to the painful realization, when it was time to get rid of an offshore drilling platform, that its reputation was being badly affected by environmental issues. It would be healthy to include in the analysis, even at this pre-project stage, the cost of having to terminate or suspend the project. This step then serves as a contingency plan for managing such termination. Like any contingency plan, it requires resources, and it is management's responsibility to keep sufficient resources on hand to be able to implement it. While such a forward-looking policy is an essential part of

[3] Subprime loans were innovative financial products with an underestimated risk component (the possibility that the real estate market could crash and many people who would not be able to honor their financial obligations was underestimated).

responsible behavior, very few project promoters in fact go to such lengths.

The fourth category of risks comprises the uncertain Collateral Damages of Tactical Moves.[4] Because Collateral Damagess do not usually affect the project itself—the primary concern of project initiators—they are rarely addressed explicitly at this stage. But Collateral Damages are bad news for Stakeholders, to whom you remain accountable, so they need to be explicitly included in your overall risk analysis. Your Stakeholders will certainly not like them, and their inclusion might even prevent them from giving your project the green light. But even if such a seeming rejection feels like a setback, it might surprisingly turn out to be a blessing for you in the end, because if the Collateral Damages were to materialize later you would have to deal with some very angry Stakeholders, never a pleasant experience!

Managing Risks means not only identifying them and anticipating their impact but also preparing contingency plans. Clearly defining your Moves well in advance is a must if you are to alleviate the impact of critical Risks. Preventive Tactical Moves can also be developed or implemented to avoid certain Risks or reduce their impact. For instance, hedging will reduce exposure to currency fluctuations.

The contingency plan sometimes turns out to be the main plan. easyJet offers an excellent example of the potential of contingency plans. In its early days, easyJet introduced flights between Geneva and Barcelona at prices substantially lower than those available from IATA companies (Swissair and Iberia). It started aggressively advertising and selling tickets for that route before it had obtained authorization from the Swiss Federal Aviation Agency (= a Factor). Swissair lobbied against the delivery of the authorization and the authorities eventually refused to give the permit. This refusal became front-page news in the media and the big question was how easyJet would handle the setback. A few days later, easyJet announced that all passengers who had booked a ticket would not only be fully reimbursed but that they would also travel to Barcelona for free. This contingency plan translated into more front-page news. But that is not the end of the story, because easyJet then announced that even

[4] See Chap. 14.

Risk Analysis

Table 15.1 Table for risk analysis

Risks	Impact on your opportunity	Preventive Tactical Moves	Contingency Tactical Moves to alleviate the impact	Triggering factors	Monitoring measures
Risk 1					
Risk 2					
...					
Risk X					

without a permit, it would continue offering flights between Geneva and Barcelona at the same price. easyJet was able to do this by selling not a transportation ticket but a package deal including one-night accommodation, which required a tour operator license rather than an aviation license. Since it already had a tour operator license, nothing prevented easyJet from selling such a package. It just "so happened" that the accommodation included in the package was camping in a tent north of Barcelona. The number of passengers who took advantage of the camping accommodation must have been very insignificant. The only thing that is sure is that during the few weeks that this episode lasted easyJet's brand recognition jumped from 50% to about 80%. Here we have a brilliant plan B that maximized the PR impact on the public, and which, by the way, is also a perfect example of non-tech innovation.

Special attention must be paid to risk analysis because it is essential to establish your credibility and show that the necessary homework has been done. A simple way of presenting risk analysis is shown in Table 15.1:

15.3 Other Recommended Verifications

A project needs a Champion and, ideally, a strong team, for experience has shown that without an extremely determined driver, it has little chance of success. Determination to win is an obvious key Factor. The human and personality characteristics of the team are not always checked out with the same scrutiny as the other parameters, and it is true that tools for assessing them are not always easily available or sufficiently effective. Nevertheless, they remain a critical Factor that should not be neglected.

Senior management support is another critical Factor that can seriously affect your ability to achieve the Definition of Success. Numerous intrapreneurial projects have failed due to a lack of sufficient support from higher-level management. Thus, securing one or more sponsors at the right level is crucial for success.

The Action Plan also needs to be aligned with corporate procedures that should be treated as Constraints to avoid painful resistance and confrontation with other departments. Developing a new market can be a very challenging exercise for a Swiss banker, for instance, if he cannot provide the required due diligence documentation. Dealing with customers who have made plenty of money in Russia may be very tempting, but the internal regulations of Swiss banks require extreme due diligence (because historically the risk of money laundering has been found to be higher in the case of Russian money). Ignoring certain procedural requirements (i.e., Constraints) can seriously jeopardize the intrapreneur's chances of success.

The strategy must respect all Constraints, not just the procedure-related ones referred to in the previous paragraph. The reason for the requirement that the IpOp Model should identify the Constraints at the earliest possible stage is precisely to ensure that by the time the Action Plan is prepared a checklist of Constraints is available to verify that they have all been thoroughly considered.

Demonstrating feasibility will also help to convince Decision-makers. Including testing or a demonstration of feasibility in the Action Plan—typical Tactical Moves aimed at reducing the level of Unknowns—will enhance the credibility of the project. The time and resources required to reduce the level of uncertainty should be outlined, as the Decision-maker may prefer to allocate limited resources for testing before committing to more substantial investments that involve more Resources and Risks. This approach offers the advantage of providing a chance for a project with high uncertainty to proceed, rather than being immediately shelved. By reducing the level of Unknowns, the decision can be deferred until more knowledge has been gathered, assuming a positive outcome from the Tactical Moves aimed at reducing ignorance.

Confirming that you can overcome potential users' Resistance to the product or service, or to making changes in their own system/process/activity chain is also important. To this effect it is useful to catalog the possible areas of Resistance from customers (who are Stakeholders), a further example of uncertainty reduction.[5]

The possibility of eliciting a "WOW" from your target audience is another key factor that will enhance your chances of success. A "WOW" response is more likely when the project is easy to communicate, highlighting the importance of the Elevator Pitch.[6]

Potential developments and related applications that offer insight to what doors the Opportunity can open in the future should also be pinpointed at this stage. Such prospects of future improvements and developments provide the "bigger picture," showing how your idea can be expanded to ensure project sustainability. Nespresso's foray into professional environments was an important development for the company. Initially successful in the consumer market, Nespresso also ventured into selling coffee to restaurants and even to airlines for their business class, showcasing the versatility and potential growth avenues of the brand.

Estimating the overall probability of success also obliges the innovator to consider the probability of failure once the project has been analyzed. The critical weakness of ignoring the possibility of failure or neglecting to factor in a contingency plan for termination is a trap into which many entrepreneurs and intrapreneurs fall. They are so infatuated with their idea that they overlook the possibility that things can go wrong. In this situation, unjustified optimism (and/or ego trips…) are unfortunately a deadly sin.

Now is the time to carefully consider whether the Opportunity is still worth pursuing. Despite its importance, many entrepreneurs overlook this step and dive into action based solely on gut feelings. While this approach may sometimes succeed, it often falls short.

[5] As indicated in Chap. 5.

[6] See Chap. 9.

Therefore, it is crucial to pause and ask yourself a decisive "Go/No-Go" question before taking the plunge. At this juncture, it is essential to review all the critical success Factors that have been identified and honestly assess whether the potential rewards justify the effort and sacrifices required.

Every opportunity has a cost. Deciding to go ahead with a project implies forsaking other opportunities that might come up in the future. This is called the "opportunity cost." Do you, the entrepreneur, have enough confidence in this Opportunity to say "No" to other Opportunities? That is the last killer question.

15.4 Two Action Plans Rather Than One

Since it is almost impossible to have an Opportunity with no Unknowns,[7] there is a high probability that some of them will serve as Go/No-Go criteria. If, even after reducing them, some insurmountable obstacles persist, it would be quite stupid to launch the project regardless. To avoid launching a project that will eventually come to a stop, savvy people begin by reducing the most critical Unknowns before giving the final green light.[8] They achieve this by identifying a set of Tactical Moves focused on reducing these critical Unknowns.

The purpose of the first Action Plan is to reduce these Unknowns. It sets the stage for a decision to be made later, once sufficient additional information has been gathered to determine that the Unknowns no longer serve as No-Go criteria. This Action Plan outlines the necessary Resources (time, money, personnel, etc.) needed to reduce the Unknowns. Failing to reduce critical Unknowns is tantamount to diving into a pool without knowing if there is enough water to prevent injury upon impact.

---

[7] As explained in Chap. 5.

[8] See step 5 in "The process from idea to launch" in Chap. 5.

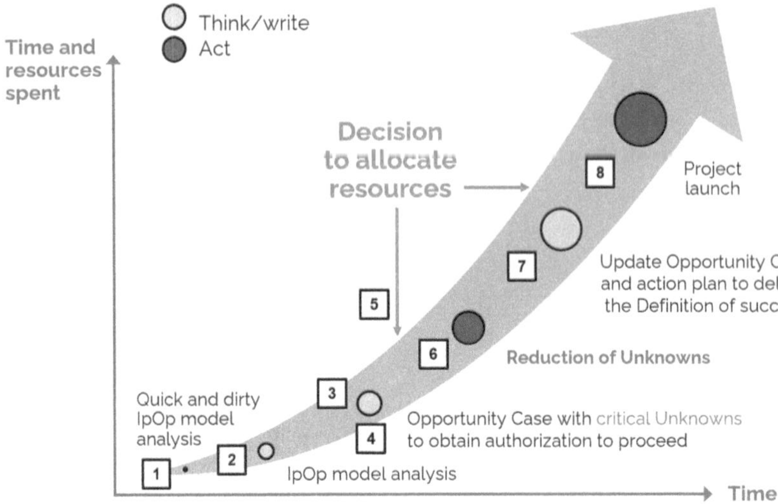

Fig. 15.1 The dual Action Plan sequence

Therefore, budgeting for reducing critical Unknowns is imperative to understand the Investment required.

The second Action Plan is designed to deliver the Definition of Success once the critical Unknowns are resolved. While it may involve reducing some non-critical Unknowns, its primary focus is on implementing the Tactical Moves to capitalize on the Opportunity (the "How"). This plan will outline the necessary Investment to attain the desired outcome (the "How much"). As indicated earlier, it necessitates a dedicated team capable of delivering the Definition of Success (the "Who").

The sequence of dual Action Plans—first tackling critical Unknowns before fully engaging with the Opportunity—is a sound strategy for managing Opportunities.[9] This approach is also recognized as a best practice by ISO 56007. However, to follow this approach, it is crucial to identify as many Unknowns as possible early on. This is where the IpOp Model proves invaluable—it aids in uncovering numerous Unknowns before committing Resources (Fig. 15.1).

[9] See steps 5–7 in "The process from idea to launch" in Chap. 5.

Link with ISO 56007 (Tools and Methods for Managing Opportunities and Ideas—Guidance)

It is noteworthy that ISO 56007 and the IpOp Model have similarities in addressing key decision criteria and risk analysis for projects.

ISO 56007 identifies "effort to reduce remaining uncertainties" and "Feasibility of the Action Plan for development" as decision criteria. The first aligns with the "Action Plan for reducing unknowns" in the IpOp Model, while the second corresponds to the "Implementation Plan" within the IpOp Model.

Risk analysis is a crucial aspect of both frameworks but with a slightly different perspective.

In the IpOp Model, risk assessment is specifically addressed in IpOp Review 3, which focuses on Influencers that can impact the project's outcome. On the other hand, ISO 56007 incorporates risk exposure into the organization alignment grouping, considering it as a criterion for strategic fit. The latter approach considers the broader implications, focusing on the risk a project poses to the organization itself—a distinct perspective that highlights the project's potential organizational impact rather than risks affecting the project's outcome.

While ISO 56007 may not explicitly mention Risks affecting the project, they are encompassed within the "acceptability of other factors that hinder or boost implementation."

Therefore, both frameworks acknowledge the importance of addressing Risks in project management, albeit with slight differences in terminology and emphasis: while ISO 56007 does not ignore project-affecting Risks, it does not specify them as distinctly as the IpOp Model does.

16

Resources Speak

Can You Afford to Implement the Plan? Resources Are the Language of Business and Cannot Be Ignored

Take-Home of This Chapter

This chapter reminds the concept of the "magic triangle," highlighting the interdependence of Resources, Action Plans, and the ultimate Definition of Success. It focuses on the need for proper evaluation of Resources and investment requirements to reduce Unknowns as well as to achieve the desired Definition of Success. Resources include not only financial aspects but also knowledge, skills, time, equipment, and networks. Having a qualified and highly motivated team is also critical. To optimize team interactions, this chapter recommends using the engaged team charter (ETC.) to optimize team interactions.

This chapter emphasizes the importance of securing early enough the necessary Investment for implementing not only the Action Plan for reducing Unknowns but also the Plan for delivering the Definition of Success. The project team should thus seek Resources from the right people and build a sufficiently large network. If the required Resources/Investment cannot be obtained, it is imperative to adjust both Action plans and the Definition of Success (and Failure) that the new plan can realistically deliver. Since ISO 56007 states that resource investment requirements and innovation capability building are two of the selection criteria, the content of this chapter can be used to refine the understanding and operationalization of these selection criteria.

R. H Cohen, *Pre-Project Excellence*, Future of Business and Finance,
https://doi.org/10.1007/978-3-031-61774-4_16

Handling resources is what distinguishes an entrepreneur from a manager. A manager has resources available and is empowered to make the best use of them to accomplish his mission. The starting point for an entrepreneur, on the other hand, is not resources, but an idea or a project. The entrepreneur plans a project (a process addressed in the previous chapters) and then looks for the necessary resources, the subject to which I shall now turn your attention.

16.1 Evaluation of Resources

The first step is to verify the Resources the Action Plans require (your series of Tactical Moves organized along a timeline). This includes evaluating how much money is needed to implement each of the two Action Plans. Without Resources, any project is a non-starter.

But Tactical Moves require more than money. Resources come in a great variety of forms: knowledge, people, skills, time, equipment, buildings, networks, and so on. Some Moves might even require partnering with third parties or a door-opener to access certain segments of the market. While acquiring most of these Resources will involve a financial cost, some may be available free of charge.

The time factor is all too often underestimated. This is particularly true of the inventor's or project promoter's time, which is rarely valued properly (understood as the time spent in hours multiplied by his or her real market hourly rate). This leads to an underestimation[1] of the real cost (and value) of the project. Underpaying key players is a common artifact that results in a nicer bottom-line (greater profit) than the painful reality would show.

Resources can be estimated either top-down or bottom-up. A common top-down approach involves using global financial projections to estimate the total resources required or using the experience of previous projects to assess the global cost of a project. The bottom-up approach

[1] The difference between the market cost and the underestimation is something of a measure of the sacrifice that the promoter is prepared to make in order to see the project materialize, in other words how important this project is to him or her.

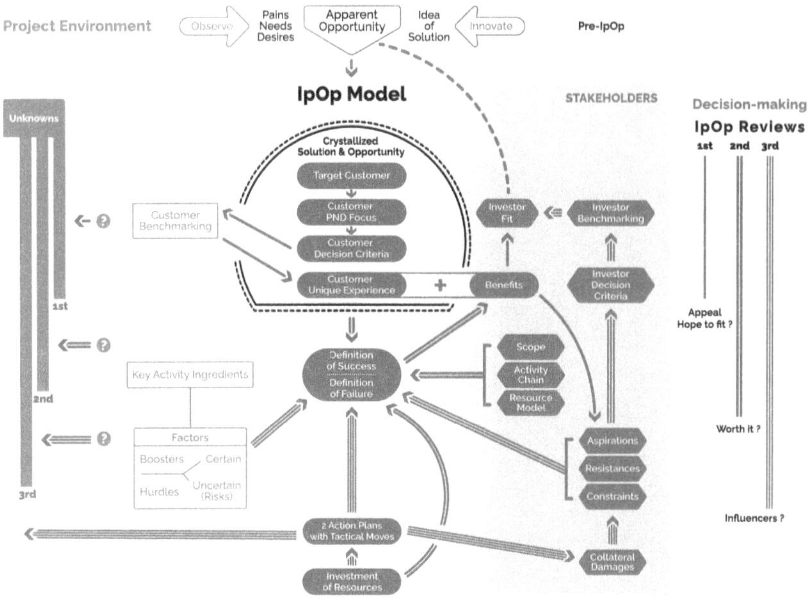

Fig. 16.1 The Investment lists the Resources required to implement Action Plans

adds a complementary perception in that it consolidates the Resources required for each Tactical Move.

This evaluation of the Resources is then consolidated into an Investment (Fig 16.1), detailing the quantity and type of Resources required to reach the Definition of Success. Pre-project analysis, such as the IpOp Model process, lays the groundwork for identifying the required Investment. Knowing that a project's success hinges on adequate Investment, many people with an idea jump straight into the budgeting without sufficient preparation. In fact, the Investment mirrors the financial consequences of the Action Plans. Since the Action Plans are fuzzy at the start of a project, the investment required is often a major Unknown. As the Action Plans become more detailed, you gain clearer insights into the necessary Investment. Rough or approximate estimates of the Investment can be misleading, leading to unexpected and expensive surprises. Without well-thought-out Action Plans, allocating time to budgeting the Investment is a risky shortcut.

Once the Investment has been defined, IpOp Review 4 is complete, and the IpOp Model is also complete (Fig. 16.2).

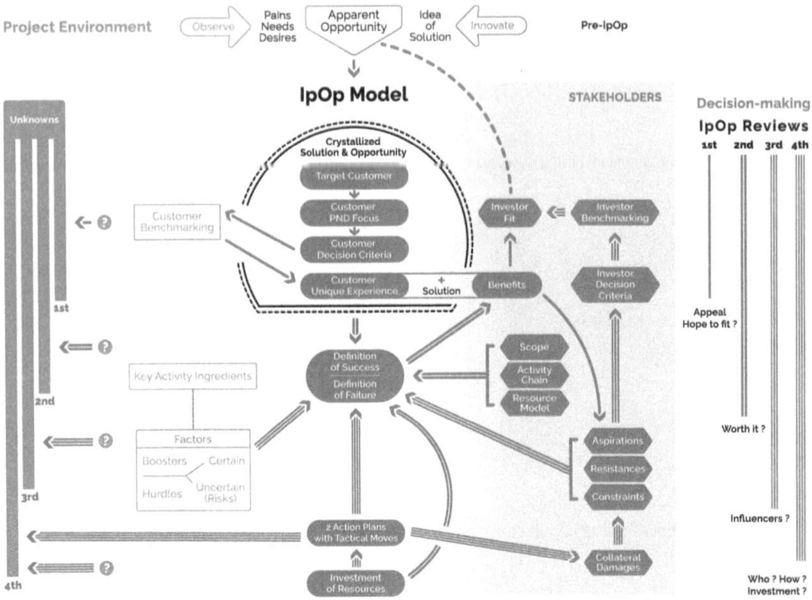

Fig. 16.2 The complete IpOp Model including IpOp Review 4 ("Who, How & with what Resources?")

16.2 The Magic Triangle

Resources provided by the Investment are the necessary fuel for executing the Action Plans, which in turn will reduce Unknowns and deliver the Definition of Success. This "magic triangle" (Fig. 16.3) serves as a reality check that needs to be well balanced to avoid the collapse of the entire project.

If the required Resources/Investment are too hard to obtain, an Action Plan must be amended until it can be reasonably executed within the limits of the Resources available. However, it should not simply be toned down into a "cheap" version of the original Action Plan with the hope of achieving the same results with less outlay.

Rather than simply toning down the Action Plan due to a lack of Investment, it is indispensable to reconsider your Definition of Success or its outcome in less ambitious terms. Achieving the same results with a

Fig. 16.3 The magic triangle: Resources to execute each Action Plan which will deliver the Definition of Success and reduce Unknowns

less costly plan would imply that the original plan did not use the Investment optimally. Such a "waste" of Resources would indicate you had not done your homework when preparing your plan (and that is bad news!). Maintaining your original Definition of Success and Failure with an underfunded Action Plan seriously affects your credibility.

Lack of money is often presented as the main obstacle to start-ups and intraprises. While there are instances where funding might be a challenge, attractive projects tend to secure the necessary funding. Of course, some people are more skilled than others in obtaining the Resources they need.

It is important that entrepreneurs seek Resources from the right people. This necessitates having a sufficiently large network to tap into.

16.3 Financial Projections

Preparation of comprehensive financial projections to identify the Resources required to implement the project Action Plans is an arduous but indispensable exercise. At the very least, the financial projections should include:

- A profit and loss statement projected over various time periods
- A projected balance sheet for the end of each of the periods considered
- A detailed cash flow analysis outlining when and how much money comes in and goes out

Cash flow projections must take the time factor into account in respect of:

- Paying suppliers' invoices
- Collecting on outgoing invoices
- Servicing the debt, etc

To ensure a realistic estimation of the money required, the cash flow should be calculated quarterly or even monthly. Longer periods could be misleading by "averaging" the flows within each period and thus hiding cash requirement peaks. The peak level of the cash deficit indicates how much money is required to avoid a cash flow problem.

Raising money is a whole other ball game, and usually presents a great "opportunity" to negotiate with fund providers. Funding can be obtained through founders' equity or loans, investors' equity or loans, bank loans, etc. Funding is not the focus of this book, but the IpOp Model is sure to contribute, because well-thought-out and properly justified Action Plans have a better chance of convincing investors than one that is not backed by thorough pre-project analysis.

Too many entrepreneurs go ahead without securing the necessary Investment, overlooking the fact that the amount of money raised must be enough to implement the plan that delivers the Definition of Success (see the Magic Triangle above). They too readily assume that the lacking funds will materialize once certain milestones are reached. Such an act of faith can be costly unless there is strong evidence that reaching those milestones will substantially increase the project's attractiveness. Failing that, prayers and hope are usually not enough to offset the risk. In the end, they would have been better off conserving their energy and resources rather than reaching a point where they have no choice but to step out of the game due to lack of resources.

Ideally, entrepreneurs should seek to obtain a conditional commitment to receive the Investment agreed upon once the objectives at the critical milestones have been reached. These milestones usually concern the resolution of key Unknowns (such as demonstrating market receptivity, PoC,[2] or MVP[3]).

Fundraising exacts an enormous collateral cost. The time spent on looking for money and convincing fund providers is unavailable for promoting the delivery of the Definition of Success. The milestone-based conditional approach suggested in the previous paragraph is much healthier than investing a lot of energy into multiple rounds of financing but is only possible with a very well-thought-out pre-project analysis.

16.4 The Who Comes Before the Cash

Last but not least, the quality of the team behind a project is more important than the money. A great project with adequate funding in the hands of a dysfunctional, incompetent, or unmotivated team will most likely fail. Conversely, a highly motivated group of competent people determined to succeed will fix the flaws of a weak project or will be lucid enough to stop the project that does not deserve to continue.

An abundance of money cannot compensate for a weak team. A weak team will never effectively utilize available Resources. Conversely, a good team facing financial constraints will often find ways to secure additional necessary Resources through persuasion and determination. While money can help, it is usually easier to acquire funds than to replace a weak team with a strong one.

First the team, then the project. Some experienced investors or business angels insist that before they hear about the project, they need to be convinced that the team is irresistible. My father who was a seasoned entrepreneur but also my mentor for many years, used to say, "Bring me good people and I will find good projects for them. Don't bring me good projects for which we have to find the team." I am convinced that he was and continue to be right most of the time.

Expertise alone is not enough. Even highly competent partners or team members can kill a project if they do not get along well orif they are

[2] Proof of concept.

[3] Minimum viable product.

not prepared to listen to others. Positive team dynamics are without a doubt a critical success factor. From my experience with numerous partners in various ventures, I have found that the key to positive team dynamics lies in shared values. When people share similar values, they are more likely to have a similar understanding and outlook on situations. This shared perspective helps them find mutually agreeable solutions to the problems they encounter.

Before diving into a project, partners should agree on an engaged team charter. This document helps ensure that everyone is aligned and committed to the same goals. While there is no one-size-fits-all charter for guaranteeing harmonious cooperation, the "engaged team charter" (ETC) has proven to deliver concrete results.[4] Why "engaged?" Because it includes characteristics that foster a higher level of engagement among team members. But beware: the ETC differs significantly, albeit partially, from the "team charters" often developed during off-site sessions with the assistance of well-meaning consultants.

The engaged team charter comprises six components and is created collaboratively with the entire team, including the manager/project manager. This approach ensures that the charter is embraced by everyone involved, making it a collective endeavor rather than a directive from the manager imposed on subordinates. Because the ETC reflects choices agreed upon by the team, there is greater buy-in and adherence to its content due to peer pressure. Peer pressure tends to be more effective than managerial pressure in fostering cooperation and commitment.

The first stage of this six-stage ETC rocket is to clearly define the finality, purpose, outcome, or raison d'être of the project. This goes beyond simply stating "what" the project is about (often referred to as the "mission") and focuses on articulating the ultimate result expected from the project. It aims to ensure that all team members have a shared understanding of what the team should ultimately achieve. While this may seem straightforward, experience shows that most people are not clear or

[4] The Engaged Team Charter has been explained in my book in French "*Les leviers de l'engagement – 54 bonnes pratiques pour entrainer, inspirer et réussir ensemble*" that means in English "The Levers of Engagement: 54 Best Practices to Engage, Inspire and Succeed Together." The following summary is an adaptation of articles that has been published by Forbes on Dec 19 2020.

in agreement on the purpose or outcome of their team's efforts. For a more detailed exploration of this concept and for the other components of the ETC, interested readers can refer to the content of "*Les leviers de l'engagement.*"[5]

Explaining the outcome for the team remains academic or theoretical if the indicators to measure how well the outcome has been achieved are not defined. These key indicators of success (KISs[6]), chosen by the team, are no longer perceived as a surveillance mechanism but as a means of monitoring the team's collective success. By making the finality/purpose/outcome tangible, KIS's ensure that each team member understands precisely what the desired outcome should entail. When the expected outcome is measured through these indicators, everyone understands what needs to be concretely delivered.

However, in line with Peter Drucker's famous quote "Culture eats strategy for breakfast," even the best finality/purpose will never be delivered if the team is dysfunctional. Before even designing a strategy or Action Plan to deliver the outcome (the "how"), the next four components of the engaged team charter must be defined. Their purpose is to optimize the smooth interaction among team members. This underscores the importance of agreeing on the engaged team charter (ETC) ideally before the team begins working on the pre-project.

The third stage of the rocket defines the imperatives the team commits to following in their interactions. These imperatives may encompass values, but they primarily consist of fundamental principles that every team member must respect, such as "The collective interest takes precedence over individual interest." These principles will define the rights and obligations applicable to everyone, similarly to the constitution of a state. Usually, such principles are implicit, but the aim here is to make them explicit.

The purpose of the fourth stage is to catalog the expected behaviors within the team. These behaviors are often derived from the

---

[5] As long as an English translation is not available, artificial intelligence can be used to translate the first 20 pages of Chap. 6.

[6] See Chap. 11.

imperatives of the third stage but are not limited to them. Based on my experience, I have observed that what may seem "obvious" behavior to some is far from obvious to others. For example, the extent to which it is acceptable for team members to check their emails during a meeting or to arrive late varies widely among individuals. As team members with different cultural backgrounds may have very different perspectives on these matters, it is important to agree on the rules of the game.

The fifth stage defines the governance rules that complement the expected behaviors. These rules may specify, for example, the right to make mistakes in good faith or how to handle certain situations, such as balancing private and professional life.

The sixth stage is indispensable, although it is often absent from the team charters I see in the field: it is the enforcement or protection mechanism that ensures all members adhere to the engaged team charter. A team charter that is not lived out is merely wishful thinking to soothe one's conscience. Those who make the effort to respect the ETC's content must be protected by a mechanism that imposes consequences on those who do not adhere to it. The team itself must agree on the consequences for not respecting the agreed rules, usually through debate to define the enforcement mechanism.

It is important to understand that the ETC operates on the same principles as the U.S. Constitution, which begins with "We the people of the United States…": voluntary buy-in by all stakeholders to the rules shaping their collective future. Just as the federal state has been successfully built on such buy-in, the same approach applies to teams. Conceptually, the six-stage ETC rocket could also start with "We the team of ….".

Link with ISO 56007 (Tools and Methods for Managing Opportunities and Ideas—Guidance)

ISO 56007's "decision criteria" within the "resource alignment" grouping encompasses "resource investment requirements," "appropriate team," and "Innovation capability building requirements."

The IpOp Model categorizes "investments," the "team," and "required external skills" under the umbrella of "Resources," as subcategories.

Though organized differently, these elements closely mirror the "Resources/Investment" concept of the IpOp Model.

The IpOp Model suggests a bottom-up approach to calculating the cost of each Tactical Move for a more precise assessment of the necessary resources, providing a complementary perspective to the conventional top-down strategy.

Given the critical role of the team in achieving success, the "Engaged Team Charter," though briefly mentioned in this book and not a direct part of the IpOp Model, serves as an effective tool for assembling an "appropriate" team. This directly supports the implementation of ISO 56007's recommendations.

Recap of IpOp Review 4

Reminder: The objective of IpOp Review 4 is to produce two Action Plans while identifying the necessary Resources/Investment for their implementation. One Action Plan, as outlined in Chap. 14, incorporates Tactical Moves focused on minimizing critical Unknowns. A subsequent Action Plan presented in Chap. 15 involves Tactical Moves designed to achieve the Definition of Success. Naturally, defining these Action Plans will specify the human, financial, and other Resources needed initially to address critical Unknowns (based on Go/No-Go criteria) and subsequently to fulfill the Definition of Success. They determine the Investment for the project.

17

The Big Picture Is on the Canvas

Capturing the Essence on Three Pages

Take-Home of This Chapter

ISO 56007 mentions portfolio management on several occasions but does not provide specific guidance on how to do it. However, the IpOp Model Canvas captures the key elements of a project and can be used to manage a portfolio of projects. Because of the complexity of projects and the limitations of one-page executive summaries, one-page executive summaries are not sufficient for decision-making. The IpOp Model Canvas consists of three pages that provide a comprehensive overview of the project, including information on the Customer adoption, organizational adoption, and critical Unknowns. While the three-page canvas is not sufficient for making decisions, it can be used for information purposes and comparing projects. The chapter also mentions the IpOp Opportunity Case, which is a document that should be used for decision-making and is described in Chap. 20.

As shown by the IpOp Model, a project is by nature complex, influenced by numerous interacting parameters. Capturing this complexity in a single document is challenging.

Many senior decision-makers make the mistake of requesting one-pagers. However, condensing the complexity of a project into a one-page executive summary is unrealistic; they should only serve as informational

R. H Cohen, *Pre-Project Excellence*, Future of Business and Finance,
https://doi.org/10.1007/978-3-031-61774-4_17

tools, not as the basis for decision-making. Ignoring critical parameters in favor of brevity can lead to misallocation of resources and overlook potential risks and other parameters that could significantly impact the project's outcome, cost, or timeline.

17.1 Capturing the Essence

Since a one-pager is not realistic, the best I can offer is a… three-pager. The three-page IpOp Model Canvas shown in Figs. 17.1 and 17.2 and Table 17.1 captures the most important information of any project. While three pages are still insufficient for making decisions, but they can nevertheless provide a decent overview for informational purposes or for quickly comparing projects.

The first page of this Canvas addresses IpOp Review 1. The left part focuses on the parameters indicating the hope of the potential adoption of the solution by Customer (assuming there is only one Customer) while

Purpose of the opportunity					Team members				
Hope with the Customer					Hope with the Company				
Profile of the target Customer					Corporate sponsor / B.U.				
Main Pain/Need/Desire(s)					Company Benefits				
Elevator pitch for the Customer					Strategic fit				
Detailed description of the Solution					Resource Model	Skills (availability)			Av.
Customer Benchmarking vs. Alternatives					**Company Benchmarking vs. other ways/BizModels**				
Number of customers									
Percentage that can be reached									

Fig. 17.1 Page 1 of the IpOp Model Canvas (mostly IpOp Review 1)

Definition of Success (KISs)				Definition of Failure (KIFs)			

Resources for full project	Resources for reducing key Unknowns
Boosters	Potential Collateral Damages
Barriers to entry	Main Risks

Key Stakeholders	Power	Support	Main possible Resistances

Fig. 17.2 Page 2 of the IpOp Model Canvas (mostly IpOp Reviews 2 and 3)

Table 17.1 Page 3 of the IpOp Model Canvas (Critical Unknowns and the effort to reduce them)

Ref	Critical Unknowns	Impact	Tactical Move to reduce the Unknown	Out-of-pocket Expenses	Man-days	Due date	Opportunity Killer
			Total resources for critical Unknowns				
			Total resources for other Unknowns				
			Consolidated total resources for all Unknowns				

the right part highlights the parameters indicating the hope that the organization/Investor will adopt the project.

The second page of the Canvas addresses IpOp Review 2 and part of IpOp Review 3. It presents the Definition of Success and Failure, demonstrating the project's viability, and outlines the role of Influencers (Factors and Stakeholders).

The third page of the Canvas recaps the critical Unknowns of the project. This list[1] provides decision-makers with insight into the effort and first Action Plan (part of IpOp Review 4) required to reduce these critical Unknowns.

The only element missing in this Canvas is the Action Plan for delivering the Definition of Success (the rest of IpOp Review 4). If needed, a fourth page could be used to summarize the second Action Plan timeline with a Gantt chart.

The IpOp Canvas can act as an enhanced and more comprehensive alternative to the traditional project charter commonly employed in organizational project management processes.

Using the canvas outlined in Figs. 17.1 and 17.2 and Table 17.1 not only standardizes the presentation of all projects but also proves useful for managing a portfolio of projects.

For actual decision-making, I strongly advocate using the IpOp Opportunity Case, described in Chap. 20, which addresses the questions posed by the IpOp Decision Tree in Chap. 19.

Link with ISO 56007 (Tools and Methods for Managing Opportunities and Ideas—Guidance)

ISO 56007 mentions portfolio management multiple times but does not elaborate on how to do it. The IpOp Model Canvas functions as both a standardized project charter and a valuable tool for portfolio management, facilitating the easy comparison of multiple projects.

[1] The same as Table 5.1 in Chap. 5.

18

To IpOp or Not to IpOp?

Pros and Cons of the IpOp Model

Take-Home of This Chapter

To help readers evaluate the pros and cons of using the IpOp Model, this chapter discusses the benefits and limitations of the IpOp Model for managing projects, concepts, opportunities, and ideas. This chapter also introduces IpOp Tools™, which is the first computer-aided software that guides users at the pre-project stage in maturing their project, idea, or opportunity. It helps them to identify more Unknowns/uncertainties but it also automatically prints a standardized concept/Opportunity Case, which is aligned with the template included in ISO 56007 annex. Thanks to IpOp Tools™, project teams no longer waste time writing a business plan

The chapter emphasizes the importance of gathering relevant information and understanding the concepts underlying the IpOp Model for successful implementation of ISO 56007 recommendations. As the IpOp Tools™ software captures all the information regarding each project, concept, idea, or Opportunity, it serves as the first and only knowledge management software comprehensively handling the pre-project stage. This chapter discusses the benefits of using the IpOp Model and Tools for start-ups, incubators, and large organizations. By using the IpOp Model and IpOp Tools™, organizations and incubators can standardize project presentations and improve their chances of success in accordance with ISO 56007 guidelines. By using the IpOp Model and IpOp Tools™, organizations can standardize project presentations and improve their chances of success in accordance with ISO 56007 guidelines.

R. H Cohen, *Pre-Project Excellence*, Future of Business and Finance,
https://doi.org/10.1007/978-3-031-61774-4_18

Is the pre-project effort worth the outcome? The complexity of the IpOp Model might seem daunting and discourage its use. This is especially true since many projects have succeeded without it.

18.1 Can You Afford to Fail?

What would be the cost of failure? If failure carries no cost, then you might have no need of a model. But if failure could have a serious negative impact, it is worth investing time and effort in a thorough pre-project analysis that can help increase the chances of success. This is where the IpOp Model comes in.

The IpOp Model is a conceptual tool. Its principal function is to help structure and guide the thought process around any project. Some people do not need a model because what is described here comes intuitively to them.[1] Others will use the model as a mental checklist to increase their chances of success and ensure they do not forget anything critical. Some will apply every component of it, while others will only take parts of it and trust their intuition for the rest. It all boils down to the ratio between effort and chances of success.

It is best to abandon a project immediately once it becomes clear that it is not worth pursuing. As we have seen, launching a project requires some kind of investment. This may be in terms of money, time, effort, frustration, credibility, or even foregoing alternative opportunities. Because people expect a return on their investment (Benefits) and a failed project produces no return, their investment might be qualified as wasted. Anything that helps to prevent failure and waste is a blessing.

[1] Reminder: The IpOp Model was developed by observing what the most successful people spontaneously do to turn a project into reality.

18.2 Completeness of the IpOp Model

What sets the IpOp Model apart is its holistic approach to project and innovation analysis. While many models exist to guide innovators, they often focus on specific dimensions while neglecting others. For example, the business model canvas overlooks Customer Benchmarking, some Stakeholders' issues, and Factors.

To compare other models with the IpOp Model, the easiest method is to overlay the components covered by each model onto the IpOp Model. For example, the black rectangle frames in Fig. 18.1 highlight the components of the IpOp Model that are fully or partially addressed by the business model canvas. This reveals any remaining components that the business model canvas does not consider. However, discovering that a model does not cover all the parameters included in the IpOp Model

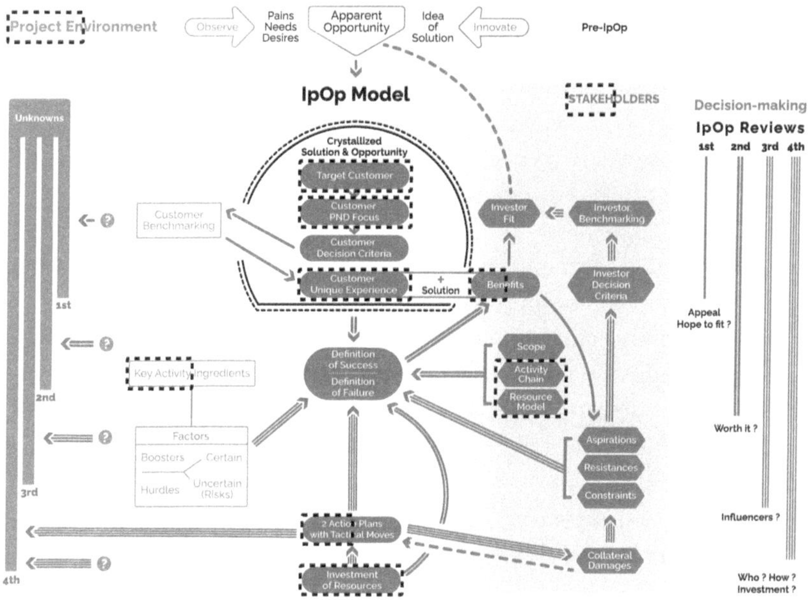

Fig. 18.1 The components highlighted by the black dotted rectangles are addressed by the business model canvas (partially covered means partially handled by the Business model canvas)

does not necessarily indicate that the IpOp Model is better. It simply suggests that the IpOp Model is more comprehensive and holistic, while the other model may analyze certain components in more depth.

This comparison with the business model canvas also illustrates that a business model comprises a combination of some components of the IpOp Model together with a selection of Tactical Moves targeting key business model-related issues (such as distribution channels, customer relationships, etc.). Essentially, the business model canvas examines the opportunity from a specific and thus restricted viewpoint, whereas the IpOp Model offers a broader, more global perspective.

The IpOp Model takes a global approach, which may result in a lower level of detail compared to other models that delve deeper into specific parameters. For example, the business model canvas includes distribution channels as one of its nine components, whereas the IpOp Model does not explicitly mention it. This omission is because managing distribution is just one of many Tactical Moves that could be part of the IpOp Model's Action Plan. Since the IpOp Model does not provide detailed descriptions of individual Tactical Moves, it does not categorize or prioritize certain Moves over others. In the IpOp Model, a Tactical Move is treated equally regardless of its significance.

Use other models to complement your IpOp Model analysis. For example, you can use the business model canvas:

- As a chebucklist to ensure that your Tactical Moves properly address the various components of the business model
- To explain the business model of your project. The business model canvas, originally designed to capture the key components of a business model on a single page, serves primarily as a descriptive tool. As such it can complement the IpOp Model to summarize the underlying… business model
- As part of your Elevator Pitch
- To explore alternative business models for your opportunity
- Etc

18.3 Benefits of the IpOp Model

One of the primary purposes of the IpOp Model is to assist Innovators and project managers in identifying and cataloging as many Unknowns as possible at the pre-project stage, before allocating significant Resources to the project. The process of uncovering Unknowns occurs as the project team members answers questions posed by the IpOp Model to mature their analysis. When the team cannot provide a verified response to a question, it signals that an Unknown needs to be verified.

Given that the IpOp Model is an iterative process, having all the answers upfront is not required. When information is lacking, simply categorize it as an Unknown. Once the information is acquired, you can integrate it into the appropriate section of the IpOp Model. The process involves cataloging all Unknowns as soon as they are identified. Following this, it is crucial to exercise the discipline needed to gather the missing information, strike the resolved Unknown from the list, and adjust your analysis based on the newfound insights.

The IpOp Model is also a validation tool, designed to filter out unworthy projects at the pre-project stage. The sooner these unworthy projects are eliminated, the better. Because the longer you wait, the more resources (time, effort, money, etc.) will have been invested and therefore wasted. The systematic approach inherent in the IpOp Model leads innovators and project managers to analyze their project with rigor at an early stage. This thorough examination helps uncover weaknesses in the project and/or confirm its potential. The initiator and the team are then equipped to decide whether the project is interesting enough to proceed before too many resources have been consumed.

In the context of joint innovation projects, this validation is critical because it aligns partners before they commit resources. By highlighting all the Unknowns that the innovation partnership needs to reduce, the IpOp Model will allow the partners to identify the resources and efforts required for the project. It will also oblige them to agree explicitly on the deliverables (the Definition of Success and Failure), which is frequently fuzzy and can translate into misunderstandings and/or frustration down the road. Using a shared model also encourages the partners to agree on a common process and vocabulary for the innovation partnership, avoiding the potential clash of trying to impose their own company jargon and methods on each other.

The IpOp Model avoids potential loss of credibility and image by eliminating unworthy projects before they are presented to the key Decision-makers. Knowing that the model can help show up the weaknesses of an idea also encourages people to take the exploration further in the safety of their own office.

The IpOp Model also serves as a maturing tool. If a project successfully survives the rigors of the IpOp Model roadmap, it is likely to have matured considerably in the process. It will also have contributed to identifying suitable Tactical Moves. More ammunition is then available for dealing with Stakeholders and the innovator's confidence level is increased (see "Convincing Stakeholders" below).

The IpOp Model prepares the innovators to face the killer questions. Many intrapreneurs-to-be harbor the fear that they will not be able to answer tough questions from their management satisfactorily: they prefer to play it safe and not submit what might in fact be a good idea. The IpOp Model addresses most of the rational issues that their superiors are likely to raise, so going through the process gives them the confidence to bring their proposal out into the open.

The IpOp Model can be used to facilitate group sessions around an innovation, because it is a simple structured process that all participants can understand, focusing their attention on the key questions. It helps the group to move forward by clarifying which points have been agreed upon and what needs further discussion, testing or investigation. It also helps members of the group understand that not all their colleagues necessarily share their own implicit assumptions.

The IpOp Model provides a standard vocabulary[2] **and language**, enabling everyone involved to be clear about the precise meaning of the terms used. Many projects fail because people do not really understand each other. A clear understanding of the terminology and the use of the same language by all concerned reduces the risk of misunderstandings. Even if some of the concepts presented by the IpOp Model are not particularly new, and may have been used elsewhere in different guises, the

[2] ISO 56000 also provides standard ISO definitions for innovation.

IpOp Model vocabulary sometimes gives them a slightly different meaning. In the SWOT analysis, for example, the factors studied are strengths, weaknesses, opportunities, and threats, while the IpOp Model simply looks at Hurdles and Boosters.

The IpOp Model makes explicit what is often merely implicit. Projects frequently fail because certain matters have not been discussed. Anything left unsaid can be interpreted in all sorts of ways or even completely overlooked. Many potential entrepreneurs and intrapreneurs who go by their intuition rely on an implicit understanding of things. When everything goes according to plan, nobody complains. But when it does not, they are in trouble. I call this the "I-should-have-thought-of-it-before" syndrome, the recognition that implicit issues have not been addressed when they ought to have been.

Using a structured process obliges group members to confront their personal perceptions. Without such a structured process, team members may be tempted to assume that others have the same perception as themselves, without bothering to check. One of the main purposes of the IpOp Model is to encourage people to spell it all out rather than letting assumptions remain in the back of their minds.

Spelling out the assumptions offers a more realistic assessment of the project's potential and the risks involved. Unknowns are a very good example. People generally do not take the time to pinpoint the Unknowns liable to undermine their project. Itemizing and analyzing them is a key success factor and will also increase the team's credibility. A presentation that explicitly spells out all the Unknowns is a sign of realism, demonstrating that the promoters are aware of what they do not know.

Explicit analysis opens the door to constructive criticism. Whatever some may say, being challenged is a positive and constructive contribution. "Yes-men" may make you feel good, but they rarely contribute to the progress of your project. Therefore, it is a fine idea to invite others to challenge your ideas, for it will oblige you to do your homework as thoroughly as possible and will lead to a more robust project. To encourage challenge is a sign of strength; evading it is a sign of weakness.

18.4 User-Friendly Software for the IpOp Model

The great strength of The IpOp Model is to connect the multiple dimensions that impact an innovation. But systematic multidimensional analysis very quickly becomes difficult to handle manually as the quantity of information increases.

IpOp Tools™[3] **is a web-based software application designed to simplify this complex task.** It has already been adopted by multinational corporations as well as start-ups and even non-profit organizations.

As a computer-aided analysis system, the software guides project initiators and innovators in organizing and structuring their ideas at the pre-project stage. Typically, innovators and project initiators use the software to mature and validate an idea until they can confirm that it has serious potential or decide to discard it. IpOp Tools™ can profitably be used individually, but groups have also reported that the questions it raises help them improve the quality of their collective analysis. The software raises questions that oblige participants to discuss each issue until a consensus is reached on the answer to be entered in the corresponding field.

The software is a time-saver, drastically cutting down the time users need to advance their ideas. By facilitating the maturation of projects in an engaging and intellectually stimulating way, IpOp Tools™ boosts users' chances of receiving approval from their decision-makers. Since it also automatically generates a concept, business or Opportunity Case, project initiators are spared the painful task of drafting a business plan or other presentation documents for their Investors or Decision-makers. The software produces a standardized Opportunity Case[4] fully compliant with ISO 56007 innovation concept case and tailors specific versions to meet the expectations of different Decision-maker profiles: senior management receives an executive summary focused on their concerns, while project management committees get access to more detailed information and reports. With IpOp Tools™, there is no longer a need for team members to spend time creating and revising numerous reports and formats for varied audiences.

---

[3] https://ipoptools.com/

[4] See Chap. 20.

IpOp Tools™ greatly streamlines the process of identifying, cataloging, and managing Unknowns, one of the central recommendations of ISO 56007. As the software prompts users with questions, they swiftly become conscious of what they do not know with confidence (their uncertainties). Whenever this occurs, the software offers an easy and fast way to capturing this lack of knowledge as an Unknown. Identifying Unknowns presents one of the most challenging tasks for project teams, a task for which ISO 56007 does not offer any specific tool or process. IpOp Tools™ eases this burden, alleviating the pain, discipline, and effort needed to capture as many Unknowns as possible at an early stage. This user-friendly approach to cataloging Unknowns sets the stage for the rigorous management of a project's Unknowns.

The list of Unknowns provides Decision-makers with a clear overview of the challenges faced by each project and quantifies the effort needed to gather the missing information or knowledge. By diminishing Decision-makers' blindness, it enables them to gain a far more thorough understanding of the issues at hand. This enhanced perspective is akin to viewing a 3D picture instead of a flat 2D image, offering a deeper, more nuanced understanding of the project landscape and roadmap.

The software displays Unknowns for each section of the Opportunity Case distinctly, allowing Decision-makers to compare what is stated against the corresponding Unknowns. Additionally, users are prompted to disclose their confidence level in their statements for each section, providing Decision-makers with a tool to assess the statements' reliability.

This functionality heightens Decision-makers' awareness of potential project pitfalls, enabling a thorough assessment of all parameters that could impact the project's outcome and reducing the chance of missing important details. The process promotes greater transparency, as it requires project initiators to explicitly distinguish between facts, assumptions, and beliefs. Consequently, the potential for misleading information to influence decisions is markedly diminished.

IpOp Tools™ is furthermore a database that stores all pre-project or innovation-related information. Since all the data are stored and labeled based on a common vocabulary (Stakeholders' Aspirations, Hurdles, Risks, KISs, Moves, etc.), the software serves as a user-friendly aid to the process of building up the network of links while identifying and storing Tactical Moves. People who thought the complete IpOp Model too complicated to apply manually have changed their perception since using IpOp Tools™. Since the software guides users through the process in an intuitive and transparent manner, they do not even need to remember each step of the model. Computer-assisted innovation or pre-project analysis can thus help to make the perceived level of complexity less intimidating.

IpOp Tools™ acts as a corporate repository for innovation-related information. Once the information has been entered by the users, the resulting database can be used to:

- Manage the process of reducing Unknowns
- Manage, prioritize, and monitor a pre-project portfolio
- Produce standardized Concept/Opportunity Cases,[5] which all share the same customized structure and logic with specific company terminology. Comparing projects that are presented this way makes project selection easier as well as much more rigorous and reliable
- Help Decision-makers truly capture the challenges of each project before allocating resources: as the Opportunity Case automatically outlines the critical Unknowns of each project, as well as the effort required to reduce them, decision-makers can have a much more realistic understanding of which parts of the Opportunity Case are reliable and which need to be verified
- Obtain a comprehensive picture of the status and evolution of innovative activity within the organization
- Provide a detailed overview of the state of innovative activities within the organization
- Compare the merits and stage of advancement of all pre-projects, given that all projects, whatever the nature of the innovation (marketing, R&D or technology-based, process, management, etc.) are structured along the same lines. This considerably helps evaluation and decision-making
- See what other innovation-related projects are being explored in parallel
- Benefit from past experience. Because all ideas, whether implemented or not, are stored in the database, any authorized person can use them

[5] See Chap. 20.

as a source of inspiration or to learn from past mistakes. In the case of projects that have been implemented it becomes possible to retroactively compare the final outcome with the original choices made. Often, people who conduct such retroactive analysis compare outcomes with what was implemented but seldom consider the Tactical Moves that were not pursued, likely because they were forgotten over time. However, software such as IpOp Tools™ makes it possible to evaluate whether the exclusion of certain Tactical Moves was the right decision

- Recycle information entered on behalf of one project in the context of another (e.g., in a family of products, many Stakeholders' Aspirations are likely to remain the same regardless of the project considered). Furthermore, ideas that have not been implemented in one project might very well be successfully used in another
- Verify whether an idea has already been explored in the past. This avoids reinventing the wheel or spending resources on exploring ideas that in fact have little novelty value
- Give credit to the right contributors. IpOp Tools™ also keeps a historical track of the paternity/maternity of each idea, allowing proper acknowledgement of the contributors to it. This management of paternity/maternity also serves to curb "idea theft," and encourages people to innovate, in the knowledge that they will be properly recognized and perhaps rewarded accordingly
- Do data mining and discover interesting trends in innovation
- Search the database to consolidate ideas, identify trends, etc.

A software-based pre-project or innovation Knowledge Management solution equips companies with a critical ingredient for project selection and managing innovation. Innovation management is no simple task, particularly when a proposal goes beyond R&D issues. The use of a single, standardized framework greatly facilitates this task. The main difficulty with Knowledge Management systems is to convince those who have information to enter it in the database. Because IpOp Tools™ saves time and effort for the team, its members are strongly motivated to use it.

IpOp Tools™ overcomes resistance to feeding the Knowledge Management system, because people can use the application for their own benefit. The more information they enter, the more their idea or project will mature and the more they will personally benefit. Because the WiiifM requirement[6] is satisfied, there is less resistance and people will use the software. This usage, in turn, automatically feeds the database with all the data related to all projects. This is further supported by the fact that the software manages the paternity/maternity of ideas. Without this feature people are poorly equipped to prove that they were the instigators of an idea. This automatic time-stamping is a great inducement for employees to use the application, for once the data has been entered, their contribution is de facto captured in the Knowledge Management system.

Harnessing innovation requires the ability to learn from past experience, which necessarily includes failures along with successes. A failure is not the opposite of a success but simply an opportunity to learn what does not work. This is why the most progressive organizations have no hesitation in rewarding failures that provide a learning experience. Because nobody likes to talk about failures, they are quickly forgotten. The ability of IpOp Tools™ to capture the thinking process associated with failure as well as success makes this learning possible.

IpOp Tools™ is a qualitative, not a quantitative, decision-making model. Because there is no reliance on numbers, there is no "black box" aggregation of data, while the occasional quantification is used only for ranking purposes. The application is not a decision-making support solution such as ThinkTools™ or certain operational research systems using mathematical models. IpOp Tools™ simply helps to organize the information without making any recommendations. Users become better equipped to grasp the relationships between the different parameters and then use their judgment to make decisions.

Startup incubators, along with government and private agencies that foster innovation, can also benefit from using the software. It is designed to tackle the issues and fulfill the requirements detailed in Tables 18.1 (for project teams and start-ups) and 18.2 (for organizations including funding agencies, R&D centers, incubators).

[6] "What is in it for Me." Motivation is largely influenced by the benefits that people get or can get for themselves.

Table 18.1 Benefits of IpOp Tools™ for project teams or start-ups

	Pain/Need/Desire(s)	Solution	Benefits
1	Skip the time-consuming task of drafting a business plan or business case	Utilize questions crafted to assist the project team in developing their project. The analysis is conducted using the IpOp Model, rather than relying on a business plan for guidance	The software automatically generates an Opportunity Case based on the responses, ensuring full compliance with ISO 56007 recommendations Different versions of the Opportunity Case are produced automatically, tailored to the detail requirements of various management levels If necessary, the generated MS-Word and PDF files can be manually customized for further refinement
2	Accelerate the process	Use the user-friendly IpOp roadmap to develop the project and create Action Plans, complete with timeline and costs	Forget about memorizing the process; the software provides all the necessary guidance The perceived complexity of the IpOp Model ceases to be a barrier
3	Ensure the project's successful implementation	Employ a suite of tools that transform an idea into a validated Action Plan	Gain a clearer comprehension of the key success factors Reduce the risk of overlooking crucial parameters
4	Identify Unknowns that could endanger the project	The challenge of answering questions through IpOp Tools™ aids the project team in naturally identifying their uncertainties and incorporating them into the list of Unknowns	Recognizing as many Unknowns as early as possible provides the team with a clearer insight into what requires verification. This understanding enables the team to realistically estimate the effort (in terms of time, skills, and money) needed to acquire the missing information and knowledge
5	Determine the project's duration and the Resources it necessitates	Securing one Action Plan for reducing Unknowns and another for achieving the Definition of Success, each equipped with its specific timeline and budget	This insight facilitates the creation of a realistic roadmap, complete with an estimate of the effort required (in terms of time, skills, and financial resources) to achieve success

(continued)

Table 18.1 (continued)

	Pain/Need/Desire(s)	Solution	Benefits
6	Having the team's responses validated by experts	The option to seek experts' opinions via email on specific sections of the IpOp Model	Easy verification of answers, enhancing the team's confidence Automated logging of consultations, including who has been consulted, their opinions, and how these have been incorporated in the team's responses
7	Facilitating communication among team members and with coaches	The ability to add comments on each page that can be shared with or kept private from the rest of the team	Ability to obtain feedback for each page from team members or coaches Functionality to annotate pages with tasks that still need completion, reminders of pertinent information, and more
9	Ensuring the team has a unified understanding	Facilitating structured discussions within the team, prompted by the software, to achieve consensus on the optimal responses	Concentrating on realistic goals rather than wishful thinking; fostering a shared vision and a common vocabulary among team members
10	Asynchronus teamwork	The capability to work remotely, contributing to a consolidated and collective outcome through groupware functionalities	The option to collaborate on the same project remotely and at different times, or to exchange ideas using shared screens during video conferences
11	Identifying who has input or altered data and the timing of these changes	Change tracking enables identifying who made specific changes and when these changes were made	No data or idea is lost. Everything is archived, offering the possibility to revisit and recycle ideas in the future
12	Mitigate the risk of someone "stealing" a team member's idea and receiving undue credit	Authorship is automatically managed, with all inputs attributed to an owner and time-stamped	A dependable system for attributing and recognizing the ownership of ideas

Table 18.2 Additional benefits of IpOp Tools™ for large organizations, incubators, and funding agencies, on top of those in Table 18.1

	Pain/Need/Desire(s)	Solution	Benefits
13	Anticipate as early as possible the multitude of issues that could influence the outcome of each project thanks to a mechanism that compels project initiators to maintain transparency	Cataloging Unknowns separately for each section of the Opportunity Case enables Decision-makers to weigh the information provided against the corresponding Unknowns Furthermore, since users are also required to indicate their own level of confidence in their assertions for each section of the Opportunity Case, decision-makers can utilize this confidence level to gauge the reliability of the information presented to them	Decision-makers become more aware of the potential pitfalls of projects. They are equipped to conduct a comprehensive evaluation of all parameters influencing the outcome of each project, mitigating the risk of overlooking crucial aspects This process enhances transparency by compelling project initiators to clearly differentiate between facts, assumptions, and beliefs As a result, the likelihood of manipulation through misleading information is significantly reduced
14	Monitoring the progression of each project and the involvement of individual team members	Since the software tracks all activity within each project, it is capable of generating detailed reports contributions and on the progress of each project	Enhanced control for management without imposing reporting burdens on the teams. No constraints
15	Minimize the waste of resources resulting from improper selection of projects	With more relevant information available, decision-makers are better equipped to make a more rigorous and reliable selection of projects	More efficient resource utilization with reduced waste. A decrease in the number of projects initiated, focusing only on those deemed worthy

(continued)

Table 18.2 (continued)

	Pain/Need/Desire(s)	Solution	Benefits
16	Early and reliable identification of the most promising projects	A universal and rigorous framework designed to validate any type of project or innovation, be it a service or a product	A more rigorous selection process The capability to assess and compare the relative strengths and weaknesses of all projects alongside their success probabilities Early termination of undeserving projects leads to fewer wasted resources Improved return on investment (ROI)
17	Rapid and uniform assessment of multiple projects at once	Standardized Opportunity Case reports featuring various levels of detail, all in complete alignment with ISO 56007 recommendations	Evaluating the potential of each project becomes significantly easier when key Unknowns are consistently positioned in the same section of the report. This approach is far more efficient than sifting through poorly crafted business cases and plans that fail to address all essential questions in a consistent manner
18	Gain insights from previous projects	Since the database archives data from all projects, it functions as a knowledge management system	A searchable repository available that contains all the knowledge pertaining to every project explored within the organization. This knowledge base is automatically updated without requiring users to exert extra effort. Because users directly benefit from using the software—through more successful projects, reduced workload, and eliminating the need to write a business plan or case—they naturally use the software, which in turn feeds the knowledge database effortlessly. The database is updated as a beneficial byproduct
19	Reuse ideas or knowledge from other projects	A searchable knowledge management system enables authorized users to access and reuse ideas and knowledge	No need to reinvent the wheel

20	Revive projects that were previously halted or suspended because they were not relevant at the time, but are now possibly feasible due to changing circumstances	With 100% of the project information stored, any project can be reactivated and updated to meet new circumstances, market needs or requirements	Quickly revive projects to address new needs
21	Learn from identifying key success factors across various projects	The knowledge management system stores data on all projects, enabling researchers to analyze it and identify relevant patterns	Identify patterns from all projects. Analyzing past successes and failures retroactively nurtures a learning organization
22	Establish a unified methodology and terminology	The user-friendly software provides guidance to everyone in the organization	Implementing best practices recommended by ISO 56007 throughout the organization
23	Lower the cost of coaching	Coaches can remotely supervise entered data and guide teams accordingly	Less coaching time is required since the team puts in most of the effort (e.g., no need to coach on writing the business case)
24	Training project teams	The tutorial teaches business skills required to use the IpOp Model	Boost business acumen to improve success rate of projects
25	Minimize the "quality gap" between senior and junior coaches	All coaches adhere to the same proven process	Achieve greater consistency and establish a shared vocabulary
26	Enhance the visibility of R&D and incubator achievements	The database stores structured data for all projects	Generating statistics on R&D, funding or incubator performance is a breeze with structured data

18.5 Limitations of the IpOp Model

The IpOp Model is not designed for people who prefer improvisation and immediate action, although it will provide them with a mental reference model. For those who like to be well prepared, it will help them build strength. It addresses most key Stakeholders' concerns and represents an effective preparation strategy. It is much less dangerous to "jump into the arena" after having worked through the IpOp Model than without the benefit of this systematic analysis.

The IpOp Model is a "garbage in, garbage out" system. As with any model, the quality of the output is only as good as the quality of the input. It is not a miracle process. For it to be effective, users must have the right information available for each step of the IpOp Model or catalog them as Unknowns. For instance:

- To be able to benchmark, you need to be familiar with what the competition is doing and is capable of
- To analyze Stakeholders' Aspirations, you must know them well what they are
- To quantify the Definition of Success, you should have a good idea of the market size and potential as well as which KISs are important for your Decision-makers
- To evaluate the feasibility of certain Moves, you will probably need to know what Resources and prerequisites they might require, etc.

Gathering relevant information is therefore critical throughout most of the process, and users will certainly benefit from using business intelligence tools. The Internet and artificial intelligence are obviously major sources of information for those trained to use them efficiently.

It is important to fully understand the concepts underlying the IpOp Model. To maximize benefits, you must understand these concepts and learn how to use them. A poor understanding will automatically translate into a poor outcome. As with any method, practice is required to master each of the concepts/tools.

The IpOp Model is not a linear process, even if it has been presented that way in this book for pedagogical reasons. In fact, using the IpOp Model starts as a linear process, but the user will quickly comprehend the need to go back and forth to amend information entered previously. At the Moves stage, for instance, it can easily happen that the user thinks of a Risk that had not been identified earlier and will then go back and add that Risk to the list of Factors. Conversely, if a user thinks of a particular Move before the relevant brainstorming stage, it can nevertheless easily be entered in the list of Tactical Moves. Clearly, using a software application greatly facilitates such a free-wheeling approach.

The IpOp Model currently does not rely on artificial intelligence, mathematical or statistical tools. It simply establishes the relationships between the various parameters that must be considered when analyzing an innovation at the pre-project stage. Quantitative models, based on (subjective) numerical data, can give the false impression that the resulting decisions are scientifically or objectively based. They may work for certain decision models, but I doubt they would be suitable for analyzing innovative ideas at the pre-project stage. I have not tried to integrate a quantitative element in the IpOp Model, but others may be successful in doing so in the future. Until I see a quantitative approach that works, I recommend avoiding the quantification trap. To understand this danger, consider how an average temperature of 37 °C does not accurately reflect the condition of someone with their head in an oven and feet in a freezer.

As artificial intelligence should soon help users of IpOp Tools™ input more relevant content, I am increasingly optimistic about the potential contribution of artificial intelligence at the pre-project stage. A.I. has the potential to take full advantage of the knowledge management system within IpOp Tools™. For example, it could use its content to identify new products, understand better key success factors, combine ideas, etc.

Link with ISO 56007 (Tools and Methods for Managing Opportunities and Ideas—Guidance)

ISO 56007 underscores best practices, such as cataloging uncertainties/Unknowns. However, due to a lack of direct methods for identifying them, it references the IpOp Model as a methodology for their identification.

Moreover, ISO 56007's annexes present the IpOp Decision Tree and the template for the "innovation concept case," both of which draw inspiration from the IpOp Model's "Opportunity Case." Utilizing a Decision Tree or a template effectively necessitates a thorough understanding of the underlying principles, which this book aims to provide.

ISO 56007 suggests an alternative to the conventional business plan by proposing a two-document presentation approach for projects: an innovation concept case followed by an action plan. The IpOp Model has long supported this dual-document strategy and details the procedure for creating these documents. Thus, the IpOp Model serves as a practical guide for implementing ISO 56007's recommendations in real-world projects.

The IpOp Tools™ software facilitates a comprehensive and rigorous analysis of projects, aiding users in listing their uncertainties/Unknowns and crafting a pragmatic Action Plan to achieve the Definition of Success.

Additionally, the software generates various versions of the innovation concept case tailored to the informational needs of different Decision-maker groups (such as top management, evaluation committees, and coaches). With IpOp Tools™ customized reports aligning with the specific concerns of each industry and with ISO 56007 guidelines, the software assists organizations in standardizing project presentations according to ISO 56007's recommendations.

19

Climbing the Decision-Making Tree

Ignoring Decision-Makers' Criteria Is Suicidal

Take-Home of This Chapter

Since selection is an essential component of ISO 56007 and with the understanding that rational Decision-makers prefer evidence-based approaches and factual information, the standard emphasizes the need to define and publish project selection criteria. By publishing their customized version of the IpOp Decision Tree organizations encourage bottom-up innovation, promote fully analyzed projects and concept, and filter out poor ideas. The only example of proven Decision Tree displayed in the annex of ISO 56007 is the IpOp Decision Tree. This chapter presents the IpOp Decision Tree and its benefits in the context of project evaluation and decision-making. The IpOp Decision Tree is a universal tool that helps project teams verify that their project, concept, or Opportunity truly addresses the unavoidable concerns of demanding Decision-makers. Knowing the 11 questions that any experienced Decision-maker should at least ask allows innovators and promoters to prepare accordingly at the pre-project stage in order to produce a compelling case for their idea or to determine that it is not worth pursuing. Heads of innovation as well as PMO's (project management offices) can also use the IpOp Decision Tree as a robust filtering mechanism to reduce the number of projects in their portfolio. Since using the IpOp Decision tree contributes to optimize the use of Resources in any organization, it fully supports the implementation of the best practices recommended by ISO 56007.

R. H Cohen, *Pre-Project Excellence*, Future of Business and Finance,
https://doi.org/10.1007/978-3-031-61774-4_19

Grasping how decision-makers select a project is crucial for successfully pitching your project. Focusing on your own decision criteria instead of theirs is as ineffective as speaking Greek to an English-speaking banker who does not understand Greek—in other words, hopeless! To communicate effectively, you must align your pitch with the Decision-makers' criteria.

19.1 Decision-Maker Profiles

Gaining the support of Decision-makers is essential to advance your project. These individuals often include Investors, board members, senior executives, business developers, and investment committee members. In the public and non-profit sectors, they could be donors or politicians. Since they control the allocation of essential resources or authorizations, Decision-makers act as crucial gatekeepers. Without their endorsement and support, progressing with your project is impossible.

Understanding the Decision-makers' evaluation criteria allows you to customize the presentation of your project to address their specific concerns. Generally, Decision-makers fall into three main non-exclusive categories:

- The "gut-feeling" group, who base their decisions on intuition
- The "rational" group, who rely on facts and analysis for their decisions
- Those who blend both approaches, applying them to varying degrees

Although there are a significant number of decision-makers who might even resort to unconventional methods like astrology, zodiac signs, blood groups, or numerology, for simplicity, this discussion will focus primarily on the first two categories.

Dealing with "gut feelers" requires a more emotional approach.[1] These individuals are driven by visions and aspirations. Using pitching and storytelling techniques that paint an exciting and attractive future

[1] All decision-makers are Stakeholders and some of their personal Aspirations, as mentioned in Chap. 6, play a significant role in driving their emotions.

can be highly effective. Many project initiators dream of seducing decision-makers into falling in love with their (brilliant!) idea. They secretly hope their passion and conviction will persuade Decision-makers to give the green light without insisting on the dreaded Business Plan or getting bogged down in "minor details". Despite their emotional approach, these Investors often still prefer to believe their decision is a rational one, offering a more reassuring outcome.

Convincing rational Decision-makers presents a greater challenge as they prioritize an evidence-based approach. They strive to maintain objectivity and rationality, relying heavily on factual information while shunning uncertainties. Dealing with this group requires thorough preparation, forcing project initiators to do their homework and gather the relevant information to justify their claims.

To adequately prepare, you must identify all the rational Decision-makers' concerns. Failing to do so can leave you vulnerable when confronted with questions you cannot answer, potentially jeopardizing the buy-in of your project. To avoid this risk, there is only one option: be fully prepared to address any potential inquiries, even if they never come up during discussions. This proactive approach is essential for safeguarding your project from being discarded.

The IpOp Model, outlined in this book, is designed to prepare you to face the Rational decision-makers. Its systematic approach helps in structuring project presentations in a highly rational manner, catering to the preferences of evidence-based Decision-makers. While some intuitive Decision-makers may utilize the model to validate or support their gut feelings, they may hesitate to undergo the rigorous process it entails.

19.2 The IpOp Decision Tree

All Decision-makers, whether rational or intuitive, use a set of criteria to evaluate projects. Experience and research indicate that it is exceedingly uncommon for Decision-makers to employ a comprehensive and reliable set of criteria for project selection. The inherent complexity of projects clashes with the human brain's capacity, which typically struggles to manage more than six or seven parameters at once. Consequently,

Decision-makers end up relying on a limited set of decision criteria, inevitably overlooking other critical parameters. This oversight leads to significant blind spots that likely contribute to the inadequate evaluation of projects, resulting in delays and cost overruns.

To mitigate these blind spots, I developed the Decision Tree shown in Fig. 19.1 after years of empirical observation, pinpointing questions that could have pre-empted issues or surprises later on. This Decision Tree is crafted as a tool for Decision-makers, who ultimately must decide whether to allocate resources to projects. Although it can assist in intermediate evaluations during the iterative process of refining an idea or Opportunity, its primary function is for the final evaluation to proceed with or terminate the project. Utilizing it beforehand aids project initiators in preparing to address these questions. The IpOp Model is an instrument for finding answers to each of these queries.

This generic Decision Tree serves as a mental guide to ensure that both Decision-makers and project initiators do not overlook any critical questions. Similar to how recruiters use a checklist during interviews to ensure they cover all bases when evaluating job candidates, the Decision Tree acts as a checklist for appraising project merits before allocating Resources.

While the sequence of questions can be adjusted to reflect personal priorities, experience indicates that these questions are relevant to a vast majority of projects, suggesting that the IpOp Decision Tree is broadly applicable across different project types, beyond innovation projects.

As this Decision Tree is recognized as a best practice, it is included in the annex C4 of ISO 56007,[2] offering practitioners a direct tool or a source of inspiration for customization.

The IpOp Decision Tree for project evaluation is pertinent not just for rational Decision-makers but also for those who depend on gut feelings. Whether operating consciously or subconsciously, individuals in both groups utilize their own criteria, with priorities influencing their parameters. Both rational and intuitive decision-makers should address similar questions and face the same issues. The primary difference is in their approach to finding answers and the importance they place on each

[2] Figure C.1.

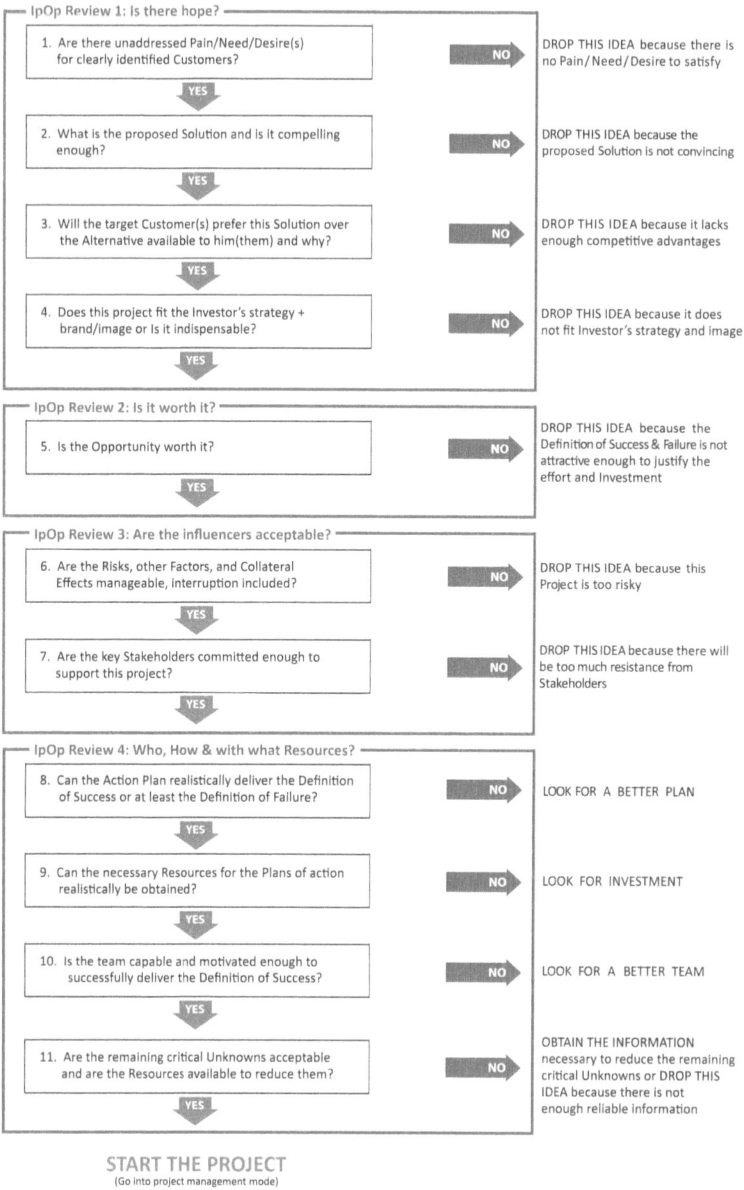

Fig. 19.1 The IpOp Decision Tree

parameter. Both categories of decision-makers usually confirm that none of the questions are irrelevant, and each demands a response.

Heads of innovation as well as PMO's (project management offices) can also use the IpOp Decision Tree as a robust filtering mechanism to reduce the number of projects in their portfolio.

Everyone is anyway free to customize this list by adding his or her own questions (and answers!) into the decision-making process. These more specific personal additional Investors' Decision Criteria may include:

- The Decision-makers' personal interests or hobbies (these could factor into the project's compatibility with the Strategic fit,[3] which stems from the Decision-makers' centers of interest)
- Compatibility of the project with the Decision-makers' values (which may be a component of the Strategic fit)
- The Decision-makers' mental readiness to invest in a new venture at that specific moment (this is a Factor[4] that can either kill or boost the project; his or her willingness to invest also reflects Stakeholders' Aspirations[5])
- The scale of necessary Resources compared to those available to the Decision-makers
- Compatibility with other ongoing projects (again, part of the Strategic fit)
- The Decision-makers' history, education, and past experiences
- The Decision-makers' confidence in the project initiator's ability to execute the project

Finally, publishing the IpOp Decision Tree within an organization yields significant benefits:

- It signals to employees that they are encouraged to explore and present new projects. By explicitly spelling out the decision-making process,

[3] For more details on the strategic fit, see Chap. 6.

[4] See Chap. 12.

[5] See Chap. 13.

management demonstrates its support for bottom-up initiatives and grants employees permission to innovate, thereby providing a powerful boost to innovation

- It encourages employees to present a thoroughly analyzed project rather than just an (often fuzzy and) half-baked idea. The questions in the IpOp Decision Tree oblige people to develop their ideas fully before presenting them to decision-makers
- It prompts employees to prepare an Opportunity Case (or business case)[6] that addresses the questions relevant to decision-making
- By helping innovators to eliminate ideas that fail to provide proper answers to the questions listed, it automatically filters out poor projects that would otherwise encumber Decision-makers' desks and waste their time

A thorough analysis is required to answer the questions outlined in the IpOp Decision Tree. As indicated above, the IpOp Model presented in this book serves as the tool to find the answers to all those questions. Figure 19.2 displays the IpOp Decision Tree, with the left column indicating where in the IpOp Model the information can be found to answer each of the 11 questions posed by the IpOp Decision Tree.

---

[6] See Chap. 20.

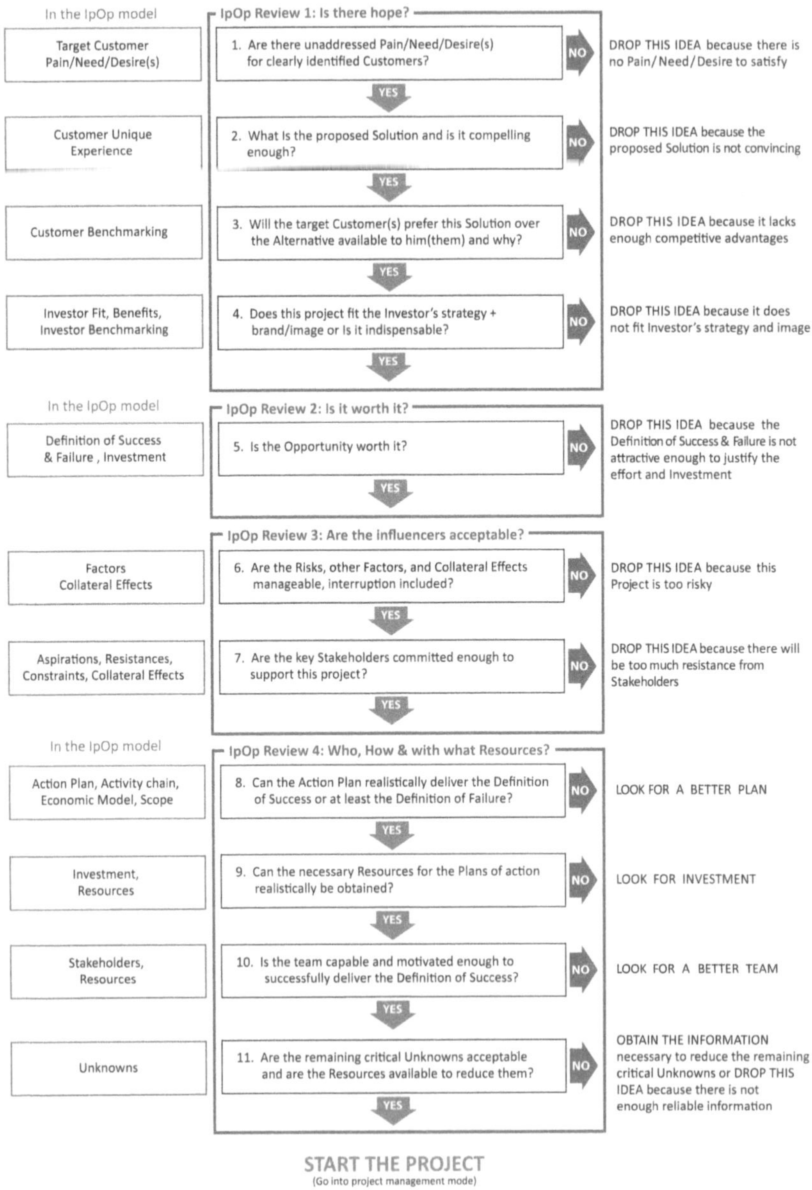

Fig. 19.2 Finding the IpOp Decision Tree information in the IpOp Model

Link with ISO 56007 (Tools and Methods for Managing Opportunities and Ideas—Guidance)

The Decision Tree located in annex C4 of ISO 56007 mirrors the IpOp Decision Tree, with only slight adjustments in terminology to align with ISO vocabulary.

For those interested in applying the IpOp Model to meet the decision criteria outlined in section 6.4.3.5.4 of ISO 56007, the following table serves as a guide:

Annex	ISO 56007 decision criteria	Correspondence in the IpOp Model	Comment
C.3.1	a) Customer/user fit	Customer Benchmarking	The Benchmarking demonstrates the customer fit
	b) Ecosystem fit	Key Activity Ingredients	The Key Activity Ingredients outline what is required to fit the ecosystem and get market acceptance
	c) Market/ mission fit	Key Activity Ingredients Factors Strategic fit	Market fit depends on Key Activity Ingredients and Factors Fit with the Mission of the organization is part of the Strategic fit

Annex	ISO 56007 decision criteria	Correspondence in the IpOp Model	Comment
C.3.2	a) Strategic fit	Strategic fit	–
	b) Scope fit	Strategic fit	Scope is a characteristic of the strategy
	c) Desired business/ mission model fit	Strategic fit	Business/mission models are characteristics of the strategy
	d) Definition of Success/Return on investment (ROI)	Definition of Success Definition of Failure	RoI (Return on Investment) is one example of KISs The Definition of Failure is not addressed in ISO 56007
	e) Innovation pipeline and portfolio objectives	Strategic fit	The innovation pipeline and portfolio aim to support the strategy
	f) Timeline expectations	Strategic fit Definition of Success and Failure	The strategy defines when the Definition of Success and Failure should be delivered
	g) Risk exposure	Strategic fit Factors	Risks are subcategories of Factors while the level of risk should be defined by the strategy
	h) IP considerations	Strategic fit Factors	IP considerations are Factors (pre-existing IP and legislation) and the strategy should include an IP strategy

Annex	ISO 56007 decision criteria	Correspondence in the IpOp Model	Comment
C.3.3	a) Resource investment requirements	Investment allocating Resources	
	b) Appropriate team	Resources Factors Stakeholders	The team is a Resource (it has a cost). It is also a Stakeholder with Aspirations and Resistances. Its members' skills, knowledge, network, and other characteristics are Factors
	c) Innovation capability building requirements	Strategic fit	The need to build capabilities is defined by the strategy
C.3.4	a) Interested parties' acceptance	Stakeholders	–
	b) Sustainability and durability	Stakeholders Strategic fit	The sustainability and durability are characteristics of the strategy while of the objectives of the strategy is to satisfy Stakeholders
	c) Collateral effects	Collateral Effects or Damages	–

Annex	ISO 56007 decision criteria	Correspondence in the IpOp Model	Comment
C.3.5	a) Acceptability of other factors that hinder or boost implementation	Factors	
	b) Effort to reduce remaining uncertainties	Action Plan to reduce Unknowns Resources	This Action Plan requires Resources (people, money, skills, …)
	c) Feasibility of the Action Plan for development	Action Plan to deliver the Definition of Success Resources	This Action Plan also requires Resources
	d) Overall coherence with innovation ambitions	Strategic fit	Innovation ambitions are part of the strategy

20

Is Your Presentation Sexy Enough? The Art of Convincing Stakeholders

Take-Home of This Chapter

ISO 56007 suggests the two-document approach as a valid alternative to the traditional business plan for presenting concepts to decision-makers innovators. The two-document approach corresponds to the approach that the IpOp Model has been advocating since 2006: one concept/Opportunity Case that gives decision-makers all the essential information they need to allocate Resources to projects except the Implementation plan that is presented in a separate document, only when Decision-makers are convinced by the merits of the project. As an example of concept case, ISO 56007 presents in its annex almost the same IpOp Model template that is described in this chapter. By mastering the IpOp Model and its key parameters, robust concept/Opportunity Cases can be developed according to ISO 56007 recommendations. By leveraging the Decision-makers drivers and psychology, the IpOp Model template uses a storyline designed to build trust, mindshare, and buy-in. This chapter provides insights into how the IpOp Model can help to provide relevant information for each component of the concept/Opportunity Case. This chapter also provides a table illustrating how the IpOp Model can be used to develop a business plan.

The best proposal in the world is doomed to remain simply a proposal if it does not have the endorsement of the key Stakeholders. Most entrepreneurs believe that the way to win over Stakeholders' minds

R. H Cohen, *Pre-Project Excellence*, Future of Business and Finance,
https://doi.org/10.1007/978-3-031-61774-4_20

is to submit a well-written business plan. This is indeed one way, but it is not the only way, and certainly not the best one.

20.1 Put an End to the Tyranny of Business Plans

The purpose of a business plan is to detail the rationale and method for implementing a project. Essentially, it addresses five critical questions:

- **What** is the project?
- **Why** is it worth implementing?
- **How** will it be executed?
- **Who** will make it happen?
- **How much**: what resources (financial, human, etc.) are needed, and what outcomes are expected?

Given the abundance of books and courses available on writing a business plan, I will not delve into this topic here.

Business plans are in fact more trouble than they are worth for several reasons:

- Studies, such as the one conducted by Babson College in Wellesley, Massachusetts,[1] suggest that having a business plan does not significantly increase the likelihood of success for a new venture
- Surprisingly, fewer than 10% of business plans are fully read. Most Decision-makers only peruse the executive summary, filtering out all but the most interesting proposals

[1] http://blog.guykawasaki.com/Bygrave.doc

This study examined whether writing a business plan before launching a new venture affects the subsequent performance of the venture. The data set comprised new ventures started by Babson College alumni who graduated between 1985 and 2003. The analysis revealed that there was no difference between the performance of new businesses launched with or without written business plans. The findings suggest that unless a would-be entrepreneur needs to raise substantial start-up capital from institutional investors or business angels, there is no compelling reason to write a detailed business plan before opening a new business.

- The process of creating a business plan often leads to delays in presenting the project to Decision-makers, potentially impeding progress and hindering timely decision-making
- Beyond those who profit from producing, teaching, or selling business plans, the majority of the business community agrees that they offer little value for start-ups and new initiatives. However, business plans remain relevant as an output of strategic analysis for coordinating the functions of existing organizations (such as marketing, production, HR, finance, etc.) to deploy the strategy
- Consequently, writing them is a waste of time and energy for innovators and project initiators!

Stakeholders are rarely interested in the level of detail found in a business plan. Decision-makers prioritize understanding the "what," "why," and "who" of a project before delving into the "how" and "how much." They will only explore the implementation details once they are convinced that the project merits further consideration. Consequently, when reviewing a business plan, Decision-makers must sift through the implementation specifics to extract the relevant points regarding the project's purpose and rationale ("what" and "why"). This process is not particularly reader-friendly, especially when seeking investment from Stakeholders.

Very few projects, if any, are implemented exactly as outlined in the business plan. One obvious reason is that the implementation plan often overlooks the potential contributions of Investors, such as their network of contacts, resources beyond capital (like equipment, expertise, personnel, etc.), or other supportive benefits. Anticipating these specific contributions in a "one-size-fits-all" business plan is challenging, unless it is tailored for a specific Investor, or a different version is created for each reader.

Furthermore, Investors typically exert influence over how a project is executed. It is rare for an Investor, whether a business angel or venture capitalist, to allow the founder to proceed without some form of (usually) monitoring and constructive intervention. As a result, the original plan, outlined in the business plan, often becomes outdated due to the input from Decision-makers or other Stakeholders. Therefore, it would be more effective to draft the Action Plan once the potential Investor's views and contributions are understood. This input should then be integrated without requiring a complete overhaul of the business plan.

The "Executive Summary" often falls short of addressing Stakeholders' specific concerns. Stakeholders typically seek answers to their questions rather than a condensed overview of the entire business plan. However, the challenge lies in accommodating this within the typical length constraint of 1–3 pages.

20.2 The IpOp Opportunity Case

A strategy more effective than traditional business plans for meeting the needs of Investors and Decision-makers involves a two-document presentation. This approach is inspired by the realization that Decision-makers first require convincing of a project's worth before they consider the specifics of its implementation. This Investor-friendly approach requires two documents:

1. **An Opportunity Case** that outlines the "what" and "why" of the Opportunity, accompanied by a list of critical Unknowns requiring further validation.
2. **An Action Plan** detailing the Tactical Moves selected to achieve the Definition of Success, addressing the "how" and the detailed "how much".

This approach implies seeking approval for the project based on its Opportunity Case before refining the Action Plan. If the Opportunity Case fails to secure approval, there is no need to proceed with preparing an Action Plan.

The first document is called Opportunity Case instead of business case because it transcends business or for-profit applications, offering a more inclusive perspective also suitable for non-profit or public sector. Due to its specific terminology guidelines, ISO 56007 refers to this presentation document as the "innovation concept case."

The following template for the Opportunity Case has proven effective for most projects, which is why it is featured in annex C.5.2.2 of ISO 56007 as an example of an innovation concept case. Its content is derived from the IpOp Decision Tree outlined in Chap. 19. While there are no strict rules regarding the sequence the IpOp Opportunity Case should answer the key questions in an order that resonates with the target audience.

It is important not to confuse the IpOp Model analysis with the Opportunity Case. The IpOp Model analysis contains details that do not need to be included in the Opportunity Case. Indeed, the analysis is conducted BEFORE writing the Opportunity Case. In the Opportunity Case, you select what is of interest to Decision-makers (thus, for instance, no details on the Aspirations of Stakeholders).

The sole purpose of an Opportunity Case is to obtain a decision. This decision might involve securing a sponsor's support (in which case, typically only IpOp Reviews 1 + 2 are needed) or getting approval to launch the project with the necessary Resources allocated (for this, completing all four IpOp Reviews is usually required). Therefore, before creating an Opportunity Case, it is indispensable to know its purpose and identify the Decision-maker targeted. In essence, if there is no one to convince, there is no need for an Opportunity Case...

The nature of the request must be explicitly stated so that the reader knows what is expected of them (preferably before reading the document). Depending on your project's stage of progress, you might need to secure:

- A sponsor's support
- Permission to reach out to business unit leaders or regional heads
- Approval to start a study
- An initial green light with Resources to reduce critical Unknowns
- The final go-ahead to launch the project on a larger scale or extend it beyond the pilot phase
- Etc.

20.3 The Opportunity Case Template

For certain sections of this template, I have included recommendations or comments in italics below to clarify what should be detailed in each section.

Start with a cover page, which must specify who the reader is as well as the type of decision expected. The cover page should of course also indicate the authors and their contact details.

1. Why should you read this document?

This section is an introduction outlining the reader's WiiifM (What is in it for Me)

The introduction should not merely present the technology, idea, or context, but rather tell the readers how the project will change their life (such as "this project can increase our market share by X% and make competition irrelevant, while doubling our profit margin...").

The context, if necessary, should be included in an appendix for readers who wish to learn more about it.

2. What could happen if we do not seize this Opportunity?

This represents the opportunity cost: the consequences of not undertaking this project.

IpOp Review 1 demonstrating the Project's viability for the Customer(s) and for the Investor/decision-maker:

3. Which Customers have which PNDs that are currently not satisfied?

Whenever you mention Pain/Need/Desire(s), you must always first specify who the Customer is.

Avoid redundant Pain/Need/Desire(s), For example, a machine breakdown inducing a Pain is the same as the Need or Desire to maximize machine availability.

If a reference to the context is necessary, it could be mentioned here, but detailed information about the context should be placed in an annex referred to in this section. This approach allows those who require more context to find it in the annex, while sparing others from reading material that may not be relevant to their needs.

4. Why these PNDs have so far not been addressed in a satisfactory manner?

This question may not be critical, but answering it reassures readers. They are curious to understand why no one before you has conceived this Solution. In essence, they want to know what makes you smarter or more insightful than others...

5. What is the proposed Solution to better satisfy these PNDs?
6. What are the Market relative advantages and weaknesses of this Solution over the Alternatives?

This section should straightforwardly present one Customer Benchmarking for each Customer. It is crucial to ensure that each Benchmarking covers ALL the Customer Decision Criteria and ALL the Alternatives. Failing to be comprehensive will indicate to readers that you lack a thorough understanding of your Customer or your market.

A comparative table that includes scores offers a much clearer and more comprehensive overview than extensive textual explanations, which could highlight strengths but neglect to address weaknesses.

If there are multiple Customers, you must specify the Pain/Need/Desire(s) (PNDs) for each customer, the Customer Decision Criteria for each Customer, and, of course, one Benchmarking table for each of them, considering the possible Alternatives for each. Combining the Customer Decision Criteria of several Customers into a single table prevents understanding how each Customer decides to buy-in.

It is recommended to rank the Customer Decision Criteria in order of importance in the Benchmarking table.

In the Benchmarking table, avoid totals or averages that could mislead the reader.

7. Does the project fit the mission, strategy, and brand essence of the organization?
8. Why this Variant is better for the Investor than other ways of executing?

This section should showcase the Investor Benchmarking, incorporating ALL the Investor Decision Criteria and ALL the Variants. This is crucial to persuade the readers that the chosen Variant optimally meets the Investors' Decision Criteria.

An Investor Benchmarking with scores is significantly clearer and more comprehensive than lengthy textual explanations, which might emphasize strengths while overlooking weaknesses.

IpOp Review 2 demonstrating that the Project is worth it:

9. What Benefits will be delivered to the key Stakeholders?
10. What are the measurable Objectives defining success for the project?
    This section should display the Definition of Success, including target Objectives for each Key Indicator of Success (KISs) at every time milestone. Merely listing the KISs without specifying the target values for each due date is insufficient.
11. What are the minimum Objectives below which the project is considered a failure?
    This section should present the Definition of Failure, detailing minimum/maximum thresholds for each Key Indicator of Failure (KIFs) that must be met by each specified due date. Simply listing the KIFs without defining the thresholds over time falls short of providing a real commitment.
    It is prudent to also outline the consequences of failure in this section, which equate to the repercussions of halting the project due to not meeting the minimum requirements.
12. What Resource Model will be used to generate Resources?
13. What skills and Resources are required to implement (the Investment)?

IpOp Review 3 demonstrating that the parameters that can influence the outcome of the project are well understood and acceptable:

14. What are the Risks and Barriers to Entry (and the Tactical Moves to manage them)?
    You should include a risk analysis table here that lists each risk, its probability, its impact on the Definition of Success, and the Tactical Moves for mitigating each risk.
    A similar table can also be added for Obstacles (Hurdles with a 100% probability).
15. What are the other important Factors?

16. What could be the Collateral Damages of this Project?
Mentioning Collateral Damages without detailing how you plan to mitigate them could deter your readers. It is advisable to specify for each Collateral Damage the Tactical Moves intended to reduce it.
17. What Barriers to entry can be implemented to block the competition?
18. To what extent are key Stakeholders committed to support this project?
The analysis of Stakeholders' Aspirations should not be included in the Opportunity Case, except possibly in the annexes. While Stakeholder analysis must indeed be conducted as part of the IpOp Model analysis, this does not mean all its components must be included in the Opportunity Case.
What needs to be presented in the Opportunity Case is a table displaying:

- *The level of power of each Stakeholder*
- *The overall level of engagement/support from each key Stakeholder. Note that the level indicated must be verified, not just assumed or hoped for. Until it has been verified/confirmed, it remains an Unknown*
- *The Resistances of key Stakeholders, also outlining what you intend to do to reduce them (Tactical Moves). Mentioning Resistances without specifying your actions to address them provides Decision-makers with ammunition to undermine your project*

IpOp Review 4 describing project tasks and responsibilities:

19. What are the remaining critical Unknowns and how can they be reduced (with which Resources)?
You should incorporate Table 5.1 from Chap. 5 here, which lists the critical remaining Unknowns. The other less critical Unknowns should be detailed in a similar table placed in an annex. Reference to its presence in the annex should be made here, along with an indication of the total Resources required to address both critical and non-critical Unknowns.
Never present assumptions as certainties. Anything that has not been formally verified should be listed among the Unknowns. Failing to mention Unknowns that arise from a lack of certainty in parts of the Opportunity Case indicates a lack of rigor and clarity that can alarm Decision-makers.

Therefore, it is crucial to maintain impeccable discipline in identifying all Unknowns and cataloging them.
Listing Unknowns without specifying how you intend to address them (Tactical Moves) and the effort (in time and money) required to acquire the missing information is also detrimental.

20. Who is behind the Project and is the team capable and passionate enough to deliver the Definition of Success?
21. What is the timeline of the Project?
22. What are the next steps and/or decisions to be taken?

Optionally, an additional conclusion could summarize the case or assess the comparative advantages of this Solution against other options, according to the Decision-maker's decision criteria.

20.4 Writing the Opportunity Case

Since the objective is to convince at least one Decision-maker, the entire Opportunity Case should be customized to consider all of the Decision-maker's concerns. As outlined above and in Chap. 6, Decision-makers are Stakeholders, and their Aspirations, Resistances, and Constraints shape their decision-making criteria. Ignorance of these criteria may prevent you from addressing their desires or concerns. This underscores the importance of being familiar with Stakeholders' (in this instance, Decision-makers') mindset to capture these criteria effectively.

To attract buy-in, the Opportunity Case needs to be reader-focused, emphasizing an understanding of the audience's motivations. As illustrated in "*Why Smart People Do Dumb Things*,"[2] decisions are not always rational. Therefore, understanding the reader's psychology and motivations can facilitate gaining their mindshare.

Plan the story line before writing up the Opportunity Case to make sure that the reader will have an enjoyable and logical reading experience. Building trust and compatibility of minds is essential for

[2] Mortimer Feinberg and John J. Tarrant, *Why Smart People Do Dumb Things*, Simon & Schuster, 1995.

obtaining mindshare, so taking the reader by the hand from beginning to end helps to make it clear that you look at things the same way. This often happens automatically, when the reader experiences "flow" as suggested by Csíkszentmihályi, enjoying the experience of being "fully immersed in what he is doing by a feeling of energized focus." A well-structured Opportunity Case will contribute to this positive feeling. Aligning with this approach will also subtly convey to your reader that you think in a similar manner, thereby contributing to the development of trust.

The answer to each of the Opportunity Case questions should be brief yet informative, offering the necessary information without unnecessary detail. It is common for individuals to feel compelled to include irrelevant information or details to demonstrate their expertise, but this can overwhelm the reader and lead to loss of attention. Readers are typically interested only in what directly concerns them. If someone requires additional information or explanations, they can always request it.

The length of the Opportunity Case need not be limited to just a couple of pages, unlike the "Executive Summary" of the business plan. Typically, the Opportunity Case is lengthier because it delves into what Stakeholders should really know before addressing how the plan will be executed. An Opportunity Case can easily run 5–10 pages, depending on the depth of information required. Moreover, it does not necessarily have to be in a report; it can be packaged in a series of PowerPoint™ slides. From my personal experience, a well-produced document or slideshow that answers the relevant questions can vary in length as long as it remains focused and avoids unnecessary repetition. Ultimately, the audience's judgment is not based on the length of the presentation but on the perceived benefits and relevant information it offers them.

Inducing Decision-makers to ask questions is also a way to build mindshare. Questions often indicate interest and provide an opportunity to better understand Stakeholders' concerns. However, it is important to avoid overwhelming Decision-makers with too many questions. There should be a balanced relationship between the content of the Opportunity Case and the questions it raises.

The main objective of the Opportunity Case is to obtain an initial conditional buy-in, subject to later verification or validation. This is a major victory, for the first battle has now been won. Additional details and explanations will of course be required to win the whole war, but first you need to get the Stakeholders interested.

The Opportunity Case should be customized in line with each Stakeholder's concerns. For instance, the concerns and Aspirations needing to be addressed in the case of a potential strategic partner will obviously not be as relevant to a business angel.

To defuse certain resistances, it might be useful to anticipate the seven traditional "killer tyrannies"[3] that people use to deflate a new idea. Such anticipation can help customize the content of the Opportunity Case. These are common challenges that businesses face:

- The tyranny of served markets: "Our current customers won't like it."
- The tyranny of established business models: "That's not how we make money."
- The tyranny of distributors: "Our distributors won't like it."
- The tyranny of current strategy: "We aren't in that business."
- The tyranny of current organizational structure: "If it can't be adopted by one of our business units, we won't be able to handle it."
- The tyranny of arbitrary financial hurdles: "If it won't generate X million within 3 years, it's not worth our time."
- The tyranny of language: "This is just so much tech (or business) mumbo jumbo to me."

Writing the Opportunity Case is easy once the IpOp Model analysis is behind you. Most of the questions raised by the Opportunity Case find an answer in one or other steps of the IpOp Model. Figure 19.2 shows in the middle column which information in the IpOp Model provides the information for each question of the Opportunity Case. Anything left over can usually be obtained from the financial projections (i.e., translating the Action Plan in terms of numbers), as shown in Table 20.1.

The Opportunity Case may be thought of as verbal packaging for the IpOp Model. As such, it should not require a huge effort, and there is no doubt that it takes much less time and energy than writing a

[3] "Radical Innovation - How Mature Companies Can Outsmart Upstarts," Richard Leifer, 2000, Harvard Business Publishing, Boston.

Table 20.1 Using the IpOp Model to write the Opportunity Case

Issues addressed by the Opportunity Case	Components of the IpOp Model that can help provide the answers	Information from financial projections
1. Why should you read this document?	Definition of Success Strategic fit Customer Unique Experience (CUE) The Solution	
2. What could happen if we do not seize this Opportunity?	Factors PNDs	
3. Which Customers have which PNDs that are currently not satisfied?	Target Customer Customer Pain/Need/Desire(s) Focus Statement (PNDs) Customer Decision Criteria (CDCs)	
4. Why these PNDs have so far not been addressed in a satisfactory manner?	Customer(s) PNDs Focus Statement, Alternatives, CDCs	
5. What is the proposed Solution to better satisfy the PNDs?	The Solution, Customer Decision Criteria, Customer Unique Experience	
6. What are the market relative advantages and weaknesses of this Solution over the Alternatives?	Customer Benchmarking based on Customer Decision Criteria	
7. Does the Project fit the mission, strategy, and brand essence of the organization?	Strategic fit	
8. Why this Variant is better for the Investor than other ways of executing?	Investor Benchmarking based on Investor Decision Criteria	
9. What Benefits will be delivered to the key Stakeholders?	The Solution, Stakeholders Aspirations, Definition of Success, CDCs, CUE	Market penetration
10. What are the measurable Objectives defining success for the project?	Definition of Success	Sales and profit
11. What are the minimum Objectives below which the project is considered a failure?	Definition of Failure	Sales and profit

(continued)

Table 20.1 (continued)

Issues addressed by the Opportunity Case	Components of the IpOp Model that can help provide the answers	Information from financial projections
12. What Resource Model will be used to generate income?	Resource Model	Sources of income
13. What skills and Resources are required to implement?	Investment/Resources Activity Chain	Investment/ Resources Cash requirements
14. What are the Risks and Barriers to entry (and the Tactical Moves to manage them)?	Factors, Tactical Moves	
15. What are the other important Factors?	Factors Key Activity Ingredients	
16. What could be the Collateral Damages of this project?	Collateral Damages	
17. What Barriers to entry can be implemented to block the competition?	Barriers to entry	
18. To what extent are key Stakeholders committed to support this project?	Stakeholders' Aspirations, Resistances, and Constraints	
19. What are the critical Unknowns and how can they be reduced (with which Resources)?	Unknowns, Tactical Moves, Resources	
20. Who is behind the project and is the team capable and passionate enough to deliver the Definition of Success?	Factors Stakeholders	
21. What is the timeline of the project?	Definition of Success Action Plan	
22. What are the next steps and/ or decisions to be taken?	Action Plan	

business plan. For my part, I can state that writing an Opportunity Case usually takes me one or maximum two days.

Ban jargon from your Opportunity Case for most target audiences. It might appeal to some consultants but as a rule it is counterproductive. Most people either do not understand the actual meaning and implications of sophisticated words or must make a mental effort to figure out what they mean. This creates an unconscious mental negative state of mind (if the writer does not use the same vocabulary as the reader, how will they possibly be able to understand one another in the future?). I recommend that instead of using vocabulary to impress the reader you write up your (convincing) Opportunity Case in a simple and attractive manner.

20.5 The Ultimate Opportunity Case

Mentioning the presence of Unknowns, especially critical ones, in each section of the Opportunity Case is essential, as they diminish the reliability of the information provided. Each section should identify all remaining Unknowns relevant to that part of the case. This allows Decision-makers to compare the section's content with its remaining Unknowns, offering a clearer insight into the information's reliability. Echoing Paul Valéry's sentiment, "There is worse than false, it is the mix of true and false," I argue that a mix of true and unverified statements is even more misleading.

For decision-makers to gain a fuller understanding of the reliability of the presented information, they should request that the authors of the Opportunity Case also express their own confidence level in their statements. This spectrum ranges from a "Quick and Dirty" understanding, rife with assumptions, to fully verified information.

This requirement encourages those drafting the Opportunity Case to differentiate clearly between what they know for certain and what remains assumed, enhancing transparency.

To ensure clarity and transparency, the IpOp Tools^{TM} software mentioned in Chap. 18 incorporates these functionalities by:

- Automatically listing the Unknowns corresponding to each section of the Opportunity Case
- Guiding the project team to express their confidence level in their declarations for each section

Contrary to potential concerns, gathering this information is straightforward and not burdensome.

For Decision-makers, understanding the reliability of a section's content provides much deeper insight into potential project challenges. This difference in perspective is akin to comparing a black and white photograph with a color one, significantly better equipping them to judge the project more accurately and make informed decisions.

Opportunity Case for Nespresso B2B Solutions

To avoid repeating the arguments given above for the concept of Nespresso Classic on the private market, here is the Opportunity Case for the new version targeting the business sector, Nespresso B2B Solutions. The objective of this example of Opportunity Case is to convince Nestlé Board of Management to launch a Nespresso concept for the workplace.

Since Nespresso B2B has already been launched, this document is of course only an illustration of what could have been presented to Nestlé Decision-makers at the time when the idea was initially brought up.

The content of this Opportunity Case is designed to demonstrate what could be included in each section, but it is not as comprehensive and detailed as the real business case for Nespresso B2B would be.

Cover page

- **Target Reader**: Nestlé Board of Management
- **Expected decision**: Conditional green light to launch Nespresso B2B subject to satisfactory reduction of remaining Key Unknowns
- **Author(s)**: XXX
- **Team members**:
  XXX
  XXX
- **Date**: X.X.20xx
- **Place**: Vevey

1. **Why should you read this document?**

This project provides a multibillion Euro opportunity. Since the projected revenues are expected to exceed XXX with a net profit of XX, this Opportunity has the potential to substantially enhance Nespresso's bottom line.

Much coffee is consumed at the workplace. The preparation of espresso coffee is time-consuming and requires a specific protocol to ensure satisfactory quality, with the result that enterprises limit themselves to offering filter coffee or installing vending machines, neither of which provide real quality and personal gratification.

The Nespresso B2B provides a Solution to the difficulties of preparing espresso coffee at the workplace while demonstrating to the employees that their employer cares.

As this solution will use different capsules from the Nespresso Classic, with new patents enjoying a much longer protection, Nespresso B2B will furthermore be able to lock in the market for the long term.

2. **What could happen if Nespresso does not seize this Opportunity?**

If Nespresso does not introduce Nespresso B2B, another market player might take the lead in the professional market, depriving Nespresso of its leadership position and of substantial sources of profit and revenues.

First mover advantage, especially with patented products, provides the chance to set a new standard and creates a significant Barrier to entry for competitors.

IpOp Review 1 demonstrating the Project's viability for the Customers and for Nestlé:

3. **Which Customers have which PNDs that are currently not satisfied?**

In the workplace, there are two Customers: the employer and the employees

The employees' Pains/Needs/Desires at the workplace may be summarized as follows:

- Coffee breaks are a cherished moment for employees who look forward to enjoying them to the fullest; unfortunately, the quality of coffee previously available does not match that offered by Nespresso
- The facilities for preparing coffee are considerably less pleasant and user-friendly than with Nespresso Classic
- It takes longer to prepare coffee with the old methods than with the Nespresso process
- Employees are dependent on their employer's choice of coffee flavor for what they drink
- Coffee consumption at work is not a gratifying enough experience and gives the staff little sense of recognition (image)

The employer's Desires are to have:

- Engaged employees who enjoy the workplace
- Employees who feels that their employer cares about them

4. **Why these PNDs have so far not been addressed in a satisfactory manner?**

The prevalent solutions for coffee in the workplace rely on soluble/instant coffee, and currently, there is no professional machine capable of delivering high-quality espresso with a meaningful market penetration.

Introducing Nespresso Classic in a professional environment might lead employees to take capsules home, increasing the cost of coffee consumption for employers. This concern could deter employers from using the same capsules at the workplace as those used for Nespresso Classic.

5. **What is the proposed Solution to better satisfy these Pain/Need/Desire(s)?**

The proposed Solution leverages a new process developed by R&D for creating pre-portioned espresso specifically for the business environment (Nespresso B2B Solutions). It utilizes different machines and capsules from those designed for household use, yet it builds upon the business model and expertise of Nespresso Classic to deliver similar benefits.

With this innovative technology, Nespresso B2B Solutions will be the only system that offers espresso coffee lovers the gratification of preparing pre-portioned coffee of guaranteed quality at the workplace in just a few seconds, using an elegant, compact, and very user-friendly machine, with the possibility of choosing the flavor and caffeine content from among a wide selection of capsules according to the whim of the moment. In short, a gratifying experience exclusive to the business community that combines pleasure, simplicity, and esthetics at reasonable cost that demonstrates to employees that their management cares about their well-being.

6. **What are the Market relative advantages and weaknesses of this Solution over the Alternatives?**

The Customer Benchmarking table below shows the superiority of Nespresso B2B Solutions over alternative solutions for the Employer. The only weak point of Nespresso B2B Solutions is cost, but this is well compensated for by the other considerations (pleasure, guaranteed quality, choice, immediate availability, ease of production, etc.).

No.	Employers Decision Criteria (CDCs)	Competition						
		Nespresso	Professional espresso machines	Instant coffee	Filter coffee	Tea	Noncompatible portioned espresso	Compatible capsules
1	Love/trust in the brand	4	2	2	2	3	2	2
2	Aroma and quality comparable to coffee prepared by top professionals	4	3	3	3	4	3	3
3	Choice of different varieties of coffee	4	2	2	3	4	2	1
4	Image	4	3	2	1	4	2	2
5	Machine design	4	2	1	1	1	3	NA
6	Ease and availability of production (fast, practical, simple, clean, individual portions, etc.)	4	3	3	2	3	4	NA
7	Ease of purchase and after-sales service	3	3	2	2	3	3	3
8	Reliability and constant quality	4	3	4	3	3	3	2
9	Price of a cup of coffee	2	3	4	4	2	3	3
10	Capsules not compatible for home use	4	4	1	1	NA	0	NA

The second Customer for Nespresso B2B is the employee. The Benchmarking table for the employee is practically identical to that of Nespresso Classic,[4] so it is not included here to conserve space and avoid redundancy.

7. **Does Nespresso B2B fit the mission, strategy, and brand essence of Nespresso?**

Nespresso aims to maintain its dominance in the pre-portioned coffee market, a status it already enjoys in the household sector. As part of its strategy to leverage its brand and technology for market expansion and diversification, Nespresso B2B targets the professional and workplace market, supporting this strategic *intent*.

All the Benefits for Nespresso outlined in section 9 below are also in alignment with Nespresso's mission and strategy.

To ensure that the branding of the B2B solution is completely in harmony with the essence of the Nespresso brand, it will be overseen by the same team responsible for Nespresso Classic.

8. **Why this Variant is better for Nespresso than other ways of executing?**

(replaced by XXX, given that the information concerning Nespresso is confidential)

The table below shows that Nespresso B2B is the best option for Nestlé. Against Nestlé Decision Criteria it performs particularly well.

	All the variants (other ways to execute the project)			
Nespresso Decision Criteria	Nespresso B2B	Using same capsules as for consumer market	Variant B	Variant C
1 Impact on brand essence	4	3	1	2
2 Profitability	4	4	3	0
3 Time to market	3	4	2	4
4 Strong barrier to entry	4	3	2	1
5 XXX	4	1	1	1
6 XXX	2	1	2	3

[4] Since each Customer must have its own Benchmarking, Table 8.3 that shows the Employees Benchmarking should normally be inserted here but to save space this table is not repeated.

IpOp Review 2 demonstrating that the Project is worth it

9. **What Benefits will be delivered to the key Stakeholders?**

Employers

- By proposing a very pleasant experience at the workplace (the availability of high-quality coffee), the company expresses a clear sign of appreciation to its employees
- By offering its staff a choice of flavors, the company shows its interest in their comfort, their freedom but also their pleasure
- Since the capsules are different from those of Nespresso Classic, employees have no incentive to steal them for home use
- Self-service preparation of pre-dosed coffee requires less labor
- If desired, the company can charge its employees all or part of the cost of the capsules, selling them in bulk (thereby also precluding the need for handling coins and small change for vending machines)
- The company has a better overview of individual coffee consumption (data mining)

Nespresso

- Increased turnover in a new market segment
- Sale of machines under the Nespresso brand (enhancing the company's notoriety and increasing the profit margin)
- Greater presence and visibility at the workplace, enticing new customers to buy the household version for their personal use
- A direct link with this segment of the clientele (greater intimacy through direct sales)
- Possibility of synergy with the water-fountain market or other Nestlé products targeting the business domain
- Diversification, buffeting any vulnerability of the household segment
- A rate of growth conducive to employee satisfaction and opportunities for promotion

Machine manufacturer

- Possibility of developing its turnover and income

Coffee producers

- Increased turnover and income

Nestlé

- High profitability

- Promotion of the Nespresso brand and increase of its valuation
- Organic growth
- Possibility of applying the example to encourage other units of the company to innovate and explore alternative business models
- A demonstration to the public of Nestlé's technological and commercial leadership
- Possible synergies for the distribution of other Nestlé products suitable for sale in business environments

All these points are aligned with the mission and the strategy of Nestlé.

10. **What are the measurable Objectives defining the success for Nespresso B2B?**

(The two tables below are based on fictitious figures, given that the information on Nespresso is confidential.)

Definition of Success

Key Indicators of success (KISs)	1 year	2 years	4 years	6 years
Turnover	100 million	200 million	500 million	800 million
Profit	10 million	25 million	70 million	100 million

11. **What are the minimum Objectives below which Nespresso B2B will be considered a failure?**

Definition of Failure

Key Indicators of Failure (KIFs)	1 year	2 years	4 years	6 years
Turnover	20 million	30 million	50 million	50 million
Profit	–5 million	–2 million	0 million	5 million
Customer satisfaction	60%	65%	70%	75%

12. **What Resource Model will be used to generate income?**

The Resource Model applied in the business sector is the same as that for the household sector. As such, no substantial investment in the infrastructure is required.

The main source of income is the sale of capsules with suitable profit margins.

The chief difference as against the household model is that the machines are sold under the Nespresso trademark without recourse to a middleman (machine partner). Thus, Nespresso must assure the sales side of the machines.

13. **What skills and Resources are required to implement?**

Except for the dedicated sales force and after sale service for Nespresso B2B, all other resources are the same as those for Nespresso Classic. To launch the project, the following resources are required (replaced by XXX, given that the information concerning Nespresso is confidential):

XXX USD including:

- XXX USD for technical development of the product
- XXX USD for the production unit
- XXX USD for marketing
- XXX USD for working capital
- XXX USD for salaries
- XXX USD for the premises

The internal rate of return for this project is XXX.

IpOp Review 3 demonstrating that the parameters that can influence the outcome of the Project are well understood and acceptable

14. **What are the Risks and Barriers to entry (and the Tactical Moves to manage them)?**

The identified risks are relatively limited.

Risks	Impact on the Definition of Success	Preventive measures	Probability
Increased cost of raw material	Reduced profit margin	Lock purchase price with futures	Low
Competitive products	Reduced market share and pressure on profit margins	Brand notoriety Patenting Rapid penetration of the market Emphasis on quality and pleasure Development of customer intimacy (positioning)	Medium

15. **What are the other important Factors?**

- The popularity of high-quality coffee
- The greater demands of employees at the workplace (better treatment)
- Hedonism in society
- Globalized competition from alternative hot drink providers
- The trend toward reduction of labor and operational costs

16. **What could be the Collateral Damages of Nespresso B2B?**

Collateral damages	Consequences	Measures to reduce the damage
Failure in the business sector	Impact on brand reputation	Launch a pilot study on a few test markets Ensure reliability of the capsule system
Cannibalization of Nescafé market share	Loss of market share for Nescafé	XXXX

17. **What Barriers to entry can be implemented to block the competition?**

- The new B2B capsules are patented with patents lasting X more years than the patents of Nespresso Classic
- Rapid market penetration

18. **To what extent are key Stakeholders committed to support Nespresso B2B?**

Stakeholders	Level of verified support	Level of power	Main Resistances	How Resistances will be reduced
Nestlé board of directors	4	4	XXX	XXX
Nescafé division	XXX	4	XXX	XXX
Nespresso	3	3	Risk of cannibalization	Different capsules for B2B
XXX	3	3	XXX	XXX
XXX	4	2	XXX	XXX

IpOp Review 4 describing what has to be done and by whom

19. **What are the critical Unknowns and how can they be reduced (with which Resources)?**

Unknowns	Consequences	Measures to reduce the uncertainty level	Man-days	EUR
Price perceived as too high	Reduced market share and pressure on profit margins	Carry out a market study in the field	20	150k
		Launch a pilot study on a few test markets	200	3000k
		Segment the market so as not to cater to price-sensitive customers	5	0
Nestlé's willingness to accept the risk of cannibalizing Nescafé and vending machine sales	Blocking of project	Discuss the matter in advance	3	0
		Organize a pilot study on a few test markets and measure the impact on other products	5	Included above
Reliability and industrialization of the new capsules	Impossibility to launch the project	Cooperate with the research and development department	20	150k
		Obtain a technological validation from external laboratories		
Reliability and cost of coffee machines	Customer dissatisfaction	Work together closely with the machine manufacturer	50	300k
		Recruit experts		
Reaction of other Nestlé units that feel threatened	Blocking of project	Concentration on less sensitive high-end markets	5	0
		Avoid proposing machines with an output comparable to that of vending machines		
……	……	……	XXX	0
		Total	**XXX**	**3600k**

The overall cost for reducing these critical as well as less critical Unknowns should be XXX, including EUR 3.6 million of out-of-pocket expenses

Less critical unknowns are listed in Annex X

20. **Who is behind Nespresso B2B and is the team capable and passionate enough to deliver the Definition of Success?**

XXX

21. **What is the timeline of the project?**

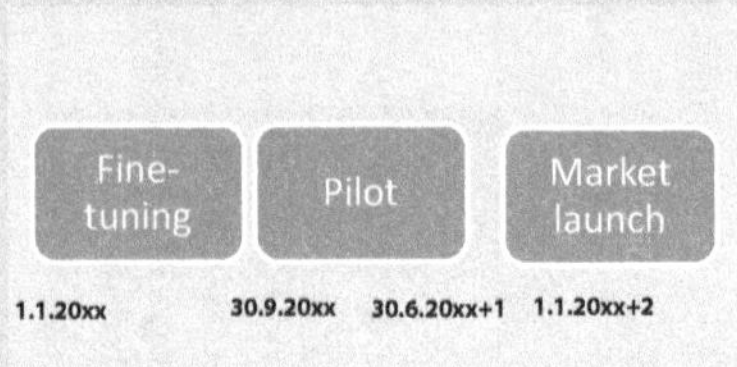

22. **What are the next important steps and/or decisions to be taken?**

- Creation of the team
- Industrialization of Nespresso B2B Solutions coffee machines
- Planning of the marketing strategy
- Establishment of the commercialization team[5]
- Setting-up the capsule production unit
- Launch

20.6 Advantages of the Opportunity Case

The Opportunity Case provides a platform for discussion between the Decision-makers and promoters of the project. The decision-makers might, for instance, want to challenge the latter on such points as:

[5] Note that the first four bullet points address Tactical Moves that are not clearly defined. Therefore, they should be considered as Unknowns to be included in the list of Unknowns (whether critical or non-critical Unknowns) of section 19.

- How the team has obtained information (e.g., that given in the Customer Benchmarking table)
- Who has been consulted to verify the accuracy of its content
- Whether the Market advantages are good enough to tilt the scale
- Whether the Customer Unique Experience can easily be communicated to Customers
- Whether the Definitions of Success and Failure are realistic
- Whether any Factors have been forgotten
- If there are Unknowns that have been overlooked
- Whether all statements have been thoroughly verified
- To what extent it is possible to reduce the critical Unknowns and with which effort
- Whether all the parameters of their own decision-making tree have been addressed[6]
- Whether the team is capable of delivering the Definition of Success, or at least the Definition of Failure, etc.

All these questions Provide decision-makers with great opportunities for a constructive and interesting discussion with the team without the need to read an entire business plan. This saves time for both parties, but particularly for those who would otherwise have to write the time-consuming business plan.

The Opportunity Case will trigger one of three reactions from the reader, who will either:

- **Not be interested**. In this case, writing a business plan would in any case have been an absolute waste of time
- **Give you the green light** because he likes the idea and trusts you and your team's ability to make it happen. It can occur, but it is not common
- **Ask to see the Implementation Plan before making a final decision** (the "how" and "how much"). Now persuaded by the "what" and "why" the Decision-makers will seek to understand how you plan to practically seize the Opportunity and whether your implementation

[6] See Chap. 19.

plan for the project is both effective and realistic. Such readiness to allocate more time and attention to the project in fact denotes a very serious interest. It may even be regarded as a conditional approval, a desire to confirm the feasibility and eliminate any remaining doubts (the condition). This alone is very encouraging.

The project initiators should have a much clearer idea of where they stand once the decision-makers have read the Opportunity Case. Because an Opportunity Case can be produced considerably faster than a business plan, much earlier contacts with Decision-makers are possible, and the project initiators will doubtless find better things to do with the time saved.

20.7 The Implementation Action Plan

The Implementation Plan complements the Opportunity Case and its Action Plan for reducing critical unknowns by including practical details for delivering the Definition of Success that are not outlined there. This is where you address the "how" and the "how much" in detail.

The Implementation Plan might contain:

- A list of the Tactical Moves
- Their timeline
- Detailed financial projections, preferably with milestones justifying further investments when the time comes
- A detailed contingency plan to deal with Risks
- Anything else that might demonstrate feasibility (e.g., buyers' letters of intent, pilot study and test results, etc.)

Tactical Moves may be grouped by function, purpose, or any other relevant structure. If you prefer to respect the underlying business plan philosophy, you can group your Tactical Moves according to a typical business plan structure (see below). But alternatives exist and you have the choice to group Tactical Moves in whatever way makes sense to you and the reader. For instance, it might sometimes be more appropriate to present Tactical Moves in a way that indicates their impact or purpose.

The Implementation Plan does not have to justify the existence of the project. Unlike the business plan, the Implementation Plan focuses only on its execution (the "how") and financial projections ("how much"). Justifying the project has already been taken care of in the Opportunity Case.

Writing the Implementation Plan is quick and easy after using the IpOp Model. Almost all of its content can be extracted from the Action Plan you have defined in the IpOp Model. But more importantly, knowing that a Decision-maker is interested in looking at the Implementation Plan will boost your energy and determination to quickly produce and deliver the Implementation plan. This is very different from writing a business plan, for its author has no idea whether anyone will read it or not. The absence of an identified reader is one of the reasons why a business plan takes so long to write. Knowing that a Decision-maker is waiting for the Implementation plan before finalizing the decision to go ahead acts as a tremendous incentive: the Implementation Plan must be produced quickly while the Decision-maker is still warm.

The Implementation Plan can be customized according to your Decision-maker's profile and characteristics. Because it can integrate any contribution[7] to the project by the Decision-maker, there is less likelihood that the Investor will want you to amend the Action Plan. This is very different from a generic business plan written *in abstracto*.

The Implementation Plan will also lead to a highly constructive discussion with the Decision-maker. Based on a concrete Action Plan, it encourages a pragmatic approach on the part of the Decision-maker to both challenge the feasibility of the Action Plan and suggest improvements. Such a constructive confrontation will also help you to improve your plan or justify its present form. Updates of the business plan or the Implementation Plan are therefore a constructive blessing.

An Implementation Plan is much easier to update or improve upon than a business plan. Updating a business plan is time-consuming because it is very difficult to amend only part of the document. The Implementation Plan is a simpler, more down-to-earth document, and is thus much less complicated to amend. Reading it will also provide the decision-maker with a more concrete perspective.

[7] e.g., access to markets, networks, expertise, equipment and other resources, people, synergies, etc.

The Implementation Plan facilitates monitoring of the actual implementation, since the justification elements included in the business plan, useless for monitoring purposes, do not need to be filtered out. Once the decision to proceed with the project has been made, the Opportunity Case can be put aside and the whole attention focused on the Implementation Plan.

20.8 For Business Plan Aficionados

If, despite all the above, a business plan is required, or if you yourself feel compelled to produce one, writing it after the IpOp Model analysis should now be pretty easy. Because the business plan combines the content of both the Opportunity Case and the Implementation Plan, some parts (e.g., the market analysis) will need to be more developed to justify the content summarized in the Opportunity Case. This will require some extra work but will be much easier than jumping straight into writing the business plan without first using the IpOp Model.

Developing the business plan from the IpOp Model is quite straightforward. Table 20.2 illustrates how this can be accomplished for various items, keeping in mind that the structure of the business plan represents the "how" within the traditional functions of a company (R & D, marketing, production, sales, HR, finance, etc.). To adhere to the structure of the business plan, the Tactical Moves should be grouped by function and referred to in the corresponding section of the business plan.

As you can see here, most items for the business plan can be extracted from the IpOp Model, particularly the selected Tactical Moves, the backbone of the Action Plan. The IpOp Model is the underlying thinking process behind the business plan. Skipping the IpOp Model analysis could lead to overlooking any number of key success parameters.

The IpOp Model replaces the business plan as a maturing tool for the project. Many proponents of the business plan claim that writing it obliges the project team to be more thorough in their analysis of the project. It is also supposed to provide a better presentation of the project for decision-makers. Writing a business plan certainly does oblige people to sit and think, but this does not mean that the result is as good as it

Table 20.2 Using the IpOp Model to write a business plan

Business plan item	Useful source of information in the IpOp Model analysis	Comments
Description of the Opportunity	PND and Solution	
Description of the technology and R&D status	The Solution, CDCs, CUE	It is the technology that makes the Solution possible
Market study	Definition of Success and Failure	Assessing the potential of the market and its condition is a prerequisite for determining the volume Objectives within the Definition of Success and Failure
Competitive analysis	Customer Benchmarking	Customer Benchmarking serves to summarize in one table your analysis of the competition
The product	CUE, the Solution	The CUE expresses what the product has to offer the customer
Product features	CDCs, the Solution	The most important features are those that can influence Customer behavior (they are expressed by the CDCs)
Risk analysis	Possible Hurdles (Factors)	Together with the corresponding Tactical Moves
Unknowns analysis (usually confused with risks)	Unknowns	Together with the corresponding Tactical Moves
Economic Model	Resource Model	
R&D strategy	Action Plan	
Marketing strategy	Action Plan	
Sales or market penetration strategy	Action Plan	
Production/partnering strategy	Action Plan	
IP strategy	Action Plan	
Outsourcing strategy	Action Plan	
Procurement strategy	Action Plan	

(continued)

Table 20.2 (continued)

Business plan item	Useful source of information in the IpOp Model analysis	Comments
HR strategy	Action Plan	
Legal strategy	Action Plan	
Funding strategy	Action Plan	
Financial projections	Action Plan + Definition of Success	
Presentation of the team	Factors	The team is a Factor (and a Stakeholder)

might be. I believe that the structure of the business plan is counterintuitive because nobody thinks according to such a structure that separates issues by function (for example, focusing on marketing, then on production, then on HR, etc.). Because the IpOp Model roadmap was inspired by the way successful people look at their projects, it is considerably more ergonomic than a business plan. It reflects the fact that people think in a more holistic manner. I have never yet met anyone who after using the IpOp Model preferred to go back to the business plan structure when analyzing the project in hand.

20.9 Project Management

Once the go-ahead for the project has been given and the necessary starting Resources made available, the next step will be to launch the project. But however good the plan and the strategy, they still must be properly implemented if they are to be successful. Implementation of the project will always be more difficult than anticipated, but good pre-project preparation can reduce the number of unpleasant surprises and Collateral Damage. At this point it might therefore be beneficial to use traditional project management techniques (see below) to increase the chances of successful implementation.

Project management tools manage Resources, time, deliverables, monitoring tools, team coordination, Constraints, Unknowns,

Tactical Moves, and more. Much of the information derived from the IpOp Model can be used for project management purposes. Project management thus follows on naturally from the IpOp Model process, dealing as it does with the execution and implementation of the plan prepared with the IpOp Model. Conversely, project management without use of the IpOp Model could mean that a project arrives at the implementation stage without a complete pre-project analysis having been done of the issues at stake. While project management does address some of the issues worked through in the IpOp Model, it does so from the angle of implementation (the "how"), whereas the IpOp Model is more concerned with justification of the project, including its purpose (the "why") and identifying the Unknowns that could affect the project to calibrate the effort.

Seamless implementation of the Action Plan furnished by the IpOp Model and project management (in the manner of an orchestral score) is the project manager's dream, but unfortunately the reality is usually a little different. While such an outcome is already rare enough in the case of well-controlled waterfall projects (such as replacing an ERP[8]) it NEVER happens with innovation projects. Most projects face surprises that force the team to adapt quickly. Key parameters affecting implementation include changes in market conditions, new offerings by competitors, a change in team composition, lack of resources, development of new technologies, new regulations, partners' change of mind, etc. Lack of time usually then leaves the project team with no choice but to improvise. Just bear in mind that good preparation is the number one success factor for successful improvisation.

Innovation projects are more akin to jazz music, where improvisation is key, rather than an orchestral score that unfolds precisely as planned. Jazz is about improvisation within certain guidelines (e.g., the Mission, Constraints) and an ear for what the other musicians are doing (Factors and Stakeholders) to achieve a collective result (the Definition of Success) that satisfies the audience (Stakeholders' PNDs and Aspirations). In the case of an innovation project, it is much easier to improvise when the various parameters (Stakeholders' Aspirations, Constraints,

[8] Enterprise Resource Planning, a system that is used to manage and coordinate all the resources, information, and functions of a business (Wikipedia).

Objectives, Factors, etc.) are well understood. The IpOp Model prepares the team to improvise in the face of changing circumstances, because all the key parameters have been analyzed and labeled and the model takes full account of the connections and interactions between them.

Link with ISO 56007 (Tools and Methods for Managing Opportunities and Ideas—Guidance)

ISO 56007 outlines two formats for presenting "proposition documents"[9] for further development of the "concept":

- The one-document approach, such as the traditional business plan
- The two-document approach, where the "Action Plan" is in a separate document while the main justification is in the "innovation concept case."

Annex C5.2.2 of the ISO standard provides a template for the "innovation concept case," illustrating the two-document approach. This template mirrors the IpOp Model's "Opportunity Case" presented in this book, with minor adjustments to align with ISO terminology. The version of the Opportunity Case template presented in this book features minor enhancements to the innovation concept case outlined in ISO 56007. These improvements incorporate new insights gained since the standard was written.

To fully take advantage of this template, it is necessary to have a complete understanding of all its components and their purpose. Since those components are based on the IpOp Model, mastering the IpOp Model helps to produce robust "innovation concept"/"Opportunity Cases."

Whether you choose a traditional business plan or an innovation concept case with a separate Implementation plan, the IpOp Model aids in preparing for both approaches. This demonstrates that the IpOp Model is a comprehensive pre-project analysis tool, versatile enough to support any proposition document and/or project management methodology.

[9] ISO 56007, section 6.4.3.6 and annex C5.

21

Bodies Matter

The Art of Pre-project Governance

Take-Home of This Chapter

ISO 56007 stresses the importance of selection and portfolio management in managing opportunities and ideas but it does not describe how to do it. To avoid wasting resources, organizations should establish a well-thought pre-project stage governance. This chapter explains how it can be done by providing best governance practices for managing ideas and opportunities, including the choice of a list of official selection criteria, publishing the criteria for transparency, using the criteria for all resource allocation decisions, and ensuring projects are screened against the criteria. Additional best practices also include creating a team of experts to coach applicants, keeping a non-earmarked budget for worthy projects outside the official budgeting pipeline, deploying the use of standardized Opportunity Case templates, training people to produce these Opportunity Cases, and establishing an evaluation board to analyze and recommend projects to Decision-makers. The chapter also recommends periodic monitoring and comparison of project results with the Definition of Success and the Definition of Failure. Overall this chapter emphasizes the role of different corporate bodies in the decision-making governance and suggests tools and methods for effective pre-project management.

R. H Cohen, *Pre-Project Excellence*, Future of Business and Finance,
https://doi.org/10.1007/978-3-031-61774-4_21

Many organizations have embraced and implemented highly effective project management methodologies, like those developed by the Project Management Institute (PMI). Some have even set up a Project Management Office (PMO) to oversee and coordinate projects within the organization. Undoubtedly, these approaches represent best practices for managing projects after the decision to launch has been made.

While these methods excel in project management, they often overlook the crucial pre-project phase, especially the need to catalog Unknowns before making a launch decision. The IpOp Model fills this gap, serving as a vital complement to existing project management tools by addressing the pre-project stage.

The introduction of new tools for the pre-project stage necessitates a reassessment of how organizations govern this initial phase. Drawing from my experience, I have identified several best practices that enhance the effective management of the pre-project stage. These practices are detailed in this chapter.

21.1 Structuring the Decision-Making

Corporate bodies play a critical role in managing ideas and opportunities. Inadequate structuring of the decision-making process within organizations can translate into significant waste of resources. To prevent this, Organizations should establish a well-thought pre-project stage governance:

Senior management or the Board of directors (*the First corporate body*) should:

1. **Establish the official list of selection criteria**, which all Decision-makers must follow when allocating Resources to projects. As mentioned in Chap. 19, this list might be a tailored version of the 11 questions from the IpOp Decision Tree. Should the need for more criteria arise, the official list should be updated accordingly.
2. **This list of selection criteria should be made accessible to everyone in the organization.** This ensures transparency and clarity regarding the criteria used for project selection.

3. **Use Unified Selection Criteria for all:**
   - **Innovation initiatives**, including open innovation, academic partnerships, etc. However, fundamental research or exploration/learning initiatives may require different or specific selection criteria and can be treated as exceptions.
   - **Requests for resources** (money, equipment, time, space, etc.)
   - **Projects**, regardless of their nature. This set of selection criteria should serve as the gatekeeper for any PMO (Project Management Office).

4. **Establish transparent decision-making rules that:**
   (a) **Prohibit the launch of any project or the allocation of resources without a fair screening against the official list of selection criteria**
   (b) **Ensure that no project can be refused or terminated without utilizing the official list of selection criteria**

   This rule promotes transparency and accountability in decision-making, preventing managers from rejecting ideas for inappropriate reasons such as:

   - Laziness
   - Fear of failure
   - Fear of finger pointing in case of failure
   - Lack of incentive to say "yes" and no accountability to say "no"
   - Focus on past success recipes
   - Lack of courage
   - Lack of entrepreneurial or intrapreneurial spirit
   - Lack of vision or anticipation
   - Etc.

5. **Customize the standardized Opportunity Case template** to address this complete list of official selection criteria. Additionally, include an executive summary as an attachment to the Opportunity Case.
6. **Make this standardized Opportunity Case the official and only document for requesting any allocation of resources** for all

projects, initiatives, or requests for resources (money, equipment, time, etc.).

7. **Train people to produce standardized Opportunity Cases with relevant content,** to enable proper judgment about the merits of each resource request. To deploy this strategy, IpOp Model training is effective. Software such as the IpOp Tools[TM1] can also be used to guide users in automatically generating standardized Opportunity Cases.
8. **Create a dedicated Evaluation Board (EB), constituting the Second corporate body, tasked with screening, and analyzing each Opportunity Case to provide a recommendation for Decision-makers.** The EB must:

   (a) Challenge the Opportunity Case content against the official selection criteria
   (b) Verify that:

   - The project warrants implementation, supported by convincing information from all IpOp Reviews
   - All identified Unknowns are appropriately listed
   - The effort for reducing the critical Unknowns has been realistically assessed
   - The statements in the Opportunity Case, which have not been identified as Unknowns, have indeed been duly verified. This reality check serves as a form of due diligence
   - Decision-makers (*the Third corporate body*) possess a realistic assessment of the challenges affecting the project before making decisions

   (c) Draft a Go/No-Go recommendation for the Third corporate body (see below), to be attached to the executive summary
   (d) Hold accountability for the recommendations provided

9. **Determine who has the final authority to decide whether each project should be launched (*the Third corporate body*). This body**

[1] see Chap. 18.

should review the executive summary and the attached EB recommendation, ask any pertinent questions to the EB and/or the team that has submitted the Opportunity Case before arriving at a decision.

10. **Task the internal audit/control or other relevant body (*the Fourth corporate body*) with periodically comparing the results achieved by each project with both the Definition of Success and the Definition of Failure.** Deliver a brief report containing this comparison for each project to senior management (*the first corporate body*). This monitoring:
    - Creates accountability for results
    - Prevents promoters from making unrealistic promises in their Opportunity Case
    - Encourages people to deliver on their commitments
    - Facilitates learning from projects that fail to meet at least the Definition of Failure

21.2 Optional Recommended Improvements

The following best practices can improve the above process. They are not indispensable, but they certainly improve the governance:

11. **Add the 'one-bullet' rule, stating that requests can only be submitted once.** This requirement ensures that applicants thoroughly prepare their Opportunity Case, knowing that they have only one opportunity to present their project. It also serves as a filtering mechanism, discouraging the submission of projects that do not meet the expectations of the Evaluation Board.
12. **Create a team of IpOp Model experts (*the Fifth corporate body*) to provide coaching and guidance to project applicants.** These experts can assist in conducting a comprehensive pre-project analysis, ensuring that Opportunity Cases are robust and convincing. A more robust Opportunity Case leads to more efficient decision-making.

13. **Allocate a portion of the budget for unforeseen but worthy projects.** This reserved funding should not be earmarked for projects already in the official pipeline but kept available for jumpstarting promising opportunities that arise unexpectedly. These may include new intrapreneurial initiatives aimed at reducing operational costs, innovative ideas to expand market share, or the development of software to enhance productivity. One corporate body (e.g., the EB or the Third corporate body) should have the authority to judiciously allocate this budget to the new intrapreneurial projects without waiting for the next budgeting cycle. This corporate body must remain accountable for the responsible use of this budget. This mechanism adds agility to the organization, reducing the constraints imposed by the budgeting cycle.
14. **Require each team to submit an IpOp Canvas as an additional attachment to the Opportunity Case.** The IpOp Canvas serves as a tool for portfolio management, providing a concise standardized overview of each project's key aspects and facilitating strategic decision-making.
15. **Use company-wise software** (e.g., IpOp Tools™) to:

    - Streamline and harmonize pre-project analysis and documentation processes
    - Speed up the IpOp analysis and the creation of Opportunity Cases
    - Enhance the quality of outputs while lowering the costs associated with these processes
    - Improve the evaluation and selection of projects
    - Manage the portfolio of projects at the pre-project stage, including requests for funding/resources and innovation initiatives
    - Benefit of a knowledge management system during the pre-project stage, aiding decision-making and fostering a learning organization
    - Professionalize the governance of the pre-project phase, ultimately minimizing the wastage of resources

Link with ISO 56007 (Tools and Methods for Managing Opportunities and Ideas—Guidance)

ISO 56007 emphasizes the importance of effective project selection. Given that this facet is often overlooked, organizations are encouraged to reevaluate their project governance framework.

This chapter does not aim to define innovation management as ISO 56002 does. Instead, it offers some best practices for the pre-project stage, once the opportunity or idea has been identified.

This chapter outlines proven best practices for implementing a cohesive and efficient governance structure for project selection and pre-project management, applicable across various projects or request for resources. It complements the general recommendations provided in Chap. 22 for promoting innovation by addressing the governance of pre-project management.

22

Managing Management

Management by Opportunity: The Practice for Institutionalizing Innovation

Take-Home of This Chapter

Both ISO 56007 and ISO 56002 provide a summary of the parameters that contribute to innovation within an organization, including culture, leadership, and other enablers. With the understanding that innovation is crucial for organizational growth and survival, and that the challenge lies in stimulating innovation without wasting resources or losing focus, this chapter introduces the concept of Management by Opportunity (MbOp) as a practice that focuses on identifying and implementing implementable innovation that delivers value to the organization. The four components of MbOp for fostering innovation are: genuine commitment by senior management, employees' motivation to innovate, an environment that supports intrapreneurship, and finally the provision of easy-to-use innovation enablers, such as the IpOp Model and intrapreneurship education. It concludes by discussing the benefits of MbOp, including increased job satisfaction, motivation, and measurable results.

Everyone agrees that innovation is important and that it is a driver for growth. The problem is how to stimulate innovation in an organization, whatever its size, without wasting resources, losing control, or becoming unfocused.

R. H Cohen, *Pre-Project Excellence*, Future of Business and Finance,
https://doi.org/10.1007/978-3-031-61774-4_22

22.1 Opportunities Are at the Heart of Innovation

The name of the game is to seize opportunities, for there are opportunities everywhere and the secret is knowing how to seize them. To accomplish this, the organization must implement a practice dedicated to identifying and capitalizing on these opportunities. I refer to this practice as "Management by Opportunity" (MbOp).

The objective of MbOp is to deliver value to the organization. An idea that is not implemented is worth no more than the ink in which it is written. Management by Opportunity is not a "suggestion box" system that just encourages people to generate ideas and rewards them with no obligation to analyze their feasibility. It is concerned only with "implementable" innovations that can translate into measurable benefits for the organization. Before an innovative idea can be implemented, it must be fully analyzed, and its true contribution demonstrated. The idea needs to evolve into a… project!

No manager can be aware of everything that is happening in his unit, unless it is a very small one. In any sizeable organization, management must rely on the brainpower of others; what can be called "distributed intelligence." This expands on the concept of "swarm intelligence," which shows how insects manage to accomplish complex things as a group in the (apparent) absence of a command center.[1] Such coordination is possible because everyone follows a set of rules. A very simple illustration of this concept can be seen with flocking rules.[2]

Management depends on every employee to identify opportunities because each of them is exposed, at his own level, to situations that could give rise to opportunities. The challenge facing management is how to entice these people to identify the opportunities and take concrete measures to seize them. Every employee needs to be empowered to look for opportunities to: improve processes, provide better service, reduce costs, improve products, ameliorate relationships, better satisfy customers' PNDs, etc. There are so many opportunities out there, and it is just a

[1] See http://en.wikipedia.org/wiki/Swarm_intelligence

[2] See http://en.wikipedia.org/wiki/Flocking_(behavior)

matter of seizing them. Such empowerment[3] stimulates innovation and pride in the work.

In real terms, this translates into empowering employees to:

- Hunt for opportunities
- Have access to information
- Be creative
- Think and analyze
- Use resources where appropriate
- Implement their idea once it has been validated and accepted

Absence of empowerment is a sign of mistrust, betraying an underlying belief that people cannot do things well enough if they are left to themselves. This is no way to motivate employees. Their natural reaction will be, "if they don't trust me, why should I do more than the minimum expected of me?" Traditional military structures used to operate that way, and the quality of their performance says it all.

22.2 Why Innovation Is Such a Managerial Challenge

Innovation is directly linked to change. Because it means doing things differently, innovation represents a threat to the "establishment," which in this context may refer to either an institution or people. While people who are in charge are not against innovation as such, they tend to resist whatever may have a potentially negative impact on them. Fear of the unknown is a major reason for the outright rejection of new ideas, however unsatisfactory the present situation may be. The adage, "the devil you know is better than the devil you don't know," has all its meaning here.

Territorial behavior is an obstacle to cross-boundary cooperation and communication. When people are intent on protecting their territory, they need to stay within its boundaries. They operate from within a shell so that nobody can bother them from outside. While this is a good way to maintain the status quo, it certainly does not encourage

[3] See the 5P formula for emPowerment below.

innovation or change, because the most powerful changes are those that go beyond unit boundaries.

As humans, we have a natural inclination to preserve our territory, and thus to resist change. People employ three basic tactics to avoid direct confrontation:

- Negotiate before war is declared
- Avoid confrontation by making moves that do not affect other people's territory
- Share a common vision/goal for which the "future victims" are prepared to sacrifice some of their own privileges. This may sound good but it does not happen very often in the "real world"

None of these options is easy. Clearly, dealing with the perceived threats of innovation, whether they are justified, is a real challenge to management.

Some managers are particularly vulnerable to change because their job is result-oriented. Their position puts them in charge of the plan. But any change, any digression from their original plan may be perceived as a threat (possibly even a personal one) to their ability to deliver the results expected. They may fear that innovation will reduce their level of control or represent a challenge to their power. They may not know how to deal with the new situation or how to answer some of the questions brought up by the innovation. Needless to say, this category of managers is not the archetype of the go-getter.

The "Not Invented Here" (NIH) syndrome is a classic innovation killer (a typical Resistance as explained in Chap. 13). It occurs when a person's ego gets in the way of accepting that others can contribute to success. These individuals subconsciously believe that good ideas can only originate from themselves; acknowledging contributions from others may suggest that others are more intelligent. Consequently, they feel compelled to dismiss ideas from others as a means of self-preservation. Some managers even choose to hire less competent people to maintain their dominance and avoid feeling threatened. In such circumstances, it comes as no surprise to witness management distrusting their employees under the pretext that they lack sufficient qualifications.

Empowerment and new ideas could be a source of risk. Delegation is one of the components of empowerment, and as such is a source of risk for people who believe that nobody can do the job as well as the boss (for why would he have become the boss otherwise?). The alternative all too often resorted to is to do everything oneself and rely on nobody. Not realistic for an ambitious outcome! The solution organizations often go for is a control system to stay on top of everything, for deep-pocketed organizations are notoriously averse to risk-taking. The richer the company, the less prepared it usually is to take risks. Because there is no pressure to make more money "play-it-safe managers" are disinclined to take any risk that could jeopardize the current level of comfort or their reputation.

Innovation might divert people away from their primary focus. The excitement and pleasure derived from a new idea could lead people to focus on new horizons rather than the job at hand. In the corporate context, this would mean people being less focused on corporate objectives. Here again, because organizations tend to be short-term-objective-driven, control systems have been devised to avoid such a deviation.

Control systems hamper innovation. Managers tend to like control systems because they further their own objectives. And because managing risk is such a major concern, control systems grow up like mushrooms. But they also reduce people's freedom and often result in stifling innovation. So, the question is: how to encourage innovation without loss of control?

Innovation demands a certain degree of freedom. Innovative people need time to explore new ideas, but it is difficult to find time to innovate when short-term objectives impose total commitment and focus. 3M and Google offer classic examples of how this issue can be addressed, by giving their employees 10–15% of free time. But not many organizations have replicated such a free-time model, and most innovators must work overtime on their projects. That requires a great deal of motivation. It also means trusting employees to come up with results rather than monitoring their time and effort. This is what differentiates result-oriented organizations from those only satisfied with managing resources.

The heart of innovation is trust. In the absence of trust, people play it safe and do not expose themselves. Innovators tend to be more vulnerable than those who play by the rules. Their vulnerability will continue until the innovation turns out to be a success. Until that stage is reached, innovators need to feel that they are in a safe and trusting environment.

In addition, institutionalizing innovation requires a coherent approach. Management by Opportunity recommends the conditions that make it possible. The four pillars of MbOp are:

- A genuine commitment by management at all levels to support innovation
- Motivation on the part of employees to innovate
- An environment that supports intrapreneurship (including intrapreneurship education)
- Provision of easy-to-use innovation tools

A whole book could be written on all these four pillars and indeed many have been devoted to each of them. Since this book focuses on the fourth pillar, innovation tools, I offer a brief description of the others further down in this chapter.

22.2.1 A Genuine Commitment by Management

Leaders at all levels must be genuinely committed to innovation and to avoiding the "Not Invented Here" syndrome. Otherwise, those below them in the hierarchy will not take the risk of trying something new but will prefer to play it safe and stay away from innovation. But being committed to innovation is not enough. Management, particularly senior management, needs not only to welcome innovation from everyone but to make sure that everyone at all levels plays the game: for if any layer blocks innovation, then the whole organization is affected. If employees feel that their ideas "are not welcome upstairs" or that the NIH syndrome is raising its ugly head, they will automatically stop coming up with new ideas. This is a vicious circle, because then the only ideas implemented come from management and this makes managers think they are indispensable, inflating their ego even further.

Self-confident managers are not threatened by innovation. They know that using their staff's skills and brainpower works to their own advantage too. They have understood that managing and encouraging a successful team contributes to the progress of their own career. Building the leaders of tomorrow should be part of any executive's job description. This means encouraging everyone to show what he can do. It behooves senior management to appoint or promote only those managers who have the maturity not to feel threatened by innovation.

Leaders must encourage innovation "across the board" to demonstrate that it is everyone's business. Recognizing non-tech innovation (e.g., by allocating resources) as well as technological innovation is an obvious way to do this. There is no point in management's claiming to support innovation when its actions demonstrate the contrary. Like everyone else management must put its actions where its mouth is. Otherwise, there is little chance of trust and credibility. An appropriate attitude is essential to get the message across and obtain results.

A culture of pride and recognition will encourage innovators. If people cannot take pride in creating Competitive Advantages, the company they work for has little chance of long-term survival. It is up to senior management to recognize that creative people make a real contribution to the success of the company, for recognition is a key motivator. There are many other cultural and behavioral factors that can influence the outcome of innovation, but I shall not address them here because they are well covered in the literature on leadership and intrapreneurship.

It is the leaders who call the tune. Their attitude and behavior dictate the corporate culture. The top boss's personality, it need not be said, will have an enormous effect on the style and culture of the whole organization and considerably affect employees' motivation to innovate. We have all seen (or experienced in our own person) how the arrival of a new leader with the right attitude can stimulate unmotivated people to become motivated. Conversely, highly motivated people sometimes lose their motivation after a management change.

Because leaders play such a critical role in the realm of innovation, everything depends on the boss's attitude. Even if all the other three pillars are in place, very little can happen without commitment on the part of management. For no management system can in the long run consistently provide the best results in respect of innovation if the leader is not genuinely committed to it. This is probably more of a theoretical issue because a boss with the wrong attitude is unlikely to establish the three other pillars or implement the governance recommendations outlined in the previous chapter.

22.2.2 Employees' Motivation to Innovate

Leadership studies cover ways to motivate people, but innovation is unfortunately often considered to be "over and above the call of duty" and to require a special effort. In fact, it should simply be part of the culture and thus the norm. But this is still something very rare in large organizations.

The central question is how to satisfy the "WiiifM."[4] When employees perceive benefits from their ability to innovate, they are more inclined to exert their best efforts to attain those benefits. Studies and books on intrapreneurship list many forms of benefits or rewards:

- Recognition
- Promotion
- A new title
- Greater freedom
- New responsibilities
- Larger budget
- More resources
- More free time
- Better pay, etc

[4] What is in it for Me.

While money holds importance, it is not the sole motivator. Drawing an analogy from the "Driver/Satisfier" concept discussed in Aspirations,[5] financial compensation often serves as a Satisfier. Though it may seem unconventional or counterintuitive, for a significant number of individuals, this rings true: once they reach a level of income that affords them a comfortable standard of living, they become more receptive to other forms of rewards. This reality is evident in many civil servants and non-profit organization employees who remain motivated to excel despite salaries that may not match those in the private sector. By combining various types of rewards, including monetary compensation, a wide range of possibilities emerges. However, money alone is insufficient to sustain long-term motivation.

The reward must be commensurate with the effort and the result, as well as fair to others in the organization. Fairness is a non-negotiable condition for trust, and there is no alternative to providing a fair reward system.

Job satisfaction, pride, and personal development get a boost from an equitable reward system. When employees have permission to demonstrate what they are capable of and their efforts are rewarded accordingly, they are irresistibly led to doing a better job. This should be the dream of any CEO and it is reasonable to suggest that a deliberate effort should be made to achieve it, but sadly this is all too often not the case.

Expecting employees to be motivated spontaneously and naturally is not realistic. A comprehensive and proactive managerial approach is a must if engagement is to be stimulated. Given the clear correlation between the motivation to innovate and the level of engagement, it is essential to focus on the levers that enhance employee engagement. The book "*Les leviers de l'engagement - 54 bonnes pratiques pour entraîner, inspirer et réussir ensemble*," referenced in Chap. 16, offers a comprehensive examination of leadership parameters that enable leaders to foster engaged employees.

[5] See Chap. 13.

22.2.3 An Environment That Supports Intrapreneurship

Leadership and motivation are not enough. The organization must also provide an environment that is supportive of innovation, so that the employees understand that the management actually means business and walks the talk.

Structural conditions can encourage innovation or get in the way of it. For instance, recruiting experienced coaches to help improve projects will contribute to innovation. Whereas certain control systems, bureaucracy, or lack of access to information and resources are obstacles to innovation. As indicated in Chap. 21 and in this chapter, "best practice environment" could include access to an innovation hub that provides resources, coaching, or advice for innovators. A structural component that can favorably influence the ultimate outcome and attitudes is the encouragement of senior corporate sponsors to help and support intrapreneurial teams. Another essential ingredient is the appointment of an "innovation champion" to promote innovation within the company.

Making the IpOp Tools™ software available to employees, for instance, is another effective structural measure that can aid the innovation process. The mere fact of giving access to the application conveys the message that management encourages innovation. Why else would management spend the money and make the effort of training people to use the IpOp Model?

Because knowledge is critical for innovation, access to it must be managed. Without accurate information people cannot make the right decisions (or even educated guesses). To avoid re-inventing the wheel, too, innovators need to have access to as much information as possible regarding what is happening on the market and what the competition is doing. Allocating resources to develop something new that is already available on the market or is being developed elsewhere within the organization can result in a costly endeavor. Although some readers might find this hard to believe, it has occurred numerous times. These instances underscore the necessity for a robust knowledge management tool. Being misinformed can lead to devastating consequences!

Neglecting the access to knowledge or information would be a significant oversight by management. I cannot stress enough the importance of ensuring that individuals have access to relevant business intelligence to foster innovation while also safeguarding in-house information from competitors. Effectively managing information entails maintaining confidentiality without stifling innovation.

Identifying trends and being aware of what is happening both inside and outside your own organization is essential. Early detection of weak (internal or external) signals can provide substantial Competitive Advantages. Market watch, technology watch, or other kinds of watch are all part of the innovation process. For example, they can certainly help to detect unsatisfied PNDs which might be turned into Opportunities. As indicated earlier, trends and their interpretation are also Factors that need to be understood.

Interpreting the information is as important as obtaining it. Not everyone will interpret the same piece of information in the same way. Interpretation is influenced by many factors, including emotions, past history, the context, personal expectations, and Aspirations. I highly recommend that managers take a step back to obtain a coherent and lucid picture of the situation. Discussing interpretation with others can sometimes avoid falling into the trap of facile judgment.

Environmental conditions are an important component of intrapreneurship research and literature. Many intrapreneurship experts and authors have focused on the conditions most conducive to increasing an organization's level of innovation and dynamism. To complement the content of Chap. 21 that gives recommendations at the governance level, I encourage readers to explore the intrapreneurship literature for valuable insights into the environmental factors that promote innovation in medium to large organizations.

But structural conditions alone are not enough (despite the common belief that "good systems can fix anything"). Because innovation is the result of human activities, the "system" needs some level of human contribution. How to get people to contribute is addressed above in the expositions on leadership and motivation above.

22.2.4 Providing Easy-to-Use Innovation Tools and Intrapreneurship Education

Offering guidance to people on the innovation road increases their comfort level. When people know how to do something, they are much more likely to do it than if they are unsure of themselves and unaware of the most suitable process. Coaching employees on the innovation process is a requirement to empower them.

The IpOp Model offers such a process. Exposure to the IpOp Model induces people to using it and start experimenting with innovation. Depending in the organization, between 33% and 56%[6] of trained with the IpOp Model expressed the desire to innovate, despite the overtime this entails. This is one more illustration of how, when people are given a hammer, everything around them looks like a nail.

Give people tools and you will see them itching to use them! But knowing how to use these tools properly is critical, because otherwise they can become counterproductive or even dangerous. A drill in the hands of a carpenter can work wonders but, in the hands of an inexperienced sailor, it can sink the boat. This is why it is important to train people on how to use the tools of innovation.

Solitary innovation is rarely effective. Successful innovation will almost always involve different parts of the organization, requiring cross-boundary activities and cooperation. The big question then is how to prevent territorial behavior, which as explained above prevents real horizontal cooperation.

Territorial behavior is usually triggered by fear. Fear of the unknown and of being challenged prevents people from being receptive. So, fear and ignorance are very closely linked. Increasing people's self-confidence and preparing them to seize opportunities is a good way to reduce their defense mechanisms.

---

[6] See Benefits of Management by Opportunity below.

The best remedy against fear and ignorance is intrapreneurship education. Obtaining a more holistic understanding of business helps people to be less territorial. MBAs are very effective in providing such a "generalist" view, but they require a lot of time and of course not every employee can study for an MBA. Such training goes way beyond what most people need to understand about the fundamentals of business and what their neighbors are doing. Intrapreneurship education can provide this generalist view to open people's mind to the "rest of the world," beyond the limits of their own realm.

Intrapreneurship education should include marketing, PR and communication, accounting, finance, negotiation skills, leadership, business intelligence, the IpOp Model, team building, presentation skills, legal issues, stress management, etc. Even if only the fundamentals are taught, they will impart business savvy, a basic business vocabulary and a global picture, while encouraging participants to obtain a more complete education in their own specific areas of interest.

Intrapreneurship education breaks down internal barriers and silo attitudes. Business education also leads people to introduce additional dimensions in respect of their own activities that they would not have considered otherwise. For instance, an expert in portfolio management in a bank can come to realize that PR techniques can promote his or her department's activities for the benefit of the employer (as well as his own!).

Intrapreneurship education has an impact on the organization's culture. It is a very effective way to convey cultural messages to a group, something that "catalog training"[7] cannot do. Cultural messages include several dimensions that are not easily taught in competence training, such as business ethics, solidarity, the intrapreneurial spirit, social responsibility, and so on. Since the participants in the intrapreneurship training program will come from different departments of the organization, they will also learn to work together while developing their internal network, a key ingredient of innovation. When employees from different

[7] "Catalog training" represents the offering of training sessions available in a large organization to people who wish to acquire certain skills. They can pick and choose items from the catalog of courses but there is usually no link between the different training sessions that do not belong to one structured curriculum. The participants must then make on their own the potential connections between the various skills acquired.

departments, such as engineers and marketing experts, gain a thorough understanding of each other's roles and responsibilities, they are better equipped to identify potential synergies and collaborate more effectively. This heightened level of cooperation leads to increased innovation and overall organizational success.

Continued business education can successfully enhance cross-boundary cooperation within organizations. For example, the AgilityBooster/MicroMBA MB™[8] training program has consistently delivered impressive results in every organization where it has been implemented.[9] This program (including IpOp Model training) has shown that education, coupled with the promotion of cross-boundary cooperation, encourages innovation among employees. By capitalizing on the diverse talents and resources within the organization and promoting a spirit of intrapreneurship, this training initiative contributes to a significant shift in corporate culture.

22.3 The Five P's Formula for emPowerment

The simple Five P's formula for emPowerment is a recipe[10] that works wonders to promote innovation within organizations:

A *Passionate* leader
+ *Permission* (to do)
+ *Protection* (in the event of failure)
+ a *Process*

= *Powerful Performance* (by emPowered People)

A Passionate leader will inspire people to be proactive. Passion is contagious and will stimulate the team. A leader who is not passionate

[8] www.MicroMBA.org or www.MicroMBA.ch

[9] Nestlé, Bühler, Microsoft, banks, industrial companies and even non-profit organizations (including several hospitals).

[10] Inspired by the 3P's of Transactional Analysis: Permission + Protection = Power.

about success is unlikely to motivate the staff to constantly look for opportunities to do a better job.

Leaders must give Permission to innovate, an encouragement to do things. Clearly stating that innovation is encouraged is of course a good starting point, but all the components of the MbOp described above contribute to conveying the message that management really desires innovation. Granting Permission should not be just a matter of lip service, and the leader's attitude in the daily operations will be essential in supporting or weakening Permission.

The leader must give Protection to those who innovate. Because of the possibility of failure, the innovator takes a personal risk for his or her career. Innovations often trigger an immune reaction from the organization which may be a killer obstacle. Leaders should therefore provide the air cover to protect innovators in case of failure of a legitimate initiative.

A Process for innovation is necessary to provide a clear roadmap for those who have an idea. In the absence of such a Process supporting emerging (bottom-up) innovation, employees will not know how to move their ideas forward. Providing a Process not only helps them mature and sell their idea but also demonstrates a sincere desire on the part of management to encourage innovation, otherwise it would not bother providing a Process. The fact that a Process for bottom-up innovation is proposed to employees clearly demonstrates that management is walking its talk. The IpOp Model has served many large organizations successfully as the Process to stimulate emerging innovation.

When these first four P's are implemented the result is the fifth double P: Powerful Performance. The four P's concretely empower employees to become proactive, and the result is high Performance.

22.4 The Benefits of Management by Opportunity

Integrating the four pillars of MbOp with the governance model detailed in Chap. 21 offers a holistic approach to innovation. While each individual pillar or governance practice has its own advantages and can yield positive outcomes, merging them creates a robust structure that becomes a far more potent source of true synergy.

MbOp is a state of mind focused on the seizing of Opportunities. It brings competitive advantages to the organization at the same time as increasing employees' job satisfaction. The possibility of seizing Opportunities is a privilege that permits them to show what they are capable of doing. This creates enormous drive.

MbOp stimulates employees' commitment. This was one of the "side effects" identified following the introduction of MbOp in the Field Marketing division of Oracle. Driven by Alfonso Di Ianni, senior VP, this initiative substantially boosted employees' motivation and job satisfaction.

MbOp delivers measurable results. Even though not all the components of its four pillars were introduced at Oracle, MbOp delivered measurable results. A survey run by Oracle Corp. stated that:

- 56% of participants initiated new projects that would not have seen the light of day if they had not attended the IpOp Model training workshop
- 87% of participants applied all or some of the tools presented during the IpOp Model training session in the 3 months following the workshop

Comparable results have been obtained in other organizations, even though no systematic measure of the outcome was implemented. So far, there is no indication that the introduction of MbOp has not been beneficial anywhere.

Intrapreneurship education was not part of the Oracle training, on the assumption that the target group already had sufficient business savvy. This demonstrates that even the partial introduction of MbOp with IpOp Model training can deliver good results, while its full introduction will of course be still more effective.

MbOp encourages emerging innovation, i.e. bottom-up innovation. This is a major difference compared with most traditional change management programs, which usually have a top-down mechanism in which the decision to change is made at the top and the objective is to convince the rest (the bottom) to buy into it.

MbOp is thus a bottom-up "change management" practice. Because MbOp empowers all employees to become Opportunity hunters, each one of them in fact becomes a change agent with the objective to contribution to the mission and support the strategy.

MbOp also reduces the level of stress within an organization. Because MbOp is a real empowering management practice, it gives employees more control over their work. Lack of control and helplessness are major sources of stress. When people must execute decisions that have been imposed on them, they feel helpless and become stressed. With empowerment, they can handle quite heavy pressure without too much difficulty. MbOp thus very meaningfully contributes to stress reduction.

MbOp is for "rightists," people who mostly focus on the right side of the P&L statement (the revenues). The left side registers expenses, so "leftists" are managers who focus on cost reduction. Innovation is mainly a rightist activity, even though some innovations lead to cost reduction. The "rightist" approach is to seize all opportunities that improve something, whether on the revenue side or the expense side. Rightists have a clear preference for the revenue side where the sky is the limit, while cost reduction is obviously limited.

MbOp complements other management practices. There is nothing to prevent, for example, implementing MbOp as a complement to MbO (Management by Objectives). MbOp focuses on proactive innovation and is not in contraindication with most other management practices. MbOp has been used in both the private and public sectors, including hospitals and non-profit organizations. In theory, and indeed in fact, there is little reason not to introduce it into every organization.

But the success of MbOp depends on a commitment to innovation and empowerment on the part of senior management, listed as the first pillar above. My experience has led me to believe that unfortunately this is the main obstacle. Not many CEO's are prepared to empower their people and encourage "across the board innovation." This could be due to inertia, the fear of change, NIH, or any of several other reasons. I unfortunately have not had a chance to run a study to figure out these reasons, but I look forward to finding out. It is certainly a very interesting area that is still open to investigation.

The IpOp Tools™ software provides a monitoring system focusing on innovation that can reduce the resistance of senior management to promoting Management by Opportunity by increasing their level of control. In today's rapidly changing environment reluctant CEO's need to realize that innovation is a must if they want to stay in business.

Link with ISO 56007 (Tools and Methods for Managing Opportunities and Ideas—Guidance)

ISO 56002 is the standard providing guidance on "Innovation management systems."

While ISO 56007 offers a condensed overview of culture, leadership, and other innovation enablers within an organization, it does not specifically mention or delve into "Management by Opportunity."

Given the absence of "Management by Opportunity" in both ISO 56002 and ISO 56007, the content of this chapter should be viewed as a practical guide for creating an environment conducive to innovation. This approach, nonetheless, aligns with the recommendations of both ISO 56002 and ISO 56007, offering a tangible framework to support innovation initiatives within organizations.

Glossary

Key Terms and Their French Equivalents

Take Home of This Section

This glossary provides the definition of terms related to pre-project management, intrapreneurship and entrepreneurship, along with their French equivalents. It covers various concepts and terminology used in the IpOp Model and their specific definitions of key terms.

This section also highlights the terminology differences between ISO 56007 and the IpOp Model.

R. H Cohen, *Pre-Project Excellence*, Future of Business and Finance,
https://doi.org/10.1007/978-3-031-61774-4

Term	Definition	French term
Action Plan	An organized set of Tactical Moves put together to reduce Unknowns or deliver the Definition of Success	*Plan d'actions*
Activity Chain	A set of activities necessary to ensure that the product or service gives complete satisfaction to the Customer	*Chaîne d'activité*
Alternatives	Other Solutions available to Customers for addressing their PND. They could result of different processes or Solutions provided by competitors	*Alternative*
Aspiration	An expectation that a Stakeholder wishes to have satisfied	*Aspiration*
Barrier to entry	A major Hurdle/Obstacle (often difficult to overcome) usually present to avoid competition	*Barrière à l'entrée*
Benchmarking	See below Customer Benchmarking and Decision-maker Benchmarking	*Benchmarking*
Booster	A Factor contributing to delivering the Definition of Success	*Accélérateur*
Business plan	Document describing (1) the plan to put the project into effect and (2) market conditions and other reasons justifying why the Project should be implemented	*Plan d'affaires*
CDC	See *Customer's Decision Criteria* below	*CDC*
Collateral damage	An undesired side effect of a Tactical Move or Action Plan	*Dommage collatéral*
Competitive intelligence, Business intelligence	Methods for obtaining information on the market, products, customers, competitors, needs, etc.	*Intelligence concurrentielle, Intelligence économique*
Competition, competitor	An alternative that is liable in some way or another to satisfy customers' PNDs or attract their attention	*Concurrence, concurrent*

Term	Definition	*French term*
Constraint	A rule that must absolutely be respected (it may be freely adopted or imposed by the organization or even the external environment, such as an authority)	*Contrainte*
Contingency plan	An alternative plan prepared in case an unforeseen event (i.e., a Risk) materializes, or if the main plan does not proceed as planned	*Plan B*
CUE	Customer's Unique Experience (see *CUE Description)*	*ECU*
CUE Description	Detailed description of the Solution designed to ensure a Customer's Unique Experience (CUE)	*Déclaration d'ECU*
Customer Benchmarking	Comparison of the relative performance of each Competitor (or alternative) for each Customer Decision Criteria (CDC) targeted	*Benchmarking du Client*
Customers' Decision Criteria (CDCs)	Criteria used by Customers to choose among the various options available	*Critères de décision du client (CDC)*
Customer PND Focus Statement	Expression of the selection of Pain/Need/Desire(s) of a defined Customer target that the Solution aims to satisfy	*Déclaration de focus SBD Client*
Decision-maker	Any person wielding the power of decision that can affect the fate of a project (Investor, founder, leader, manager, etc.)	*Décideur*
Definition of Failure	The list of minimum objectives for each Key Indicator of Failure that must at least be met at the various milestones to avoid terminating the project	*Définition de l'échec*
Definition of Success	The list of objectives for each Key Indicator of Success that must be met at the various milestones if the project is to be rated as successful	*Définition du succès*

Term	Definition	*French term*
Driver	An Aspiration that has no ceiling (upper limit); the more it is satisfied, the happier Stakeholders will be (the other category of Aspiration is the *Satisfier)*	*Driver*
Effort model	The combination of the Activity Chain that will be mobilized + the Resource Model for a certain Scope	*Modèle d'effort*
Elevator pitch	A concise outline of the Project (not exceeding one minute) designed to capture the listener's attention	*Elevator Pitch*
Empowerment	The act of giving employees the freedom to take the initiative and make certain decisions	*Autonomisation*
Entrepreneur	The initiator of an entrepreneurial project in the context of a start-up	*Entrepreneur*
Entrepreneurship	Entrepreneurial activity aimed at launching a start-up	*Entrepreneuriat, entrepreneurship*
Factor	A parameter over which one generally has little influence, but which can have a (positive or negative) impact on the likelihood of a project's attaining its Definition of Success	*Facteur*
Hurdle	A known difficulty intervening on the path to the Definition of Success (it is a Factor)	*Frein*
Influencer	Parameters that can influence the ability to deliver the Definition of Success and Failure: Factors and Stakeholders	*Influenceurs*
Intrapreneur, corporate entrepreneur	The champion of an entrepreneurial project in the context of an existing organization	*Intrapreneur*
Intrapreneurship, corporate entrepreneurship	Entrepreneurial activity aiming to launch an innovative project within the framework of an existing enterprise	*Intrepreneuriat, intrepreneurship*

Term	Definition	*French term*
Investment	The allocation of Resources to jumpstart the project until the Economic Model makes the Opportunity or project self-sustainable	*Investissement*
Investors	The Stakeholders who can provide the Investment. As they include anyone who invests one way or another in the Opportunity they can be the owner, the team, shareholders, external fund providers, top management, or any Decision-maker	*Investisseur*
Investor Decision Criteria (IDC)	The criteria that the Investor uses to assess an opportunity in her/his own perspective	*Critères de Décision Investisseur (CDI)*
Investor Benchmarking	Comparison of the relative performance of each Variant for each Decision-maker Decision Criteria	*Benchmarking Investisseur*
IpOp	Innovation by Opportunity	*IpOp (Innovation par les opportunités)*
IpOp Reviews	The four fundamental questions for eliminating as early as possible Opportunities or projects. They should first be addressed sequentially but future iterations will allow a deeper analysis	*Revues IpOp*
KIFs	Key indicators of Failure, indicators used to terminate a project that does not deliver the Definition of Failure	—
KISs	Key Indicators of Success, indicators used to measure the success of a project (its ultimate purpose defined by the Definition of Success)	*Indicateurs clés de succès*
KPIs	Key Performance Indicators: indicators used for management purposes to measure the performance of a unit or an activity that contributes to delivering the target end result	*Indicateur clé de performance (ICP)*

Term	Definition	French term
Market advantage	A feature or combination of features of the project that the competition cannot copy	*Avantage concurrentiel*
Milestone	Key moments after launch of the Project when KISs and/or KIFs are measured to verify progress (used in the Definition of Success and Failure)	*Jalon*
Mission	Expression of the realistic intentions to be achieved when implementing a strategy	*Mission*
MbOp	Management by Opportunity	*MpOp*
Objective	The value attributed to an indicator at a given moment	*Objectif*
Opportunity	Combination of an innovative Solution with at least one Pain, Need, or Desire that could be addressed better	*Opportunité*
Opportunity Case	A short document of a few pages setting out the reasons why the project deserves to be realized; specifically, it serves to verify the apparent interest of Decision-makers	*Dossier d'opportunité*
PESTEL	An analysis of the political, economic, social/sociological, technological, environmental, and legal Factors	*PESTEL*
PND	Pain/Need/Desire(s) that the Customer would like to have satisfied	*SBD Souffrance/Besoin/Désir*
Pre-project	the period before a decision has been made to launch a project	*Préprojet*
Resistance	Something that a Stakeholder wants to avoid	*Résistance*
Resource Model	The mechanism(s) for obtaining the Resources necessary to satisfy Stakeholders	*Modèle de ressources*
Resources	The means (included in the Investment, such as money, personnel, premises, equipment, etc.) required to implement each Action Plan. Resources can also be generated by the Resource model	*Resources*

Term	Definition	*French term*
Risk	An uncertain Hurdle that may or may not have to be confronted (it is a Factor)	*Risque*
Satisfier	An Aspiration for which it is sufficient to attain the defined threshold in order to satisfy Stakeholders (the other category of Aspiration is the *Driver)*	*Satisfier*
Scope	The limits of a Project (geographic, market segment, etc.)	*Envergure*
Solution	A manner (usually innovative) of satisfying one or more PNDs	*Solution*
Stakeholder	A person or entity to whom or which the project team/promoter is accountable (and thus whose Aspirations and Resistances must be taken into account)	*Partieprenante*
Start-up	A budding new business	*Start-up*
SWOT	Strategic analysis of the strengths, weaknesses, opportunities, and threats of an existing entity	*SWOT*
Tactical Move	A concrete action designed to deliver a certain result (e.g., reduce an Unknown, achieve the Definition of Success, etc.); component of an Action Plan	*Action tactique*
Terminators	Indicators used to kill a project if a predetermined threshold is not reached	*Terminators*
Unknowns	Situations where there is a lack of information or knowldedge. Obtaining all or part of the missing information through appropriate Tactical Moves can eliminate or reduce Unknowns. Unlike Risks and other Factors, Unknowns do not have a probability of occurrence	*Inconnues*
Variants	Other ways or processes to deliver the same Customer Unique Experience or Solution	*Variante*
WiiifM(T)	What is in it for Me (Them)	—

Link with ISO 56007 (Tools and Methods for Managing Opportunities and Ideas—Guidance)

While the terminology differences between ISO 56007 and the IpOp Model are minimal, two key distinctions stand out:

What the IpOp Model calls "Unknowns" are referred to as "uncertainties" in ISO 56007.

The IpOp Model explicitly focuses on "Stakeholders" (those interested parties to whom you are accountable) while treating other interested parties as Factors, whereas ISO 56007 does not make such differenction: it treats stakeholders as a subcategory of "interested parties."

Another notable difference is in categorization: ISO 56007 includes "strategic fit" within the "organization alignment" category, among other criteria. Conversely, the IpOp Model treats "strategic or Investor fit" as encompassing all aspects of "organization alignment."

Recommended Reading

In addition to the books mentioned in the text, I recommend the following selection:

Carsrud, A., & Brännback, M. E. (2007). *Entrepreneurship*. Greenwood Press.

Chesbrough, H. (2003). *Open innovation: The new imperative for creating and profiting from technology*. Harvard Business School Press.

Cooper, R. G. (2001). *Winning at new products: Accelerating the process from idea to launch* (3rd ed.). Basic Books.

Gumpert, D. E. (2002). *Burn your business plan!: What investors really want from entrepreneurs*. Lauson Publishing.

Heath, C., & Heath, D. (2008). *Made to stick: Why some ideas survive and others die*. Random House.

Katz, J. A., & Green, R. P. (2011). *Entrepreneurial small business* (3rd ed.). McGraw Hill Higher Education.

Kawasaki, G. (2004). *The art of the start: The time-tested, battle-hardened guide for anyone starting anything*. Portfolio Hardcover.

R. H Cohen, *Pre-Project Excellence*, Future of Business and Finance,
https://doi.org/10.1007/978-3-031-61774-4

Kim, W. C., & Mauborgne, R. (2005). *Blue ocean strategy*. Harvard Business School Press.

Leifer, R., et al. (2000). *Radical innovation*. Harvard Business School Press.

McKnight, T. K. (2003). *Will it fly? How to know if your new business idea has wings...before you take the leap*. FT Press.

Mullins, J. (2004). *The new business road test: What entrepreneurs and executives should do before writing a business plan*. FT Press.

Pinchot, G., & Pellman, R. (1999). *Intrapreneuring in action*. Berrett-Koehler Publishers.

Pinchot, G. (1985). *Intrapreneuring: Why you don't have to leave the corporation to become an entrepreneur*. HarperCollins Publishers.

Trías de Bes, F., & Kotler, P. (2011). *Winning at innovation. The A-F model*. Palgrave MacMillan.

www.ingramcontent.com/pod-product-compliance
Lightning Source LLC
Chambersburg PA
CBHW062003250926
51852CB00008B/2
* 9 7 8 3 0 3 1 6 1 7 7 3 7 *